"Attention must finally be paid to such a writer as Donald Margulies."
—Jan Stuart, *New York Newsday*

"A playwright of most unusual imaginative power."
—Clive Barnes, *New York Post*

"Manages to transform what might have been kitchen-sink drama into theatre that is unsettling, imaginative and quite hilarious."
—Howard Kissel, *New York Daily News*

"Diabolical ingenuity and rueful tenderness . . . dark wit and gentle lyricism . . . lovely and devastating . . . at a crucial moment in Margulies's career, a glowing reminder of the particular pungency and intelligence of this playwright's vision."
—Ben Brantley, *New York Times*

"Margulies has taken the naturalistic approach—and pipe-bombed it. . . . Much as Margulies parodied Neil Simon-esque writing in *What's Wrong with This Picture?* to find emotional truths in the Brooklyn-apartment Jewish comedy, and much as he turned Arthur Miller inside out in the mordantly hilarious *Loman Family Picnic,* in *The Model Apartment* he skews the angle on Holocaust plays. . . . *The Model Apartment* is among the most complex and daring Holocaust plays I've seen."
—Alisa Solomon, *Village Voice*

"Somber and questioning, brash and funny in their assertiveness, these plays create an arena where public and private mingle, an American reality that is like the world of our daily lives but not of it, a distorting mirror where we can see, maybe a truer reflection of our selves."
—Michael Feingold, from the Introduction

SIGHT UNSEEN

and other plays

SIGHT
UNSEEN

and other plays

Donald Margulies

THEATRE COMMUNICATIONS GROUP

8/25
Margulies

Sight Unseen and Other Plays is published by Theatre Communications Group, Inc.,
355 Lexington Ave., New York, NY 10017-0217.

Margulies, Donald.
Sight unseen and other plays / Donald Margulies.
ISBN 1-55936-103-4
I. Title.
PS3563.A653A6   1995
812'.54—dc20
95-45984
CIP

The author wishes to thank Joachim Neugröschel for providing the Yiddish
translation in *The Model Apartment*.

Book design by Lisa Govan

First Printing, January 1996

In memory of my parents

CONTENTS

DONALD MARGULIES,
or
WHAT'S AN AMERICAN
PLAYWRIGHT?

by Michael Feingold

When I see one of Donald Margulies's plays, I always end up thinking about my cousin Abe. He and his wife were among the lucky ones. They had been in Theresienstadt, which was not one of the worst camps, and they had survived to settle here after the War. They had actually married in the camp, their wedding solemnized by the first Jewish chaplain to arrive with the Allied forces. They took a solemn vow, as part of the ceremony, never to reveal to their children what they had seen and endured. Abe and Ella did well here; they had a comfortable house and two adorable daughters. But daughters growing up in America come home from school and want to know why Mommy doesn't talk like all the other mommies, why she has a funny accent, so eventually—after going to a rabbi and being ceremonially released from their vow—they told the whole story to their daughters, who cried a lot at learning they were part of vast nameless historical events on the other side of the world. It made Abe, an intelligent, fastidious man who had always carried the secret sorrow deep inside himself, start to wear it more openly; he began to fret more outspokenly about politics, about the state of America. In the late '60s, he took Ella and the kids and emigrated to Israel, because, he said, "It is going to happen again. It is going to happen here. And I want to be with my own people when the time comes."

Back then I thought Abe was funny, a bit cracked. We all did. (My mother, always worried about my eyesight, said, "You see what happens to people who read too much?") Nowadays I'm not so sure: Israel, where Abe's family still lives, is slowly struggling toward peace with the Palestinians. Meanwhile, I sit here in New York, flanked by Louis Farrakhan on one side and Pat Robertson on the other. Maybe it is going to happen here, but I was not born in Europe, and don't find it so easy to say who my own people are. I always told Abe, "If it happens in this country, it will happen to the blacks, not to us. They are hated worse than we are." In that respect I find it easier to understand Farrakhan's hatred than Robertson's psychopathy; at least Farrakhan has something to be angry about, however wrongheaded his choice of targets.

Anyway Jews, like blacks, are used to being hated; once you have met the hatred, you never get over it. Your consciousness is always marked by a sense of being in some way separate. And your history—like the Holocaust history that sneaks or strides into all of Donald Margulies's plays—hangs over you, a permanent cloud in even the sunniest sky. There is no escape; what you believe to be permanent and comforting can be taken from you in a second, can vanish with a word. When I was Literary Director of the Guthrie Theater, in the late '70s, we gave the world premiere of a beautiful, somewhat erotic play by Isaac Bashevis Singer, with a wonderful performance by the then-unknown F. Murray Abraham. Somehow, my office ended up having to answer the angry letters—there were only a few, awkwardly written on crude lined paper—that said, "How dare you put this Jew pornography on our beautiful stage." Nowadays—that damn word again—I would not be so surprised. The American resistance to the concept of art as a sensual pleasure, art as a salutary shock, art as a revelation of the Other, is in full cry.

And this, too, hangs over Margulies, who very properly uses his plays to test the validity of such concepts, sorting out what it means to be creative along with what it means to be a Jew: In *Sight Unseen*, we weigh, and watch the artist-hero weigh for himself, the question of whether the sensationalism that brings media success is a spiritual impulse or merely a money-making ploy. One of his attention-getting paintings shows a black man and a white woman making love—or is she being raped?—in a cemetery defaced by graffiti'd swastikas. When the German art critic who is interviewing the hero suggests that this image may be the product of a clever Jewish mind, and gets called a Nazi in return, it's hard to tell which party to the conversation is being touchy—especially when one recalls that, if the image is indeed the product of a clever Jewish mind—Margulies's—so are the art critic and her disturbing question. His gift for raising troublesome issues subtly (notice how the Holocaust has worked its way into the play's discussion of art and artists' tactics) comes with a concomitant gift for ironizing his way around them, for seeing them from all sides. Because troublesome questions don't have simple answers; that's why, like history, they never go away.

In *The Loman Family Picnic*, *What's Wrong With This Picture?* and *The Model Apartment*, the troublesome questions are about family ethics; in *Found a Peanut*, they're about friendship and money; in *Sight Unseen*, about love and art. But in all five plays, the underlying question that is more deeply troublesome is about Jews and identity in America, and the real beauty of Margulies's work is that he's managed to create an ethnic theatre without the tub-thumping self-consciousness that often mars ethnic-minority art. In art the things you assert are your identity; the questions you raise are your way of transcending it.

Pretending that you have no ethnic identity is no use for purposes of transcendence. *Death of a Salesman* is a Jewish play too, for all of the little impulses on Arthur Miller's part to make it more universal by making it abstract. No wonder the salesman's son in *The Loman Family Picnic* identifies with it; no wonder, too, that he feels the impulse to turn it into something it isn't—a musical with a happy ending. The American ending, you might say, that every ethnic group looks for and that none of us, as a group, can find. What Miller wrote, in effect, was the story of the Jewish spirit's failure to find a home in the American system; everything Margulies writes, one step further on, is an implied critique of the system on that basis, the chronicle of a land which is all model apartments and no home for anybody's spirit.

It shouldn't escape notice that O'Neill's *Long Day's Journey into Night*—an Irish Catholic play the way *Death of a Salesman* is a Jewish play—has seeped into the consciousness of *The Loman Family Picnic* too, in the bridal-gown speech. What's not a home for my spirit is not a home for yours, either. The cruel banality of American life, with which both Miller and O'Neill are at war, is a kind of terrifying wonder-world to Margulies: twisting the kids' language in *Found a Peanut*, where the brand of rubber ball you possess is both a status symbol and a revelation of character; weirdly muddling the family's historical memories in *The Model Apartment*; knocking the hell out of the Greek myth at the structural bottom of *What's Wrong With This Picture?* Imagine—if Alkestis came back from the dead today, she'd be a Jewish mother, and clean house. What a long way we've sunk from the time of gods and heroes, when the land of the dead was a place people communed with, and the brave journeyed to.

Miller and O'Neill, with their obsessive focus on the family, represent one American approach to art; the other is that consolation of displaced souls, the desire to include everything: Walt Whitman, Gertrude Stein, Thomas Pynchon. (Both O'Neill and Miller made forays in this direction too: *The Iceman Cometh*, *The American Clock*, *Marco Millions*, *The Crucible*—family problems transjected into a social landscape.) Margulies, coming after so many such efforts and sensitively aware of them, seems to be struggling to strike a balance between the two modes. The American everything is in his plays: street slang and Greek myth; the form of naturalism and a determined stylistic disruption of it (the scenes "hung" out of sequence in *Sight Unseen*); the assertion of ethnic identity and a systematic effort to see around it. (School assignment for dramaturgs: List the verbal changes required to make *What's Wrong With This Picture?* playable by an all-Black, an all-Irish, an all-Italian and an all-Pakistani cast. Not too many, I bet.) Somber and questioning, brash and funny in their assertiveness, these plays create an arena where public and private mingle, an American reality that is like the world of our daily lives but not of it, a distorting mirror where we can see, maybe, a truer reflection of our selves, the way adults past and to come are eerily reflected in the children of *Found a Peanut*.

What America was we know, or can learn; what's to come is a little harder to determine, which is probably where Margulies's plays get their somberness. After I had given *Sight Unseen* a very favorable review in the *Village Voice*, a colleague from the paper's Art section went to see it and complained that it was an "obvious" story about a painter struggling to decide whether or not to sell out, with an "obvious" happy ending. But that is not at all what happens in *Sight Unseen*. The hero's struggle is to determine whether he has already sold out without realizing it. (For comparison, look up another speech in *Long Day's Journey*—James Tyrone Sr.'s last-act monologue beginning, "That goddamned play!") At the end of the play he regains, not his integrity, but a piece of his past, in a compromise that discomfits everyone involved and leaves the best behind him; his future—for all the play's time disruptions—is an empty canvas.

As so is America's, unless it is like the ravings of the concentration camp survivors' schizophrenic daughter in *The Model Apartment*, where Hitler and the terror of the Six Million keep coming back, mixed up with junk food and medical technology and life in a now-crumbling Brooklyn. The relatively mild Jewish-Gentile tensions of *Found a Peanut* are the past; the closest thing to a spokesman for the future, so far, is a retarded teenage black boy who sleeps on the streets. (His absence from the last scene of *The Model Apartment*, without a word of explanation, is far more disturbing than the blank canvas.) The brutality that has lately become a prevailing trend in our politics (let's hope it's only temporary) may, if it keeps up, send us all, artists and marginalized ethnics alike, onto the streets with him. It was a playwright—O'Neill, in fact—who told *Time* magazine, when he was named "Man of the Year," that for him America was "the greatest failure in the world" because it had all the resources imaginable and it squandered or brutalized them in the pursuit of material gain instead of using them to nourish the spirit. His words ought to be tattooed on the wrists of all newly elected congressmen . . .

Fortunately, there is another America: the one artists have always sought and all immigrants have come here to seek; the America that nourishes, cherishes, accepts and includes. An American success story: A blonde girl named Hedwall and a dark-haired boy named Boutsikaris get married and star in a Donald Margulies play Off Broadway. What ethnic group do their children belong to? Americans, I suppose. In the absence of other possibilities, we have to call them that. I am an American, you are an American, he or she is an American. If each of us has a consciousness of also being something separate, maybe we have to say that that too is an American phenomenon, and Donald Margulies's "Jewish" plays mixed up with pagan myths and European history and Florida condos and Broadway musicals and old plays and young black homeless people are American plays. Ours is this country of endlessly unreeling possibilities, where anybody's misery can be made into a musical (though this is probably not the best thing to do with it), and everything great can still happen— even if a small group of powerful people who are frightened by endless possibility try to choke it off.

So Donald Margulies's plays remind me of all the reasons why I am not, despite the premonitions of my cousin Abe, going to leave America, to which my father came as an eleven-year-old, in 1922, to learn English from Tin Pan Alley songs about flappers rolling their stockings down. I am going to stay here "because I was born here, and my great-great-grandmother baked bread for George Washington's troops when he crossed the Delaware, and I am going to stay here and have a piece of it just like you." The part about my great-great-grandmother isn't true. I didn't say those words; Paul Robeson did, to a session of the House Un-American Activities Committee, which was trying to deprive him of his passport because of his political beliefs. And when they asked him why he liked Russia so much, he said, among other things, "the great poet of Russia is a Negro," which is true; he was speaking of Pushkin. Well, the great playwrights of America are African and Latin American and Irish and Italian and Chinese and Eastern European. And Jewish. And when I see Donald Margulies's plays, I see America. And I like America. And I fear for America. And I smile at America. And I decide not to emigrate.

FOUND
A PEANUT

□ □ □

CHARACTERS

JEFFREY SMOLOWITZ, 11, skinny; a loner who believes in fairness and struggles for acceptance

MIKE, 11, a sturdy, emotional kid

MELODY, 8, Mike's sister; sunburned; engaged in an active love-hate relationship with her brother

JOANIE BERNSTEIN, 8, Melody's playmate whom Melody shamelessly dominates; freckled, fat

LITTLE EARL, 4, the youngest member of the group who because of his age and size is most protected and most abused and manipulated; his older brother, JAY, ordinarily the group's leader, is absent today

SCOTT, 12, charismatic, manly but an inept and opportunistic group leader

ERNIE, 14, and his brother SHANE, 12, who together form a syndicate of harassment and violence; sinewy and angular, crewcuts; their knees and elbows wear the emblems of their volatile boyhood

At rise: The back of an apartment building in Brooklyn. 1962. The last day of the summer; school starts tomorrow. A muggy, humid day. Clouds intermittently break up the hazy sun. Occasionally there is the sound of distant thunder. The scale of the brick building is slightly oversized to help diminish the size of the players. We see perhaps only one or two stories of what is a six-story building. The major access to the yard is a ramp which leads to the unseen front entrance of the building; between the ramp and the building is hidden access to the basement and alongside the corner of the building is an alley. Bordering on the alley is a rusted metal fence through which a hole has been cut to permit entrance into the neighboring yard. The surface of the yard is mostly concrete; there are no trees. A patch of dirt tangled with weeds and trash figures prominently in the play's action. In the center of the yard, Mike, age eleven, is on his knees meticulously drawing on the pavement with chalk a court for Skelly, a game that's played with bottle caps. Jeffrey Smolowitz, also eleven, is practicing bouncing a ball, perilously close to Mike; he doesn't catch well so he's repeatedly chasing after the ball.

SMOLOWITZ: Want to play catch?

MIKE: Do I look like I want to play catch?

SMOLOWITZ: You want?

MIKE: No. I'm doing something, Smolowitz, do you mind? Move. Come on, Jeffrey, move!

SMOLOWITZ: I was here first.

MIKE: God, Jeffrey, when will you learn there's a time and a place for everything? Move your foot!

Smolowitz stays put defiantly; Mike glares at him, Smolowitz giggles.

Baby . . .

Mike traces the chalk around Smolowitz's shoe. Melody, Mike's eight-year-old sister, skips down the ramp as he continues to draw the grid.

Melody, did you find Jay and Scott?

A beat. Melody skips up the ramp, exits.

SMOLOWITZ: What are you making, a Skelly court?

MIKE: Yes.

SMOLOWITZ: Who's playing? You and Jay and Scott?

MIKE: Uh-huh.

SMOLOWITZ: And who else?

MIKE: Just us.

SMOLOWITZ: Can people watch?

MIKE: Yeah, but you can't play.

SMOLOWITZ: I don't want to play.

MIKE: Only the best can play. It's like the World Series of Skelly.

SMOLOWITZ: I don't want to play.

MIKE: Ernie and Shane better not crash it.

Melody skips down the ramp.

Did you see them?

MELODY: No.

MIKE: Did you look?

MELODY: Yes.

MIKE: And?

MELODY: They weren't there.

MIKE: Where'd you look?

MELODY: In the front.

MIKE: Not Jay *or* Scott?

MELODY: No, I lost my keys.

MIKE: How, Melody.

MELODY: I don't know, I lost them.

MIKE: Why weren't they around your neck?

MELODY *(Playing with a costume-jewelry necklace)*: Because I *lost* them.

MIKE: Mommy's gonna be mad.

MELODY: Shut up.

MIKE: She's not gonna be home when you come home from school anymore, Melody.

MELODY: I know. You'll be home three o'clock.

MIKE: No I won't. I've got Hebrew, Melody, remember? I've got Hebrew school *four* days.

MELODY: Don't tell Mommy.

MIKE: Find them and I won't.

MELODY: I don't know where they *are.*

MIKE: Look around. Ask Jeffrey.

SMOLOWITZ: Ask Jeffrey what?

MELODY: Jeffrey, did you see my keys?

SMOLOWITZ: What kind of keys?

MIKE *(Continuing to draw with chalk)*: Keys, Jeffrey, keys.

SMOLOWITZ: I mean, were they just keys?

MIKE: On a string.

MELODY: A lanyard. A pink and white lanyard.

SMOLOWITZ: When'd you take them off your neck? *(He's in Mike's way again)*

MIKE *(Drawing; overlap)*: Jeffrey, your *foot!*

MELODY *(Overlap)*: If I knew *when*, Jeffrey, I'd know where I put them!

MIKE: Start looking for them, Melody!

MELODY: Don't yell!

MIKE: Mommy's gonna be at work.

MELODY: I know.

MIKE: We have to let ourselves in now.

MELODY *(Sadly)*: I *know*.

MIKE: What are you gonna do?, wait in the hall? You can't.

MELODY: I'll go to Mr. Schuster next door.

MIKE *(A beat)*: You *can't* go to Mr. Schuster next door.

MELODY: No?

Mike shakes his head. A beat.

So I'll go up to Joanie's.

MIKE: You can't go up to Joanie's every day.

MELODY: Mike, I don't want any keys . . . *(She touches Mike's arm tenderly)*

MIKE: Don't be a baby, Melody. Find them. Look over there. Weren't you playing over there? *(Meaning the weeded area)* Look. *Go!*

He nudges Melody; she lethargically goes to the weeded area. Mike continues drawing the Skelly court with great care.

SMOLOWITZ: Mike?

MIKE: All the lines got to be neat . . .

SMOLOWITZ: Yes . . .

MIKE: Like, you don't want one box thicker than another . . .

SMOLOWITZ: Uh-huh. . . . All the boxes have got to be identical . . .

MIKE: That's right.

MELODY: Mike . . . can't find it . . .

MIKE: What if your bottle cap lands on the line *here* . . .

SMOLOWITZ: Yes.

MIKE: You want the line just as thick over *there*.

SMOLOWITZ: Of course.

MELODY: No keys . . . *(Continues to look)*

SMOLOWITZ: You have to be fair.

MIKE: That's right. It's hard . . .

MELODY: Oh, well . . .

SMOLOWITZ: Of course.

MIKE: You have to make it *exact.*

SMOLOWITZ *(A beat)*: So why don't you use a ruler?

Mike looks at him, both annoyed and impressed by Smolowitz's pragmatic suggestion. Before he can respond, Melody suddenly runs in fright from the weeded area.

MIKE: What's the matter?!

MELODY: There's something over there.

MIKE: What?

MELODY: I don't know. Something scary.

MIKE: What?

Melody shrugs. Mike moves to investigate but hesitates.

Jeffrey, come with me?

SMOLOWITZ: She says it's scary.

MELODY: It's dis*gust*ing . . .

MIKE *(To Smolowitz)*: You want me to go all by myself?

SMOLOWITZ: Yes.

MIKE: Okay, Smolowitz, be scared. *(He starts to go, stops)* You don't have to look at anything, Jeffrey, I'll look. I'll do the looking.

Smolowitz shrugs.

Thanks a lot, Smolowitz. *(He steps into the weeds)* Where did you see it?

MELODY *(Holding Mike's arm)*: No.

MIKE *(Looking cautiously)*: Where did you see it, Melody?

MELODY: Don't find it . . . Mikey, please, it's disgusting . . .

MIKE *(Overlap; makes his discovery)*: Oh, God!

Melody screams and jumps.

Mel-o-dy . . . !

SMOLOWITZ *(Overlap)*: What?! What?!

MIKE *(Kneels and examines his find, out of view)*: A bird. A baby bird.

7

SMOLOWITZ: Is it dead?

MIKE: I don't think so.

MELODY: Mike, let's go up . . .

MIKE: I think it's alive. *(He looks around for a stick, finds one, and gently probes the bird with it)*

MELODY *(Overlap)*: Mi–ike . . .

SMOLOWITZ *(Slowly approaches)*: Is it breathing?

MIKE: I think its chest is moving up and down.

SMOLOWITZ: Maybe you should leave it alone. Maybe it's diseased.

MIKE: No. It's hurt.

MELODY: Is it gonna die?

MIKE: I don't know.

MELODY: Like Mr. Schuster next door?

MIKE: Go ride your bike or something, Melody . . .

SMOLOWITZ: What does it look like?

MIKE: Come here and look.

SMOLOWITZ: Hold it up.

MIKE: No, Jeffrey, if you want to see what it looks like. . . . Its wing moved!

Smolowitz tentatively goes to the weeded area and sees the bird.

SMOLOWITZ *(Pleasantly surprised)*: Oh. . . . It's not so bad . . .

MELODY *(Trying to ignore the bird)*: We can't go to the beach anymore.

SMOLOWITZ: What if you roll it over?

MELODY: Mommy says it's gonna pour.

MIKE: Melody, go in the front and look for Jay and Scott.

MELODY *(Picking at her sunburned shoulder)*: My skin is peeling and we can't go to the beach anymore and we have to go to school tomorrow.

SMOLOWITZ: Is its chest still going up and down?

MIKE: Yeah, I think.

MELODY: Better not bring that thing upstairs, Michael.

MIKE: I'm not bringing it upstairs.

MELODY: No more animals in the house.

MIKE: Shhh . . .

MELODY: Your turtle stunk up the whole house.

MIKE: Go ride your bike!

MELODY: You drive me crazy, Michael, you know that?

MIKE: Go to the storage room and take out your bike.

MELODY: I can't! I lost my keys! Remember?!

MIKE *(Reaching into his pocket)*: Use my key and if you lose it . . .

MELODY: Your key's no good.

MIKE: What's the matter with my key?, it's the key to the storage room . . .

MELODY: Yeah but it doesn't open my lock, Mister Genius.

SMOLOWITZ *(His eye still on the bird)*: Mike!

MIKE: What.

SMOLOWITZ: I think it moved!

Melody shrieks, Mike slaps her arm lightly.

MIKE: Don't scare it!

Joanie skips on carrying her doll.

MELODY: Michael, you hurt me on my sunburn!

MIKE: Joanie Bernstein is here. Go play with Joanie Bernstein.

MELODY: I'm telling Mommy you hit me on my sunburn on purpose.

MIKE: Good. Joanie, play with Melody.

Joanie nods and dutifully goes to Melody.

SMOLOWITZ *(Still on the bird, to himself)*: It stopped.

JOANIE: Melody, you want to go up and get your doll and we'll play?

MIKE: Good idea.

MELODY: I don't want to go up. I want to stay and watch.

JOANIE: What are they doing?

MELODY: I found it. It's a bird.

SMOLOWITZ: Mike, I think it's dead.

Joanie moves close to the bird to get a good look; she's quietly fascinated and unafraid.

MIKE: No it's not.

SMOLOWITZ: Its chest stopped moving.

MIKE: It's moving, a little–little bit. See?

JOANIE: What are you gonna do with it?

MIKE: We're gonna make you eat it.

Smolowitz and Melody laugh.

JOANIE *(Blushing)*: Ha. Ha. Very funny.

Melody pushes Joanie in order to get closer to Mike.

MELODY: Mike? Mike, I'm gonna go up and get my doll, okay?

MIKE: Thank God.

MELODY *(To Joanie)*: Come up with me.

The girls begin to exit.

MIKE: If you see Jay and Scott . . .

MELODY: I know, I know . . .

JOANIE *(To Melody)*: Your skin is peeling.

MELODY: No kidding.

Joanie shyly waves goodbye to Mike and Smolowitz. Smolowitz waves back as the girls exit up the ramp.

MIKE: I hate it when Jay does this and I have to wait.

SMOLOWITZ: I know what you mean.

MIKE: They got me to draw the court and I did.

SMOLOWITZ: I know they're nice and everything but they can be real mean sometimes, Jay and Scott. To me, I mean.

MIKE: Hey, we're friends.

SMOLOWITZ: Oh I know.

MIKE: Scott's like my best friend.

SMOLOWITZ: I know.

MIKE: And I really like Jay.

SMOLOWITZ: Jay's great. And Scott, I like Scott a lot. *(Refers to the bird, without missing a beat)* This thing is not moving.

MIKE: It's breathing softly. It is.

SMOLOWITZ: I don't think so Mike.

MIKE: Oh yeah? Well, you ever see anything dead before?

SMOLOWITZ: No.

MIKE: I have. Last night. Mr. Schuster next door.

SMOLOWITZ: Oh, *him*. People were talking about him in the elevator coming down.

MIKE: Oh yeah? Well, my mother was the one called the cops.

SMOLOWITZ: The sirens woke me up.

MIKE: You were sleeping?

SMOLOWITZ: Not really.

MIKE: Well, I was right there. Like two inches away. There was this stink coming from next door.

SMOLOWITZ: Ich. What did it smell like?

MIKE: Like if you have a turtle and you don't wash out the bowl?

They laugh, Smolowitz hysterically.

So, anyway . . . Jeffrey, shut up, do you want to hear this?

Smolowitz stops laughing. A beat.

SMOLOWITZ *(Matter-of-factly)*: Yes.

MIKE: Everybody was in the hall. I was like two inches away when the cops broke down the door.

SMOLOWITZ: Wow, they really broke it down? And then what?

MIKE: I saw what they found.

SMOLOWITZ: What.

MIKE: Mr. Schuster. Sitting at his dinette table reading the paper. Only it looked like he fell asleep. His head was down like. He was dead, though.

SMOLOWITZ: Really.

MIKE *(Reflectively)*: Yeah.

SMOLOWITZ: So where was the smell coming from?

MIKE: Him.

SMOLOWITZ: What do you mean?

MIKE: My mother says that smell happens when you're not alive anymore.

SMOLOWITZ: Oh, wow.

MIKE: He'd ask me stuff and we'd talk.

SMOLOWITZ: Like what?

MIKE: How's school?, stuff like that.

SMOLOWITZ: Hm.

Little Earl, four years old, enters the yard quietly alongside the apartment building; he's playing with two plastic dinosaurs, a toy horse and soldiers. He's wearing Bermuda shorts; there are bruises and Band-Aids on his knees.

MIKE: And he buys me all these comics, Jeffrey.

SMOLOWITZ: Yeah?

MIKE: I come over, we read 'em, talk . . .

SMOLOWITZ: That's *nice*.

MIKE *(Seeing Little Earl for the first time)*: Hey Little Earl.

LITTLE EARL: Hi.

SMOLOWITZ: Hi, Earl.

LITTLE EARL: Hi.

MIKE *(To Smolowitz)*: Piles of 'em. Classics Illustrated . . . *Treasure Island* . . . *(To Little Earl)* So. Little Earl. Jay coming down?

LITTLE EARL: No.

MIKE: What do you mean, no?

LITTLE EARL: My father came before. Took Jay to the city with him.

MIKE: To the city?!, what's he doing in the city?! We have a game!

SMOLOWITZ: I'll play if you want . . .

MIKE: When's he coming home?

LITTLE EARL: I don't know.

MIKE: Boy, I'm really glad I made a new Skelly court.

LITTLE EARL *(Showing off his dinosaurs)*: Mike! Look what I got!

SMOLOWITZ: What should we do with the bird, Mike? I think it's dead.

MIKE: It's not!

SMOLOWITZ: Yeah, I think it is.

Mike bends and looks closely at the bird and sees that Smolowitz is right.

MIKE: Yeah.

LITTLE EARL: Mike! Look what I got!

MIKE: Uh-huh.

LITTLE EARL: Tyrannosaurus. *(He moves to the ramp, settles beside it, and plays with his toys: a Slinky and an abandoned pair of rusted roller skates)*

SMOLOWITZ: Is it gonna smell?

MIKE: I don't know if birds smell.

SMOLOWITZ: So what do we do?

Scott, age twelve, runs down the ramp.

SCOTT: Sorry my mom made me clean my room.

MIKE: The game's off.

SMOLOWITZ: Hi, Scott.

SCOTT: What do you mean, off?

SMOLOWITZ: Hi, Scott.

MIKE: Jay's not here. Little Earl says he's not coming.

SMOLOWITZ: Scott, hi.

SCOTT: Not now, Smolowitz. Where'd you see Little Earl?

LITTLE EARL: Here.

SCOTT: Oh, shit, Little Earl, where's your brother?

LITTLE EARL: My father took him.

SCOTT: What does that mean? Speak.

LITTLE EARL: My father came and took him to *his* house.

SCOTT: Shit. When?

LITTLE EARL: Before.

SCOTT: When? Like an hour ago?, two hours ago?

MIKE: Little Earl doesn't know.

LITTLE EARL: I don't know.

MIKE: I redid the Skelly court and everything.

SCOTT *(Looking over the new court)*: What happened here?

MIKE: Smolowitz was in my way.

SCOTT: Great, Smolowitz.

Mike glares mockingly at Smolowitz for Scott's benefit and corrects the imperfection.

MIKE: Do you want to play anyway?

SCOTT: What, you and me?

MIKE: Yeah.

SCOTT: What about Jay?

MIKE: He's not coming.

SCOTT: It's not the same thing, you and me.

MIKE: We could . . .

SCOTT: Yeah, but Jay's the one to beat. I mean, no offense or anything, I beat you all the time.

MIKE: You don't want to? Just for fun?

SCOTT: This is supposed to be like the biggest game.

SMOLOWITZ: I'll play, Mike.

MIKE (*Annoyed*): Shhhh . . .

SCOTT (*Overlap*): There's no game without Jay, let's face it. This
is really great of him, doing this. No Jay, no game, and I just
saw Ernie and Shane.

MIKE: Oh, no. When?

SCOTT: Outside.

SMOLOWITZ: Oh, no . . .

MIKE: Were they gonna crash our game?

SCOTT: They were mad about something.

SMOLOWITZ: God . . .

SCOTT: I know . . .

MIKE: *Now* what?

SCOTT: Jay said something, got them mad.

SMOLOWITZ: Oh, no . . .

SCOTT: Are you gonna pee in your pants, Smolowitz?

MIKE: What did Jay say?

SCOTT: Something about them getting left back again.

SMOLOWITZ: Oh, no!

MIKE: I can't believe Jay did that!

SCOTT: I don't know, it was something like that. I asked them if
that's what it was, they got mad.

SMOLOWITZ: Oh, God . . . Ernie and Shane . . .

SCOTT: Remember in school the fire drill they hit Jay?

SMOLOWITZ: Why don't they leave us alone?

SCOTT: Smolowitz, nothing is easy.

SMOLOWITZ: I wish they'd move or go to jail or die or something. They make fun of me.

SCOTT: Of *you*? Why would they do that?

Scott and, to a lesser degree, Mike laugh. Scott goes to Little Earl who has been pretending the Slinky is a telephone.

Little Earl. Be useful. When you see your brother? I mean the split second he comes home?

LITTLE EARL: Yeah . . . ?

Scott takes one end of the Slinky and he and Little Earl talk into it like a phone.

SCOTT: Tell Jay Scott is really mad he did this to me. Mike is p.o.'d too tell him.

LITTLE EARL: They went to Radio City.

SCOTT: Oh shit, no really? *(He disgustedly drops his end of the Slinky)* Well, now you're talkin', Little Earl. What else?

LITTLE EARL: My mother yelled at my father he has to bring him back. Jay can't sleep over my father's 'cause of school. They yelled.

SCOTT: Great. So he'll be back tonight. We'll all be dead tonight.

LITTLE EARL *(Shows dinosaur)*: Scott, look what I got.

Scott ignores him; Little Earl makes the dinosaur bite Scott's arm. Scott continues to ignore him.

SMOLOWITZ: Scott, what are we gonna do? If anything happens, my mother'll kill me . . .

MIKE: God, Smolowitz . . .

Little Earl's dinosaur is now nibbling at Scott's foot.

SCOTT: Okay, we should have a meeting.

MIKE: Without Jay?

SCOTT: Well, is he here?

MIKE: We can't have a meeting without Jay.

SCOTT: *I'm* here.

MIKE: What kind of meeting?

SCOTT: To talk about what we're gonna do about this.

SMOLOWITZ: What can we do?

SCOTT: I don't know, that's how come I'm asking you want a meeting.

MIKE: I feel funny having a meeting without Jay.

SCOTT: Yeah, but Jay is the reason for the meeting.

MIKE *(To Smolowitz)*: Do you feel funny?

Smolowitz nods.

SCOTT: I'm here, I'll run it, what's the big deal?

MIKE: You'll run it?

SCOTT: Do you want me to? I will if you want me too.

MIKE: Okay.

SCOTT: Okay? I will if you want me to.

MIKE: Okay.

Scott begins to lead Mike and Smolowitz to their meeting place, hesitates, then continues.

SCOTT: Okay.

Mike sits, traditionally, on the pavement. Smolowitz, unwilling to get his pants dirty, remains standing.

Jeffrey, we're gonna have a meeting. Please, Jeffrey, sit. This is a meeting.

Smolowitz reluctantly squats.

Thank you.

Little Earl, toy horse in hand, sits beside Mike.

So we're all here, right?

A beat.

Who wants to talk first?

Pause. Little Earl's attention is waning. Long pause. Mike is un-

certain of what to say, Smolowitz is bored, and Little Earl simply falls back on the pavement with his horse in his mouth.

MIKE *(A beat)*: I don't know, Scott, maybe we should wait till Jay's here.

SCOTT: Is that what you want?

MIKE: I think so.

SCOTT: If that's what you want . . .

Mike nods, Smolowitz does, too.

Okay.

MIKE: Is that okay?

SCOTT: Hey, I don't care. I just thought maybe we'd give it a shot without Jay for a change, but if you want to wait . . .

LITTLE EARL: Mike.

He offers Mike a Life Saver. Mike rejects it. A beat.

Mike. Last week my father came and took *me*. Jay was sick. I didn't want to go with him again. Jay went. My father went.

SMOLOWITZ: Scott.

SCOTT: Jay, thank you for doing this to me. Risks everybody's life, breaks up the game, and his dad takes him to the movies.

SMOLOWITZ: Scott.

SCOTT: Radio City.

SMOLOWITZ: Hey Scott look.

SCOTT: The Rockettes, a stage show, a movie. Shit.

SMOLOWITZ: Scott.

SCOTT: What, Smolowitz?

SMOLOWITZ: Look what we found.

SCOTT: What.

SMOLOWITZ: Come here.

SCOTT: Hey, Rosen, what you find?

MIKE *(Proudly)*: Go look.

Scott goes to the weeded area, Smolowitz points out the bird. Mike joins them, followed by Little Earl.

SMOLOWITZ: It died.

SCOTT: A dead bird?

MIKE: Yeah.

SCOTT *(Genuinely)*: *Great.* Hey Mike I heard about the old guy next door.

MIKE: I was there you know.

SCOTT: Yeah so was my dad.

MIKE: I was like two inches away.

Little Earl resumes playing by himself.

SCOTT: Oh well my dad knows one of the cops from bowling. Told him stuff nobody else knows.

MIKE: Like what?

SCOTT: Can't tell.

He coyly walks away from them. They follow.

SMOLOWITZ: Please?

MIKE: Come on . . .

SCOTT: Okay you know what?

MIKE AND SMOLOWITZ: What?

SCOTT: Well, first of all, you know rigor mortis?

MIKE: Yeah . . . ?

SCOTT: That's when you go stiff when you're dead.

MIKE *(Overlap)*: I know . . . yeah . . . so?

SCOTT: When they put the old guy on the stretcher?

SMOLOWITZ: Yes . . . ?

SCOTT: They had to do it sideways. 'Cause he was shaped like he was sitting down.

SMOLOWITZ: You mean like he was frozen?

SCOTT: Yeah, like in a cartoon.

Scott demonstrates by falling over and shrieking. He and Smolowitz laugh.

MIKE *(Overlap; upset)*: No he wasn't. Smolowitz, it's not funny. He was not . . .

SCOTT *(Overlap)*: Yes. That's what the cop told my dad. They couldn't bend him to lie him straight. They put him on like that. Threw a sheet on him.

Scott falls over again. Little Earl imitates him.

LITTLE EARL *(Overlap; laughing as he falls over)*: Scott, look . . .

MIKE *(Overlap)*: He was not frozen.

SCOTT: He was stiff. He was.

MIKE: I saw when they wheeled him out. His shoe was hanging out.

SCOTT: So?

MIKE *(Shrugs)*: I don't know . . . I wanted to maybe take the laces out and save 'em. Something . . .

SCOTT: Oh and you know the best part?

SMOLOWITZ: What?

SCOTT: In the old guy's house?

SMOLOWITZ: Yes . . . ?

SCOTT: You know what they found?

SMOLOWITZ: What?

SCOTT: They found—all over the place—

MIKE: Comics. I know. He gets them for me. He knows I like 'em.

SCOTT *(Overlap)*: No, no, not comics. Money.

SMOLOWITZ: Wow.

MIKE *(Overlap)*: What?

SCOTT: Money. Moola.

MIKE: Money?

SCOTT: Everywhere. *Ev*erywhere. In the toilet like where it flushes from?

SMOLOWITZ: Yes . . . ?

SCOTT: A thousand dollars.

SMOLOWITZ: Wow.

SCOTT: In his pillow?

SMOLOWITZ: Yes . . . ?

SCOTT: Like with all the feathers?

SMOLOWITZ: Yes . . . ?

SCOTT: *Two* thousand.

SMOLOWITZ: *Wo-owww!*

MIKE: Jeffrey! *(To Scott)* How do *you* know?

SCOTT: I told you, Mike, my dad, he bowls with one of the cops. And you know what?

SMOLOWITZ: What?

SCOTT: Under the bathtub thing you stand on so you won't slip?

SMOLOWITZ: Yes . . . ?

SCOTT: *Hun*dreds they found. In a plastic bag with mold in it.

SMOLOWITZ: Ich.

SCOTT: You ever heard of penicillin?

SMOLOWITZ: Yes . . . ?

SCOTT: They get that from bread mold. It's medicine.

MIKE: I know.

SCOTT: They went through his closet?

SMOLOWITZ: And . . . ?

SCOTT: Every pocket they found some. In his bed? A hole this big they found, stuffed with moola.

MIKE: You're lying, Scott.

SCOTT: Am not. Ask my dad.

MIKE: I live next door!

SCOTT: So?

MIKE: We can hear his TV through the wall!

SCOTT: What're you getting so upset about?

MIKE: He always gives me and my sister little Bit-o-Honeys. And Carvel flying saucers. I was in there all the time! I never saw any money sticking out anywhere.

SCOTT: Ask my dad you don't believe me. The cops said the old guy was nuts. That's what happens when you get old. He acted like a kid. Comics all over . . .

MIKE: He knows I like them!

SCOTT: Oh and you know what they found in the thing in the freezer you make ice in?

SMOLOWITZ: What.

SCOTT: Diamonds!

SMOLOWITZ: Diamonds, wow!

Mike glares at Smolowitz.

SCOTT: Diamond rings from his dead wife.

MIKE: So where is all this stuff?

SCOTT: The cops.

MIKE: Bullshit they can't take it.

SCOTT: Can too. They're the cops, they're the police. They get to put the stuff in a safe place.

MIKE: Where?

SCOTT: I don't know, City Hall. The 60th Precinct maybe?

MIKE: You mean they took all the comics to the police station?

SCOTT: I don't know, I think so.

MIKE: What are they gonna do with 'em?

SCOTT: I don't know, this is what I heard. I'm not lying, Mike, I swear. Are you gonna cry?

MIKE *(Fighting back tears)*: Jeffrey, we have to do something with this bird.

SCOTT: Just leave it. Let it rot.

MIKE: We're not gonna leave it, we're gonna dig a hole.

SCOTT: Mike, you mad at me? I'm not lying. I swear. Why would I lie? Want me to call my dad? *Ask* him.

MIKE: No . . .

SCOTT: I'll call my *dad* you don't believe me . . .

MIKE: No, Scott.

SCOTT *(Calls to an unseen window up above)*: HEY, DAD!!

MIKE: Don't! Jeffrey, I'm going up and get a box. Make sure nothing happens to the bird.

Smolowitz nods.

SCOTT: Why don't you just dig a little hole if you want, cover it up.

MIKE: That's not the way you do it, Scott. You need a box. Jeffrey, I'll be right back. *(Starts to exit via the ramp)*

SCOTT: Hey Mike.

MIKE: Yeah.

SCOTT *(Following Mike out)*: Whenever you want, I'll call that meeting. Jay's a traitor, right? We should kill him when we see him.

MIKE: I'm going, Jeffrey, the bird.

SMOLOWITZ: I am.

MIKE: Thank you.

SCOTT: See you later.

MIKE: Bye.

He exits. Little Earl, meanwhile, has created a "train" with the dinosaurs, the horse and the roller skates. Greatly amused by it, he calls for Scott's attention.

LITTLE EARL: Scott . . .

SCOTT: Touchy-touchy. What did I say? I told him the truth. Oh, well . . .

Scott playfully grabs Little Earl and tickles him; Little Earl is cackling hysterically.

I'm gonna tickle you to death!

LITTLE EARL: Don't, Scott!

SCOTT: I'm gonna tickle your armpit and you're gonna die, Little Earl!

LITTLE EARL *(Beside himself with glee)*: Stop, Scott, stop!

Scott releases him after a couple of beats.

More!

SMOLOWITZ *(Further examining the bird)*: I think it's starting to smell.

SCOTT: That's your b.o.

He and Little Earl laugh.

SMOLOWITZ: Sc-o-ott . . .

SCOTT: When you're dead you rot, you know. Remember in *Psycho*?

SMOLOWITZ: Didn't see it. Wasn't allowed.

SCOTT: Oh. *(He puts his arm around Smolowitz)* There's this part at the end? She taps the mother on her shoulder?

SMOLOWITZ: Yes . . . ?

SCOTT: And the mother turns around? You hear this already?

SMOLOWITZ: No go ahead what.

SCOTT: The mother turns around and . . . AHHHHH!!!!

He screams, a horrifying scream. Smolowitz jumps, Little Earl squeals.

She's a skull! Her face is a skull and the light bulb is going back and forth and everybody's screaming and the music is going eek! eek! eek!

A beat.

SMOLOWITZ: Why was her face a skull?

SCOTT *(Exasperated)*: She was a skeleton! Her son Anthony Perkins goes nuts when she dies and keeps her in the house so she rots and shrivels up.

SMOLOWITZ: Does she smell?

SCOTT: I don't know. Probably. *(Refers to the dead bird)* Wow look at the bugs going at it now. The thing's rotting up. You leave meat out in the air, it rots. Like once my mom?

SMOLOWITZ: Yes . . . ?

SCOTT: She was cooking franks and a frank fell behind the stove?

SMOLOWITZ: Yes . . . ?

SCOTT: A long time went by and there was this funny smell in the kitchen every time you walked in.

SMOLOWITZ: Ich.

SCOTT: She didn't know where it was coming from. My mom, she washed the floor, she washed under the refrigerator like where the blood drips down?

SMOLOWITZ: Yes . . . ?

SCOTT: It still smelled, though. We even ate out pizza, it got so bad. Then I said, Mom, remember the frank that fell that time? And she said, Oh my God! And my dad moved the stove. There it was on the floor. This frank. With hair on it? And dirt?

SMOLOWITZ: Ich.

SCOTT: It looked like a rotten dick.

He and Smolowitz laugh. Scott suddenly snatches up the dead bird and chases Little Earl who shrieks gleefully.

LITTLE EARL: AHHHHHHHH!!!!!!!

SMOLOWITZ *(During the above action)*: Scott! Put it down! Sc-o-ott . . . !

SCOTT *(Overlap)*: AHHHH!! Watch out Little Earl!!—

SMOLOWITZ: Sc-o-ott! *Please?!*

SCOTT: —The bird's gonna contaminate you with death!! AHHH!!

Little Earl runs shrieking, up the ramp and out of the yard. A beat. Scott looks at the distressed Smolowitz, forces a laugh to make light of what he did.

Watch the birdie, Smolowitz. *(He tosses the bird into the air, it lands on the Skelly court)* Ooops.

SMOLOWITZ: Very smart, Scott.

SCOTT: Come on, I'm playing. *(A beat. A giggle. He starts to exit via the ramp)*

SMOLOWITZ *(Suddenly panicked that Scott is leaving)*: Where you going?

SCOTT: I'm gonna go see if my dad's up.

SMOLOWITZ: Wait till Mike gets back? Please? I have to stay and watch the bird . . .

SCOTT: What's the matter?, you scared to be by yourself? *(Deliberately ominous)* Don't be scared . . .

A beat. Scott laughs diabolically. Meanwhile, Little Earl stands at the foot of the ramp flirting with Scott.

Is that you, Little Earl? Hm? Hm? Is that you?

Scott chases after Little Earl, who is giggling. They exit.

SMOLOWITZ *(As Scott exits)*: No! Scott, wait! *(To himself)* Oh, God. . . . What if they come? *(He sighs, looks around nervously, then uncomfortably stands guard over the dead bird. He thinks he hears a sound and darts a glance to the ramp)* Uh-oh . . . *(No one is there. He's frightened. Soon he begins to sing "Found a Peanut" —sung to the tune of "My Darling Clementine"—the first stanza of which is barely audible)*

Found a peanut, found a peanut,
Found a peanut last night,
Last night, I found a peanut,
Found a peanut last night.

(Gradually becoming louder. During the song, Smolowitz, re-pulsed by the bird, figures out a way to return it to the weeded area without touching it with his hands)

It was rotten, it was rotten,
It was rotten last night,
Last night it was rotten,
It was rotten last night.

(A beat)

Ate it anyway, ate it anyway,
Ate it anyway last night,
Last night I ate it anyway,
Ate it anyway last night.

(He picks up a skate and one of the dinosaurs and approaches the dead bird)

Got a bellyache, got a bellyache,
Got a bellyache last night,
Last night I got a bellyache,
Got a bellyache last night.

(He picks up the bird with the skate and dinosaur and, while holding his breath, drops the bird in the dirt. He composes himself before resuming the song)

When to heaven, went to heaven,
Went to heaven last night,
Last night I went to heaven,
Went to—

During Smolowitz's song, Melody, closely followed by Little Earl, appears at the top of the ramp eating an ice cream pop. She sees Smolowitz and laughs mockingly; Smolowitz stops singing mid-

verse, darts a frightened glance in her direction and is ultimately embarrassed at being discovered in a private moment. Joanie enters, messily eating ice cream.

JOANIE *(Entering)*: Melody, I don't *want* to play "Slave"!

LITTLE EARL *(Overlap)*: Gimme a bite?

JOANIE *(Overlap)*: I'm always the slave. I don't want to be the slave! I want to be the master if we're gonna play "Slave"!

LITTLE EARL *(Overlap)*: Gimme a bite?

MELODY: Gimme a bite *what*?

LITTLE EARL: Gimme a bite, Melody.

MELODY: Drop dead.

Melody runs down the ramp to the weeded area; the others follow.

LITTLE EARL: Joanie, let me have a bite.

JOANIE: Let me have a bite *what*?

LITTLE EARL: Let me have a bite pleeasse.

JOANIE: No. *(She giggles mischievously)*

SMOLOWITZ: Excuse me, you kids better move. You're too close to the bird.

MELODY: So?

SMOLOWITZ: So, you might step on it.

MELODY: God, Jeffrey, mind your own business.

SMOLOWITZ: Mike'll be mad if you squish it.

Joanie, meanwhile, is taunting Little Earl with her ice cream.

JOANIE *(Overlap)*: Melody, watch . . .

MELODY: You're such a stupid jerk, Jeffrey.

SMOLOWITZ: Oh, great.

JOANIE: Why can't we play "Mommies"?

MELODY: I hate playing "Mommies."

SMOLOWITZ *(Demonstrating)*: Just move over here, everything'll be great.

MELODY *(Overlap; to Joanie)*: Let's play "School."

JOANIE *(Woefully)*: I don't want to *play* school. Tomorrow's school.

LITTLE EARL: Let's play "Monster"!

MELODY *(Disapprovingly)*: "*Mon*ster"?

SMOLOWITZ: If anything happens to that bird, Melody . . .

MELODY: Why are you talking to me? Hm? What about him? What about her? *You* were the one playing.

SMOLOWITZ: You're right, Melody. I shouldn't play here and you shouldn't play here either. Let's go over there and play.

MELODY: You're not playing with us.

SMOLOWITZ: I know. I don't want to play with you. You're little.

LITTLE EARL *(Overlap)*: Please please please, Joanie. . . . Please?

MELODY: Joanie, let him have.

JOANIE: No, *you*.

MELODY: He's just a little boy, come on, give him. You're so fat, you shouldn't eat any at all.

Joanie's face flushes. Melody and Little Earl laugh. Joanie struggles to keep her melting ice cream from dripping down her hand.

MELODY: Ich, look what she's doing . . .

JOANIE: You better eat yours before yours drips on *you*.

MELODY: How dare you talk to me like that, young lady.

JOANIE *(Offering the ice cream)*: Take some, Little Earl. . . . It's dripping anyway.

He bites the whole pop.

Hey! Not so big! God, Little Earl! I didn't say eat the whole thing!

Little Earl has ice cream all over his face.

MELODY *(Laughing)*: Look at you, Earl. Joanie, look what a disgusting mess.

Little Earl beams at all the attention he's getting. During the above, Ernie and Shane enter through a hole in the rusty fence.

ERNIE: Hey. Any you seen Jay?

SHANE: We're looking for Jay.

ERNIE: What about that kid Scott?

SMOLOWITZ: Nobody's here.

ERNIE: Nobody's here? What you doing, Smolowitz? Bouncy ball?

Smolowitz, frozen in fear, doesn't respond.

SHANE: My brother axed you something. Faggot.

ERNIE: You playing ball, Smolowitz?

No response.

Must be deaf.

SHANE *(Screams into Smolowitz's ear)*: DEAF, SMOLOWITZ?! *(He convulses with laughter)*

ERNIE: Let's see how you bounce a ball. You know how he bounces a ball?

SHANE: Like a girl.

ERNIE: Bet you girls bounce a ball better than him.

SHANE *(Laughing, refers to Joanie)*: Look at the fat one with the ice cream on her.

ERNIE: Give me the ball, Smolowitz.

SHANE: You want his "ball"?

ERNIE: Yeah, let me play with your "ball," Smolowitz.

Shane is beside himself with laughter.

Give you a free lesson how to bounce a ball. Give me, I'll show you.

Smolowitz stands silently.

You hear what I said? Free. Won't cost you.

Still, no response.

You're a dumber Jew than I thought. Your old man'll slap your ass passing up something free. Give me the ball.

SHANE: What you got, Smolowitz?, a Spal*deen*?

ERNIE: Nah, it's got to be a Pensy Pinky.

SHANE *(Looks at the ball)*: Yeah it is! *(Laughter)*

ERNIE: Use a faggot ball, play like a faggot.

SHANE: Pensy Pinky . . . shit . . .

ERNIE: You can keep your Pensy Pinky.

Shane pushes the ball at Smolowitz, who takes it back.

SHANE: Yeah we don't want your Pensy Pinky.

ERNIE *(Beginning to exit)*: So what about you girls? You seen Jay?

Joanie shakes her head timidly.

MELODY *(Very softly)*: No.

ERNIE *(Not having heard her)*: Jesus you kids wear me out, can't I get a straight answer out of you?!

MELODY *(Overlap)*: I said, "No."

ERNIE *(Testily)*: Oh.

SHANE *(Meaning Joanie, who is blushing in fear)*: Look at that girl. I don't believe her face.

ERNIE *(Overlap; spotting Little Earl)*: Hey. You're the little brother, ain't you?

LITTLE EARL: Yeah.

ERNIE: Where is he?

LITTLE EARL: The movies.

ERNIE *(Charmed)*: The movies? *(He squats beside Little Earl)*

LITTLE EARL: My father took him Radio City.

SHANE: Coward. Going to the movies with his father . . .

ERNIE *(Overlap; meaning Little Earl)*: This kid cracks me up, he's so fucking cute.

Shane playfully wrestles with Little Earl for Ernie's benefit; Little Earl is beaming.

SHANE *(While wrestling)*: You think you're so cute, hm? You think you're so cute?

LITTLE EARL *(Showing off his dinosaurs)*: Look what I got.

ERNIE: What you got?

LITTLE EARL: Dinosaurs.

ERNIE *(Takes the toy from him, looks it over)*: Wow. Dinosaurs.

LITTLE EARL: Tyrannosaurus.

ERNIE: Tyrannosaurus *Rex*.

Shane laughs.

Where'd you get it?

LITTLE EARL: My father. I'm this guy and you're this guy.

They play for a moment, making dinosaur sounds. Then Shane forces Little Earl to face Joanie.

SHANE *(Awkwardly holding Earl's head)*: Hey, you see that girl over there? Look at her belly.

LITTLE EARL: I know. She's fat.

SHANE: You hear that? This kid is great.

ERNIE: Leave him alone. Let go of him.

Ernie pulls Little Earl out of Shane's clutches.

SHANE: I'm fooling around with him.

ERNIE *(Overlap)*: I don't want to hang around here with these little kids all day, all right?

SHANE: Doesn't that kid crack you up?

ERNIE: Yeah.

SHANE: So fucking cute.

ERNIE: Smolowitz, I got a message you give to Jay, y'hear?

SMOLOWITZ: Yes . . . ? *(He's blinking his eyes out of nervousness)*

ERNIE: Tell him school has nothing to do with intelligence. Tell him that.

SMOLOWITZ: I will.

ERNIE: Fuck that dogshit. Tell him I don't want none of his remarks.

SMOLOWITZ: I will.

ERNIE: I.G.C. means shit to me. *(Ernie blinks his eyes in imitation of Smolowitz)*

SMOLOWITZ: I'll tell him.

A beat. They start to exit.

(Glibly) Goodbye.

Ernie and Shane run back and corner Smolowitz.

ERNIE: You in a hurry for us to go or something?

SMOLOWITZ: No.

ERNIE: Huh?

SMOLOWITZ: Un-uh.

ERNIE: Don't open a mouth like that to me.

SHANE: Yeah.

Ernie threatens Smolowitz with his fist.

ERNIE: Smart aleck. I'll knock out your *teeth* you talk to me like that, y'hear me?

SMOLOWITZ: Yes.

ERNIE: Nobody cares how smart you are, Shmaltzenstein.

SHANE: Brain-o.

Ernie, annoyed with Shane, hits his shoulder; Shane, in turn, hits Smolowitz's.

ERNIE: We'll go when we feel like. You understand?

Pause. Ernie and Shane glare menacingly at Smolowitz.

Let's go.

SHANE: Wave bye-bye, Smolowitz.

A beat. They start to exit in the direction of the fence. Shane suddenly pokes Smolowitz in his stomach and grabs the ball.

(To Ernie) SALOOGIE!!

Laughing, Shane throws the ball to Ernie. Smolowitz, depressed, watches them as they exit through the fence.

SMOLOWITZ: HEY! Dibs on the ball! Hey, please?! Give it back! *(He looks off at them, his frustration building to rage)*

LITTLE EARL *(Runs to the fence, watches Ernie and Shane go)*: Be your best friend!

JOANIE: Those boys are so mean! I hate them!

Smolowitz suddenly screams but Ernie and Shane are too far away to hear him.

SMOLOWITZ: YOU'RE MEAN!! YOU'RE OBNOXIOUS!!!

During the above, Mike comes down the ramp. He's holding a cigar box.

MIKE: Who's obnoxious?

SMOLOWITZ *(Furious)*: What took you so long?

MELODY: Mike! Mike! Ernie and Shane!

SMOLOWITZ: I'm standing here watching this stupid bird for you.

MIKE: Thank you, Jeffrey.

MELODY: Ernie and Shane took Jeffrey's ball.

SMOLOWITZ: Stole it.

MIKE: What did they want?

SMOLOWITZ: Looking for stupid Jay.

MIKE *(Overlap)*: Are you okay, Melody?

Joanie is disappointed Mike didn't ask after her.

MELODY: Joanie's mother said you should keep an eye on us.

LITTLE EARL: Mike . . .

MIKE: *I* should?

JOANIE: My mother said.

LITTLE EARL: Mike, you have to watch *me*!

MIKE *(Ignoring Little Earl)*: That's not fair. I can't keep an eye on you and Joanie.

LITTLE EARL: You have to watch me, too.

MIKE: I'm busy, Melody.

MELODY: We'll be good.

JOANIE *(Chiming in)*: We'll be good.

MIKE: Go play where I can see you. Play over there.

They gradually move to a corner of the yard and play together. Little Earl plays alone, putting his dinosaurs into the fence.

SMOLOWITZ: If I didn't have to stand here and watch your stupid dead bird . . .

MIKE: My mother wouldn't give me a box so I had to empty out my baseball cards, do you mind?

SMOLOWITZ: I was practicing. . . . Now I'll never learn . . .

MIKE *(Takes tablespoons from his back pocket)*: Look: I remembered spoons.

SMOLOWITZ: What for?

MIKE: To dig.

SMOLOWITZ: We have to dig in the dirt?

MIKE: Come on, Jeffrey, use your brain . . .

SMOLOWITZ: I can't get dirty. These are school pants.

MIKE: They don't look like school pants.

SMOLOWITZ: Well, they are.

MIKE: So if they get dirty your mother'll wash them. Jeffrey, take a spoon and help?

SMOLOWITZ *(Woefully)*: Oh my ball. . . . I just bought that ball. . . . I want it back!

MIKE: So go ask them for it.

SMOLOWITZ: Ernie and Shane? Are you kidding? *(Pause. He suddenly yells in Ernie and Shane's direction)* FUCK!!

MIKE *(Amused)*: Jeffrey . . . *(He has begun to prepare the box for the bird's burial by placing weeds inside)*

MELODY *(Approaching)*: Mike, what are you doing?, burying the bird?

Joanie and Little Earl follow.

MIKE: Yes please don't breathe down my neck? Jeffrey, pull those weeds? We have to make room.

Smolowitz does so, gingerly, to avoid messing his clothes.

LITTLE EARL *(To Melody)*: The bird's gonna go in there?

MELODY: Uh-huh.

LITTLE EARL: What's the stuff in it for?

MELODY: It's like a little bed.

LITTLE EARL: Oh.

MELODY: Right, Mike?

MIKE: Yeah Melody why don't you kids give us a little room. *(He lifts Little Earl's hands out of his way)*

LITTLE EARL: Mike, I'm helping.

MIKE: Don't.

LITTLE EARL: God!

Little Earl walks away, dejected, as Smolowitz pulls a stick out of the ground.

MIKE: No, leave the Popsicle stick.

SMOLOWITZ: Why?, it's garbage.

MIKE *(Replacing the stick)*: No, that's where my turtle is.

SMOLOWITZ: Oh. *(He aggressively tugs at weeds)*

MIKE: Easy. Why you in such a hurry all of a sudden?

SMOLOWITZ: I don't want to do this all day. I want to play! Before you know it, it's gonna be bedtime and we're gonna have to go to sleep and when we wake up the summer'll be over and we'll have to get dressed for school.

JOANIE *(To Melody)*: I don't want to go to school.

MELODY: Me neither but we have to.

JOANIE: Why? I don't understand that.

Mike and Smolowitz begin to dig.

MELODY: Those are our spoons! Does Mommy know you took our spoons?

MIKE: Melody do you want me to hurt you very badly?

SMOLOWITZ: How deep does it have to be?

MIKE: Just dig, Smolowitz, and stop being such a pain in the ass.

MELODY: Mike said "ass"!

Melody and the younger children titter.

SMOLOWITZ *(Overlap)*: If that's the way you're gonna be, I don't have to help you at all . . .

MIKE: Smolowitz . . . Jeffrey. . . . Come here . . .

SMOLOWITZ *(Overlap)*: Sometimes you treat me just like Ernie and Shane and Jay and Scott and everybody else . . .

MELODY *(During the above; playing with a spoon)*: Mike, I'll dig. Jeffrey says he's not gonna.

MIKE: He's gonna.

SMOLOWITZ: You just want me to do the dirty work.

MIKE: I'm digging too, aren't I? Hm? If we both dig, it'll go faster.

A beat.

SMOLOWITZ: Okay but I can't get dirty.

JOANIE *(Beckons)*: Melody . . .

SMOLOWITZ: This isn't funny.

Smolowitz and Mike are digging. Melody comes closer to Joanie, who covers her mouth and whispers in Melody's ear.

MELODY: I can't hear you; you're too close.

SMOLOWITZ: Ich, it's muddy . . .

MIKE: You're doing good.

MELODY: Ask him yourself.

SMOLOWITZ: Oh no look at my pants.

MIKE: Forget it.

MELODY: You want *me* to?

Joanie nods.

Mike?

Melody pushes Joanie forward, putting her on the spot. She giggles.

Joanie wants to ask you something.

MIKE: What.

MELODY *(To Joanie)*: Ask him.

JOANIE *(With difficulty)*: Mike? Melody said when you were our age you had Mrs. Appelbaum, right?

MIKE: Yes, Joanie.

JOANIE: Was she good or bad?

MIKE: She was okay.

JOANIE: I heard she yells.

MIKE: She likes good hygiene. There's a chart at the back of the room she checks things off. Like, are your nails clean?, when was the last time you used Q-tips . . . stuff like that. For boys, white shirts for assembly or *then* she yells.

JOANIE: Oh no.

MIKE: Don't worry. How's your penmanship?

JOANIE: Ugh not so good.

MIKE: There you better watch out. She's not like Mrs. Kantor. Mrs. Kantor didn't care *how* you wrote.

JOANIE: Do you have good penmanship?

MIKE: Yes, Joanie, I do.

JOANIE: Oh God.

MIKE: Jeffrey, we hit a rock.

MELODY: My penmanship is good.

SMOLOWITZ: I don't think it's a rock. Feel it? It's soft.

MIKE: Yeah it is.

MELODY: Maybe you hit China!

MIKE: It's a bag.

MELODY: Buried treasure!

Melody and Joanie giggle.

MIKE: It's a paper bag. Let's dig it out.

They dig vigorously.

Don't rip it.

SMOLOWITZ: I'm trying. The bag says something.

MELODY: Ooo!

SMOLOWITZ: Can you read it?, "something-VEL?"

MIKE *(Reading the bag)*: "Car-VEL." Carvel.

MELODY: Oh! Ice cream!

The younger children laugh.

MIKE: Melody . . .

MELODY *(Justifying her remark)*: It says.

SMOLOWITZ: Maybe it's garbage. Maybe we should leave it alone. Maybe there's something dead in it.

A beat.

MIKE: You think so?

SMOLOWITZ: Who knows, Mike, just leave it.

JOANIE: Open it!

MELODY: Open it!

LITTLE EARL: Open it!

SMOLOWITZ: There could be something in it disgusting.

MELODY: Urine!

MIKE: Melody. . . . What if there *is* something dead in it?

JOANIE: When my grandmother died?

MIKE: What?

JOANIE: When my grandmother died?

MIKE: Yeah . . . ?

JOANIE: I touched her hand.

MELODY: You have a grandmother who died?

JOANIE: Uh-huh.

MELODY: How many grandparents do you have?

JOANIE: Three.

MELODY: Wow. I have four.

MIKE: So . . . ?

JOANIE: When nobody was looking I touched her hand.

MELODY: You touched her?

JOANIE: Uh-huh.

MELODY: Where?

JOANIE: In her coffin. On her veins.

MELODY: Ich, you touched your grandmother on her veins when
   she was dead and you weren't scared?

Joanie shakes her head.

MIKE: So . . . ?

MELODY: What did it feel like?

JOANIE: Like . . . *(She thinks a moment)* It felt like chicken roll.

MIKE: So? So, Joanie?

JOANIE: So, you want me to open the bag?

MIKE: You?

JOANIE: I will if you want me to. . . . I mean, I don't care . . .

MIKE *(Overlap)*: But you're just a little girl, Joanie, why would
   you want to open the bag?

Joanie shrugs nonchalantly.

SMOLOWITZ: If she wants to, let her.

MIKE: I'm supposed to be keeping an eye on her. She's just a little
   girl.

SMOLOWITZ: Well, then maybe we should get Scott.

MIKE *(Outraged)*: Why Scott?!, Smolowitz?, *I'm* here.

SMOLOWITZ: Because, I don't know, he's bigger, older . . .

MIKE: Big deal, a year!

JOANIE: I'll do it.

SMOLOWITZ: Scott would just do it.

MELODY: Yeah.

Mike glares at Melody.

MIKE: God, Smolowitz, you're always running to Scott . . .

SMOLOWITZ: Scott wouldn't be scared.

MIKE: Who said I'm scared?!

JOANIE *(Overlap)*: I'm not scared . . .

SMOLOWITZ *(To Mike)*: Then open it!

MIKE: OKAY!! *(He tentatively moves toward opening the bag but loses courage)*

SMOLOWITZ: Melody, better go find Scott.

MIKE: No!

SMOLOWITZ: Go see if he's in front.

Melody starts for the ramp.

MIKE: Melody, no! Don't boss my sister around, Smolowitz, she's *my* sister! Who do you think you *are*?!

MELODY *(Overlap)*: Yeah, Smolowitz . . .

MIKE: How would you like it if I did something like that if *you* had a sister *or* a brother.

SMOLOWITZ *(Overlap)*: Okay, okay, I'm sorry, I'm sorry . . .

LITTLE EARL *(Teasing)*: Mike, I'm gonna get Scott.

MIKE: You're staying right here. Forget about Scott. We don't need Scott.

Wincing, Mike snatches up the bag. The others are rapt in antici-pation. Joanie, giggling with excitement, covers her mouth with her hand. Mike takes a deep breath, then using just the tips of his fingers, peels open the bag. As he looks into the bag, his mouth drops open in amazement.

Ho-ly shit!

SMOLOWITZ: What?!
MELODY *(Overlap)*: What! What!

Joanie is jumping up and down.

MIKE: Money!
SMOLOWITZ: What?!
MIKE: Money!

Mike pulls a rolled wad of money out of the bag; the others gasp and squeal.

MELODY: Money!
JOANIE: Ooooooo!
LITTLE EARL: Money money money!
SMOLOWITZ: Wow!

Mike pulls another roll of bills from the bag. Smolowitz claps his hands, the others giggle and jump with glee.

MELODY: Mike, my brother, I love you! We're rich!!
LITTLE EARL: We're rich! We're rich!
MIKE *(Overlap)*: I do not be*lieve* this! There must be hundreds!
MELODY: Ooo!
SMOLOWITZ: Count it!
MELODY: Yeah, Mike, count it!

All, except Smolowitz, excitedly sit on the pavement as Mike begins to count the money.

MIKE: One, two, three, four, five, six, and five . . .
SMOLOWITZ: Eleven.
MIKE: And five . . .
SMOLOWITZ: Sixteen.
MIKE: And five. . . . Twenty-one.
SMOLOWITZ *(Overlap)*: Twenty-one.
MIKE: And five. . . . Twenty . . .
SMOLOWITZ: Six.
MIKE: I know. And ten.
SMOLOWITZ: Thirty-one.

MIKE: *Ten.* Thirty-six.

SMOLOWITZ: Thirty-six.

MELODY: Wow! Thirty-six!

MIKE: And . . . *(He removes the rubber band from the second wad of bills and counts)* One, two three, four, five, six, seven, and five. . . . Seven and five is . . .

SMOLOWITZ: Thirteen. Twelve.

MIKE: Which is it?

SMOLOWITZ: Twelve.

MIKE: And five . . .

SMOLOWITZ: Seventeen.

MIKE: And five, ten, fifteen . . .

SMOLOWITZ: Seventeen and fifteen?

MIKE: Yeah, you should know that.

SMOLOWITZ: Seventeen and fifteen is . . . seventeen plus fifteen equals. . . . Wait, twenty . . . thirty-two.

MIKE: Okay, so thirty-two dollars and thirty-six dollars is . . . sixty-eight dollars!

SMOLOWITZ *(Overlap)*: Sixty-eight!

MELODY: Wow! Sixty-eight dollars!

Ad lib celebration which quickly dies down. A beat.

SMOLOWITZ: It looked like more.

MIKE: Yeah, it did.

SMOLOWITZ: It's still a lot, though.

MIKE: Oh, yeah, are you kidding? Sixty-eight dollars? You know how much money that is? That's a lot.

SMOLOWITZ: What are we gonna do with it?

MIKE: What do you think? Keep it.

SMOLOWITZ: And do what?

MIKE: What do people do with money, Jeffrey?, use your brain. Spend it.

MELODY: Yeah!

SMOLOWITZ: Like on what?

MIKE: Like, you know what I could do? I could go into Jack's, buy every single comic . . .

LITTLE EARL: I want a Humorette.

MIKE: . . . double issues, superhero annuals . . .

LITTLE EARL: I want my own.

MIKE: . . . pile 'em up in my room, I wouldn't have to go next door anymore!

JOANIE: I want Chatty Cathy 'cause I love her . . .

MELODY *(To Joanie)*: I want Mister Machine. I don't care what my mother says, I want him. More and more.

MIKE *(Overlap, to Smolowitz)*: Or you could buy out all the baseball cards!

SMOLOWITZ: I don't care about baseball cards, or . . .

MIKE: Well, some of us do, Smolowitz. You could buy yourself a new ball. Don't you want a new ball?

SMOLOWITZ: Yeah, but that's twenty-five cents, so what? What would I do with the rest? Save it?

MIKE: If you want.

SMOLOWITZ: For college?

JOANIE *(To Melody)*: You know what I would do? I would buy a teacher to come over to my house.

MELODY: Yeah!

MIKE *(To Smolowitz)*: How about you could buy pants for school?

SMOLOWITZ: My mother gets me pants.

JOANIE: Wouldn't that be great?

JOANIE AND MELODY: We wouldn't have to go to school!!

MIKE: Melody, go over there. I can't hear myself think. This is just between me and Jeffrey Smolowitz.

MELODY: No, we want to play with the money, too.

MIKE: You can't. You're too young.

SMOLOWITZ: Maybe we should tell our mothers.

MIKE: Why?! This has nothing to do with mothers, Smolowitz.

MELODY: I'll go tell Mommy.

She starts for the ramp, Mike follows her.

MIKE: No! Melody, this is none of Mommy's business.

MELODY: I'm tell-ing . . .

MIKE: Melody . . . if I give you a dollar, will you promise not to tell Mommy?

She stops. A beat.

MELODY *(As if saying, "What a good idea")*: Yeah.

Mike gives her a dollar bill.

MIKE: Now go over there and leave me and Jeffrey alone.

SMOLOWITZ: Mike, I got this feeling maybe we should've left it in the hole.

MELODY: Gimme a dollar first.

MIKE: I just gave you!

MELODY: That was for not telling Mommy. This is for playing.

MIKE: God . . . *(He gives her another dollar. To Little Earl, who awaits a dollar)* Go!

Melody leads Little Earl and Joanie to another part of the yard where they inaudibly continue talking about their individual plans for the money; eventually they engage in ad libbed games.

SMOLOWITZ: Mike, I think we should've left it in the hole.

MIKE: Why?

SMOLOWITZ: Well, do you think it's stolen or something? How did it get there anyway?

A beat.

MIKE: Oh God, you know what . . . ?

SMOLOWITZ: What?

MIKE: *I* know what it is.

SMOLOWITZ: *What?*

MIKE: Mr. Schuster.

SMOLOWITZ: What?

MIKE: Remember what Scott said about Mr. Schuster and the money?

SMOLOWITZ: Yes . . . ?

MIKE: He dug a hole and put money in it on purpose 'cause he knew I would find it!

SMOLOWITZ: How would he know that *you* would find it?

MIKE: Because. 'Cause he knows where I bury things. I told him I put my turtle here and he said that was a great idea.

SMOLOWITZ: Mike, that doesn't make sense.

MIKE: Yes it does.

SMOLOWITZ: Is your name on the bag? No. Did he put a note in or something?

Mike checks.

No. So what makes you think it's yours?

MIKE: 'Cause I know Mr. Schuster. Why else would he put it in a hole right next to where I told him I buried my turtle, hm? 'Cause he knew sooner or later I would find it next time I had something to bury.

SMOLOWITZ: Yeah, but I found it, too, and I didn't even know the guy!

MIKE: That was a mistake. I was supposed to find it myself. You weren't supposed to be there.

SMOLOWITZ: You asked me to help you!

MIKE: I know. *(A beat)* You're absolutely right. *(He hands a dollar to Smolowitz)* Buy yourself a new ball. You can buy four with this.

SMOLOWITZ: I don't want a dollar.

MIKE: Take it, Jeff.

SMOLOWITZ: I want half! Half is mine!

MIKE: I'm sorry. I admit it was my mistake: It's not yours *and* mine, it's just mine. Take the dollar.

SMOLOWITZ: No!

MIKE: I thought you wanted a new ball.

SMOLOWITZ: It was supposed to be half and half!

MIKE: Who said?

SMOLOWITZ: Oh, come on, Mike . . .

MIKE: Look, I'm giving you a dollar. . . . If you don't want any money at all . . .

SMOLOWITZ: No, no, I didn't say that . . .

MIKE: . . . you don't have to have any.

SMOLOWITZ: Finders keepers. We both found it, we both keep it.

MIKE: But, Jeffrey, I have to have it. It was a surprise for me, something special for *me*. A present.

SMOLOWITZ: You're crazy, Mike.

MIKE: Shut up.

SMOLOWITZ: Now I'm really gonna tell Scott.

MIKE: What.

SMOLOWITZ: That you're selfish, that you took it all.

MIKE: But it's mine!

SMOLOWITZ: Are you gonna give me, or what?

MIKE: Who's holding it? Me. Whoever's holding it gets to keep it.

SMOLOWITZ *(Nearly frustrated to tears, makes a futile grab for the bag)*: Who says?!

Mike runs from Smolowitz.

MIKE: Baby Jeffrey.

SMOLOWITZ: Fine.

Smolowitz starts to exit via the ramp. Mike blocks him.

MIKE: Baby run to Scott.

SMOLOWITZ: Get out of my way!

MIKE *(A final plea)*: Jeffrey, please take the dollar . . . ?

SMOLOWITZ *(Overlap)*: Mike, let me go!

MIKE: Please, Jeffrey . . . ?

A beat. Smolowitz takes the dollar from Mike.

(Relieved) Good.

A beat. Smolowitz crumples the dollar.

Hey! What are you doing?!

Smolowitz throws the crumpled bill to the ground. Little Earl sees it and scurries to it; Melody briefly scuffles with him over the dollar but he holds onto it and goes off. Melody follows.

SMOLOWITZ *(During the above action)*: I don't want your little dollar.

MIKE: That's a dollar!

SMOLOWITZ *(Nearly trembling)*: I'm not stupid, you know. You can't treat me like one of the little kids. I'm just as smart as you. My reading level is *higher* than yours! I mean, come on, Mike, this isn't fair! I deserve more! *(Starts up the ramp)*

MIKE *(Following Smolowitz)*: That's right, Baby Jeffrey, run to Scott . . .

SMOLOWITZ: I thought we were getting to be friends!

Pause. The boys, both hyperventilating, are looking at one another. Suddenly, Mike shoves Smolowitz.

MELODY: Mike's fighting!

SMOLOWITZ *(On the verge of tears; quietly)*: I don't want to play with you *any*more.

Smolowitz runs up the ramp and exits. Mike takes a few steps after him.

MIKE *(Yelling at the top of his voice)*: GOOD!!

MELODY *(Sing-song)*: Ooo-ooo, Mike's in troub-le . . .

Mike runs back up the ramp and chases her.

MIKE: Melody, shut your mouth. What did you do with that dollar?

MELODY: What dollar?

MIKE: The one Jeffrey threw away.

Mike grabs Melody and tries to pry her fingers open.

MELODY: I don't have it! Little Earl took it!

MIKE: Open your hand!

Melody screams, opens her hand; there is no dollar bill. At this moment, Joanie notices Ernie and Shane approaching their side of the fence.

JOANIE *(Whispers)*: Ernie and Shane.

Mike releases Melody, turns and sees them.

ERNIE: What you doing?, beating up your baby sister?

MELODY: Yes. You hurt me, Michael.

MIKE: Shhh . . . *(He tries to conceal the money while Ernie and Shane approach)*

SHANE: You beat up girls?

ERNIE: Hey.

MIKE: What.

ERNIE: Where's the faggot was playing ball with himself?

MIKE: Jeffrey? Smolowitz?

ERNIE: Yeah.

Mike shrugs.

Borrowed his ball.

Ernie playfully grabs Little Earl, who's playing with the dollar bill he snatched earlier.

SHANE: Giving back his Pensy Pinky.

ERNIE *(To Little Earl)*: Hey, where'd you get that dollar?

JOANIE *(Warning)*: Little Earl . . .

MELODY: You know what Mike found?

MIKE *(Through gritted teeth)*: Melody, get out of here.

ERNIE: What you find, Mike?

MELODY: You hurt my hand, Michael.

MIKE: I'm sorry, now go in front, the three of you.

ERNIE: Your baby sister said you found something.

Joanie whispers in Melody's ear, prompting her.

MIKE: Go, Melody . . .

MELODY *(Suddenly)*: Mike found a dead bird. No, I found it.

MIKE: Melody . . .

Ernie presses Smolowitz's ball into the fence, where it remains for the rest of the play.

SHANE: Leave her alone, what you bossing her around for?

Ernie scares Joanie off, then whispers to Little Earl, who, grinning, exits.

MIKE: She's got to go in front. My mother's waiting for her there. Go ahead, Melody.

Mike and Melody exchange looks, then she runs off.

SHANE: You got her trained, hm?
MIKE: Yeah.
ERNIE: Hey. Jay back yet?

Mike shakes his head. He's trying to conceal the money from them.

Why you standing like that?
MIKE: Like what?
SHANE: What you holding? What's he got, brother?
ERNIE: Come here a minute.
MIKE: What?
SHANE: He said, come here.
ERNIE: Turn around, what you got in your hand?

Mike turns in a full circle, still trying to shield the money from their view.

SHANE: Looks like money.
ERNIE: You hiding money?
SHANE: That's what it looks like.
ERNIE: That your money, Mike?
MIKE: Uh-huh.
ERNIE: Where'd you get it?
MIKE: Somebody gave it to me.
SHANE: Bull*shit* somebody gave it.
ERNIE *(Climbing down the fence)*: Let's see.
SHANE *(Following Ernie)*: Yeah, show us what you got.

A beat. Mike smiles nervously, suddenly flaunts the money at them and runs out of the yard. Ernie and Shane dash after him.

ERNIE: Now he's dead!
SHANE: You hear that, Mike? You're dead!!

They're gone. The yard is empty for a beat, until Little Earl runs on from behind the ramp shrieking gleefully, proudly clutching his dollar bill. No one is there to share his excitement. He runs to the fence, looks out, but he doesn't see anyone. He runs to another part of the yard, but he can't see any of the other children from there either. A beat. He addresses the dead bird.

LITTLE EARL: Where'd everybody go, bird? Hm? *(Pause)* Where'd everybody go? *(He goes to the weeded area, kneels beside the bird)* They left you? Did they leave you home? You have to be by yourself now. Your daddy left and everybody left. You were bad. . . . They all went 'cause you were bad. You did something bad. You can do whatever you want now. Do you want a pillow? Hm? I'll make you a pillow. *(He looks around him, gathers some weeds and crumples his dollar bill to use as a pillow. He props the bird upon it, then sniffs his finger to see what a dead bird smells like. Then he puts one of his toy soldiers inside the box to keep the bird company and he leaves his dinosaurs nearby)* There. . . . This guy's a guard. *(He discovers an old book of matches in the weeds)* Oooo. . . . Look what *I* found! Matches! Oooo . . .

He tries to strike a match but it rips. Suddenly, Mike runs through the hole in the fence, breathless, sweaty, disheveled. Little Earl shoots to his feet the moment Mike enters.

Hi, Mike.

Mike, standing in a corner of the yard, tries catching his breath while reorganizing the money into all of his pockets; the moment Little Earl greets him, Mike furiously puts his finger to his mouth, indicating "Be quiet."

MIKE: Shhh!
LITTLE EARL *(Whispers)*: Hi.

Pause. Little Earl, feeling so privileged to be a part of this moment, continues looking at Mike, who is out of breath; he mimics Mike's panting. A beat.

You're sweaty.
MIKE: Shhh!

The money stashed in his pockets, Mike starts to leave cautiously. Little Earl follows.

LITTLE EARL: Whatcha doing? *(He pulls on Mike's shirt)* Do you want to play something?

MIKE: No.

LITTLE EARL: Can I come?

MIKE: No.

LITTLE EARL: Yes.

He tugs on Mike's shirt again, Mike pulls away.

MIKE: No.

LITTLE EARL: I'm coming with you.

MIKE: *No.*

Mike suddenly shoves Little Earl, who falls to the ground on his already bruised knee. Mike is regretful, but he must run. Little Earl, alone, gets up; his knee is smarting.

LITTLE EARL *(As if about to say something, but doesn't know what to say)*: Um . . . *(To his hurt knee)* Shut up.

Little Earl kneels again by the bird and throws handfuls of dirt into the box. He then successfully lights a match. His eyes widen as he looks at the flame. He throws the lit match onto the bird, lights another and does the same. He "peeps" with each throw of the match and repeats the action a few more times. Melody enters from behind the ramp, followed by Joanie.

MELODY *(Entering)*: Mike . . . ? Mike . . .

JOANIE: If we're gonna play "Monster" let's get it over with.

MELODY: You can't run from the monster if you're holding your doll.

JOANIE: Yes-yes.

MELODY: No-no. What if the monster's chasing you and you drop your doll?

JOANIE: I'm not gonna drop her.

MELODY: How do *you* know?

Joanie clutches her doll defiantly. Melody sees Little Earl playing with matches.

What are you doing, Little Earl? Are you trying to set that poor little dead bird on fire?

LITTLE EARL: No.

MELODY: Are you?

LITTLE EARL: No.

MELODY: Bad boy. We're gonna play "Monster." *(She pulls Little Earl to his feet)*

LITTLE EARL: We're playing "Monster"?

MELODY: Yes.

LITTLE EARL: Ooo, good.

MELODY *(Overlap)*: Lie down.

He does, on the Skelly court.

Okay. You're the monster. I'm the mad scientist.

JOANIE: Naturally.

MELODY: You can be the hunchback.

Melody prompts Joanie to bend over as if she has a hump; Joanie reluctantly complies.

JOANIE: I'm always the hunchback.

Little Earl, reveling in being the center of attention, is nearly hyperactive with excitement.

MELODY: Lie still, Little Earl.

JOANIE *(Straightening up)*: They're gonna get Mike, I think.

MELODY: Sssh. We are starting *now*.

Joanie resumes hunchback position.

Monster!

Melody lifts Little Earl's arms; he holds them straight out. Melody speaks in a make-believe voice.

I put you together . . . from dead people . . . pulled out their eyeballs . . .

JOANIE: Ich . . .

MELODY: . . . popped 'em in your head . . . scooped out the brains . . .

Little Earl grunts monstrously, Melody nudges him to play correctly.

. . . and zipped open your hair . . . and put all the gooey brains inside . . .

JOANIE: Uck. Melody . . .

Little Earl grunts gleefully. Joanie groans in mock disgust. Melody holds an imaginary glass.

MELODY: Okay, now here's the special monster drink I'm gonna give you to drink—

Little Earl jumps the gun and swallows his own imaginary potion.

No! You can't drink yours, you have to drink mine! Yours doesn't count!

JOANIE *(Overlap)*: Could we please do this already please.

Little Earl shrieks at Joanie.

MELODY: You're not the monster yet, Earl, only when you drink it!

JOANIE: So let him drink it already.

MELODY *(Exasperated)*: Okay! God!

LITTLE EARL: God!

MELODY: Drink this, Monster! *(Mimes sprinkling ingredients into drink)* Bit O' Honeys that fell in the dirt and you can't eat them anymore . . . and . . . bird doody . . . *dead* bird doody . . .

Little Earl howls with laughter; Joanie smiles despite her feigned disapproval.

. . . and broccoli . . .

JOANIE: Ick . . .

MELODY: . . . and . . . bugs in the bathtub . . . and keys . . . and no television . . . and going to bed early . . .

JOANIE *(Suddenly depressed)*: Oh no, school . . . *(She walks away from the game)*

MELODY: Where you going?

JOANIE: I don't want to play this.

MELODY: Joanie, I can't play just me and Little Earl. There's gotta be three.

LITTLE EARL *(Overlap)*: Joanie, play. . . . Joanie, come on, play.

JOANIE: I don't feel good.

MELODY *(Exasperated)*: What's the matter? You sick?

JOANIE *(Nods)*: Yes.

MELODY *(Goes to Joanie)*: God, Joanie. . . . All right, lie down. I'll take care of you.

LITTLE EARL: Let's play "*Mon*ster."

MELODY: Shhh . . . *(To Joanie)* Lie *down*.

Joanie does.

LITTLE EARL *(Pulls up Joanie's dress)*: Deedle deedle.

JOANIE: No deedle deedle. *(She slaps Little Earl)*

MELODY *(Perfunctorily)*: Okay, I'm the nurse. What's the matter, little girl?

JOANIE: I don't feel good.

MELODY: Where does it hurt?

JOANIE: Everywhere.

During the following, Melody tickles Joanie's underarms and stomach until Joanie writhes in pleasure, giggling.

MELODY: Does it hurt *here*?

JOANIE: Yes . . .

MELODY: Does it hurt *here*?

JOANIE: Yes . . .

MELODY: Does it hurt *here*?

JOANIE *(Convulsed with laughter)*: Yes . . .

MELODY: Okay, all better. Now, get over here.

Melody moves away to resume the game. Joanie remains reluctant.

You want to give him the drink?

Joanie shyly nods "yes."

Okay. You can give him the drink.

Melody mimes handing Joanie the drink; Joanie relishes being given the task.

Okay, Monster. . . . When I count to three, you drink this. . . . Before you turn into a monster, you have to give us time to hide first, okay?

Joanie hands the "cup" to Little Earl.

Okay?

Little Earl hits Melody.

Hey! No hitting! You're gonna get a good slap if you start hitting.

LITTLE EARL: You're not my *moth*er . . .

JOANIE *(To Little Earl)*: Hey! Bad!

MELODY: You better behave. *(She hands Little Earl the imaginary glass)* On your mark . . .

Melody and Joanie slowly walk backward away from Little Earl during the countdown.

. . . get set . . . and a-one Mississippi . . .

MELODY AND JOANIE: . . . two Mississippi . . .

JOANIE *(In defiance of Melody)*: . . . two and a *half* Mississippi . . .

Melody and Joanie, now several feet on either side of Little Earl, wait expectantly for the final count.

MELODY AND JOANIE: . . . *three!* Drink it!

Little Earl downs the imaginary potion; his gestures and growls become more monster-like. Melody and Joanie scramble about the yard in mock terror, shrieking.

MELODY: Oh, no, Joanie! Look! The monster's turning into the monster!

JOANIE: Oh, no!

Little Earl intentionally falls to the pavement and lies still for a beat. Joanie, perplexed, looks to Melody.

What?

Suddenly, Little Earl shrieks and jumps to his feet. The girls scream with delight as he chases them around and out of the yard as Scott and Smolowitz come down the ramp.

SMOLOWITZ *(Breathlessly, as they enter)*: . . . I found the money, Scott. *Me.*

SCOTT: Easy, Smolowitz, you're spitting on my cheek.

Smolowitz leads Scott to the weeded area as Little Earl runs back screaming and puts his hands around Scott's neck, pretending to choke him.

Hey! Big Earl!

LITTLE EARL: What.

SCOTT: Stop! *(He pulls Little Earl's hands away)*

LITTLE EARL: I'm the monster.

SCOTT: I don't care you're the monster, I got a headache from you . . .

Little Earl runs off again, in monstrous pursuit of Melody and Joanie. Smolowitz, meanwhile, has gingerly picked up the Carvel bag and shows it to Scott.

Mike is an idiot.

SMOLOWITZ: I like him.

SCOTT: Yeah, but this isn't smart, Smolowitz. This is not a bright thing.

SMOLOWITZ: What if Ernie and Shane get him? You know they took my ball?

SCOTT: Forget about your ball, Smolowitz. We're talking a potentially lot of money. We have to plan strategy.

SMOLOWITZ: I know. What?

SCOTT: There are decisions to be made, questions to be answered.

SMOLOWITZ: Like?

SCOTT: Like: Where's Mike.

SMOLOWITZ: Maybe he went up.

SCOTT: To his house?

SMOLOWITZ: Yes.

SCOTT: Why?

SMOLOWITZ: To hide the money?

SCOTT: Doubtful.

SMOLOWITZ: Why?

SCOTT: He wouldn't want his mother to find out.

SMOLOWITZ: What would you do?

SCOTT: Well, I wouldn't tell my mother. My dad? Maybe.

SMOLOWITZ: I wish Jay was here.

SCOTT: What?

SMOLOWITZ: Jay would know the right thing.

SCOTT: I know the right thing, Smolowitz. You better watch it, 'cause up against Ernie and Shane *or* Mike, even, I'm telling you, you need assistance. I'm bigger than you, Smolowitz.

SMOLOWITZ: I know . . .

SCOTT: I know how to handle these things. I'm older.

SMOLOWITZ: Big deal, a year.

SCOTT: All right, if you think you're so wise and you don't need me, great, 'cause I don't need you either, Smolowitz. *(He starts for the ramp)*

SMOLOWITZ *(Overlap)*: No, Scott . . .

Scott stops.

SCOTT: Okay, if I get your money, what'll you give me?

SMOLOWITZ: I have to give you something? I thought you were doing me a favor.

SCOTT: Un-uh, no favors. Are you kidding? What do you think I am, UNICEF?

SMOLOWITZ: What do you want?

SCOTT: What do you think? Some of the money. A percentage.

SMOLOWITZ: How big?

SCOTT: Fifty.

SMOLOWITZ: What!?

SCOTT: What do you think, Smolowitz, am I gonna risk my life if there's nothing in it for me? Think about it.

SMOLOWITZ: *Half* of my half?

SCOTT: You want help, yes or no?

SMOLOWITZ: Yes.

SCOTT: Then you got to pay, Jeff, this is life. I'm very sorry, life is hard.

SMOLOWITZ: Jay would do it for nothing.

SCOTT: Oh yeah? You don't know Jay like I do. He would not. Jay would take faster than anybody.

SMOLOWITZ: No he wouldn't . . .

SCOTT: Oh yes he would! I'm telling you, you don't know!

SMOLOWITZ: But, Scott, I'm the one who found it!

SCOTT: Yeah, and then you lost it, Jeff, you got to pay the price. Now: Do I get a percentage or what?

A beat. Smolowitz is mulling it over.

SMOLOWITZ: No.

Joanie, giggling uncontrollably, runs on; in pursuit is Little Earl, growling as the monster. He chases her around the yard. Joanie escapes; Little Earl exits after her.

SCOTT: I could go right now—by myself—find Mike, get the money, and you wouldn't even have to know about it, I wouldn't even have to tell you. Right? Couldn't I?

SMOLOWITZ: Yes . . .

SCOTT: But I say to myself, do I want to do that to Jeffrey Smolowitz?

A beat.

SMOLOWITZ: Do you?

SCOTT: I don't know, don't make me do this to you . . . *(Starting for the ramp)*

SMOLOWITZ *(Following)*: Scott, wait . . .

SCOTT: I'm offering my assistance . . .

SMOLOWITZ: Scott . . .

SCOTT *(Nearly up the ramp)*: Try this on your own and *you* know and *I* know you will die. See you in heaven, Smolowitz . . .

SMOLOWITZ: Wait . . .

SCOTT: I'm being honest with you. Believe me: I know.

SMOLOWITZ: You'll find Mike and get him to give me my money?

SCOTT: Uh-huh. Fifty-fifty, right?

SMOLOWITZ *(Resignedly)*: Yes.

A tin can is heard rolling, off.

Oh, God . . .

Scott panics for a beat, not knowing what to do.

(Whispers) Deal?

SCOTT: Deal.

Smolowitz hurries Scott along the side of the building; they hide by the ramp. In a beat, Mike runs into the yard from the alley, thinking he'll be able to get a moment's refuge while he catches his breath. But Scott sees him and, followed by Smolowitz, dashes from behind the ramp and grabs Mike.

Okay, Michael, this is the end . . .

SMOLOWITZ *(Overlap)*: Scott . . . don't hurt him . . .

MIKE *(Overlap)*: Let go of me . . .

SMOLOWITZ: Scott, you don't have to hurt him . . .

MIKE: You better let me go or Ernie and Shane are gonna get you, too.

SCOTT: Where's the money, Mike?

MIKE: Let me go, they're gonna come. I lost them in Waldbaum's.

SCOTT: That's where you ran?, you ran into Waldbaum's?

MIKE: Yeah. Down the aisles.

SCOTT: Smart, Rosen!

MIKE: I know. I lost them by the meat.

SCOTT: Smart.

MIKE: There was a line.

SCOTT: Very wise.

MIKE: They're gonna come . . .

SMOLOWITZ: God, maybe we should go up . . .

SCOTT: *Go* up, Smolowitz, I'm tired of hearing your voice. Your mother's waiting. *(Turns his back on Smolowitz)* You want my help, Mike?

MIKE: You'll help me?

SCOTT: Yeah. . . . Give me some of your money, I'll help you . . .

MIKE: Oh, I *see*!

SMOLOWITZ *(Overlap)*: Now wait a minute . . . *I* was giving you . . .

MIKE: What?

SCOTT: I'm not talking *yours*, Smolowitz, I'm talking *his*.

SMOLOWITZ: You can't take from both . . .

MIKE: Yeah, why should you get *any*?

SCOTT: I'm helping *you*, right? If I'm helping him, too, why shouldn't I get from *each*?

MIKE: No!

Mike tries to flee but Scott sits on him.

SMOLOWITZ: Oh, yeah? Well, you didn't *find* him . . .

SCOTT: What do you call *this*?

SMOLOWITZ: Yeah, but Mike *came*, you didn't *find* him . . .

SCOTT: I've *got* him . . .

SMOLOWITZ: He *came* . . . you didn't have to *look* . . . that was the deal.

SCOTT: Fuck you, I got him like I said. Who cares how?

Suddenly, the sound of a garbage can lid falling.

MIKE *(Whispers)*: That's them. . . . Thanks a lot, Scott . . .

SCOTT *(Whispers; overlap)*: Oh, shit, what do we do?

SMOLOWITZ: We should run!

As they agree to run, Little Earl runs through the hole in the fence making monster noises.

SCOTT: Jesus H. Christ, Little Earl, what the hell you doing?

LITTLE EARL *(Breaking character from the monster)*: Scott, what do you want from my life?

Scott suddenly pushes Little Earl to the ground, knocking the wind out of him, as Melody appears in the alley.

MELODY *(Taunting Little Earl)*: Nyah-nyah nyah-nyah-nyah . . .

But Little Earl is hurt and angry and isn't playing anymore. He gets up and exits through the fence. Melody follows him out, wondering if the game is still in progress.

Monster . . . ? *(She's gone)*

SCOTT: The mouth on that kid! Fuck him, fuck his brother.

MIKE: He's just a little kid.

SCOTT: I know he's a little kid, he still gives me a pain in the butt, all right?

SMOLOWITZ: Mike, why don't you just give me back my half? I'll forget the whole thing ever happened.

SCOTT *(Beckoning)*: Mike . . .

Mike and Smolowitz step closer.

Just Mike, Smolowitz. I have to talk to him. Why don't you stand guard by the fence?

SMOLOWITZ: Why me? Why don't you?

SCOTT: Because I'm asking you.

MIKE: Come on!

SMOLOWITZ: What do I do if I see them?

MIKE: You tell us.

Smolowitz tentatively walks toward the ramp and stops.

SMOLOWITZ: I'm gonna stand here.

SCOTT: Good. That's real good. *(Whispers to Mike)* Level with me, Mike: You got it on you?

MIKE *(Whispers)*: Un-uh. Scott, I'm not telling . . .

SCOTT: You can trust me. I'm not gonna tell anybody . . .

SMOLOWITZ: What are you talking about?

SCOTT: Don't worry about him. This is between you and me.

MIKE: Forget it . . .

SMOLOWITZ: Are you talking about me?

SCOTT *(Overlap)*: Hey, how am I gonna help you if you don't tell me what's what?

MIKE: Then don't help me.

Scott gets Mike in a headlock.

SCOTT: Hey . . . I'm your friend . . . I just want to point out to you . . . Ernie and Shane . . . and if you're in this by yourself . . .

MIKE: What do you want?

SCOTT: I'm not asking much . . . considering I'm saving your life . . .

MIKE: What.

Scott releases the lock but continues to hold him.

SCOTT: Honestly?

Mike nods wearily.

Half.

MIKE: No way!

SMOLOWITZ *(During the above; a warning)*: Shhh . . .

SCOTT: Is it them?

SMOLOWITZ: I don't know . . .

Mike tries to escape. Scott blocks him.

MIKE: Scott. . . . Get out of my way!

SCOTT: Tell me where it is, I'll stick up for you, Mike.

MIKE *(Teeth gritted)*: Get out of my way!!

Little Earl suddenly scrambles through the hole in the fence, leading the way for Ernie and Shane, who follow.

SMOLOWITZ *(During the above)*: Oh, God . . . *now* what?

Mike pulls himself from Scott's now-relaxed hold and makes no attempt to run.

ERNIE: Well, well, well. . . . Lookee who Little Earl brung us to.

Scott pushes Mike toward Ernie.

SCOTT: I kept him here for you.

Mike looks at Scott in disbelief.

ERNIE: So? You want a medal? *(To Little Earl, praising him)* What a good spy!

SHANE: Yeah, you did good, Little Earl.

Ernie approaches Mike.

ERNIE: How ya doin' there, Mike.

MIKE: Hi.

ERNIE: Long time no see.

MIKE: Yeah.

ERNIE: We come to collect our allowance.

SHANE: Yeah, Pop, give us our allowance. *(He laughs while roughing up Mike)*

MIKE: Too late.

ERNIE: What do you mean too late.

MIKE: I got rid of it.

SHANE: Bull. Shit.

SCOTT: You didn't get *rid* of it. . . . How come you were running if you got rid of it?

MIKE: I hid it somewhere.

SHANE: He's so fulla shit his eyes are brown.

ERNIE: Do we got to feel you up to check?

SCOTT *(To Ernie)*: I can talk to him, you want me to get it out of him?

MIKE: Fuck you, Scott.

LITTLE EARL: Fuck you, Scott.

Ernie and Shane laugh. Scott goes toward Little Earl with his fist raised.

SCOTT: I'm gonna kill that kid . . .

Ernie intercepts, protecting Little Earl; Scott backs off.

(Referring to Mike) You want me to give it a try? I got a *way* with him, y'know? I get him to talk, maybe we can work out a deal?

ERNIE: A *deal*? Who the fuck you think you're talking to? *(To Shane)* I do not *believe* this guy . . .

Ernie rolls his eyes. Shane pushes Scott. Ernie stands threateningly close to Mike.

Well . . . ? You gonna hand it over nice? Hm? Do we got to torture you, Mike? *Hm?*

Shane spots Melody watching the confrontation in the alley. She tries to get away but Shane goes after her.

SHANE: Lookee, it's Kid Sister . . .

Shane grabs Melody; she resists as he pulls her to the center of the yard.

MELODY *(Overlap)*: Get your hands off me . . .
MIKE *(Overlap)*: Hey, let go of her!
ERNIE: What you do with the money, Mike?
MIKE *(Overlap)*: Let go her arm!

Mike reaches out to help Melody. Shane hits Mike's hand.

MELODY: Mike, they're gonna hurt me . . .
SMOLOWITZ: Mike, you better tell them . . .
SHANE: She's gonna die you don't tell us . . . *(He pins Melody's arm behind her)*
MELODY *(Whining in fear)*: Mike . . . help me!
ERNIE *(Overlap; to Shane)*: Hey, easy . . .
SCOTT *(Overlap; to Mike)*: Are you gonna stand there like a stupid idiot?
MIKE *(Near tears; helpless)*: Help me!
ERNIE: You gonna talk, Mike? Or what?
MIKE *(Overlap; to Scott)*: You're the one's supposed to be in charge . . .

SCOTT: Not me, *Jay* is.

MIKE: Oh, *now* Jay is.

SCOTT: Don't give me this shit. She's *your* sister . . .

SMOLOWITZ *(Overlap)*: Mike . . . you have to tell them . . .

ERNIE *(Overlap)*: Jesus, is this gonna take all day?

SCOTT *(Overlap; to Mike)*: Tell them where the money is, Mike, they're gonna rip her arms out.

LITTLE EARL: Rip her arms out.

ERNIE: You're a great big brother, ain't ya?

MIKE *(Starts crying)*: It's not fair . . . I don't know what to do . . .

Shane and Ernie mock Mike.

SCOTT: You started this whole thing, now do something! STOP CRYING!

Scott punches Mike. Mike howls as they continue hitting each other.

ERNIE: Aw right! Fight!!

Ernie jumps into the fight and hits both Mike and Scott. Shane throws Melody into the scuffle and pandemonium ensues; he moves her arms so that she also strikes Mike.

SHANE: Hit him! See what he did to you?

Smolowitz stands clear of the fight but Little Earl throws handfuls of dirt on the others. Amid the melee Ernie discovers a dollar bill and picks it up.

ERNIE: He's got the money on him!

SHANE: Take off his pants!

Scott tries to help restrain Mike as Ernie attempts to pull down Mike's pants. Before Ernie can succeed, Mike, crying, pulls the money out of his pockets and tosses it into the air.

MIKE: HERE! TAKE IT!!

As all the kids except Mike and Smolowitz scramble for the money, Joanie enters the yard, thinking some kind of celebration is going on. Shane, exhilarated by the violence, sees her and wantonly turns on her.

SHANE *(Restraining Joanie)*: Hit her, Little Earl! Hit her!
JOANIE *(Screaming)*: No! Stop!
SMOLOWITZ: What are you doing?!
SHANE *(Overlap)*: Hit her in her tits, Little Earl!

Little Earl punches Joanie several times in her stomach as she screams.

Look at this, big brother!
LITTLE EARL: Ernie. . . . Look . . .

Little Earl continues to pummel Joanie. Smolowitz suddenly grabs his fists.

SMOLOWITZ: You can't *do* this! We *live* here! *(He throws Little Earl off Joanie)* Stop that! There's more money!

Shane goes after Smolowitz.

The guy who put the money?, there's more . . .

Shane grabs Smolowitz by his collar.

SHANE: Oh yeah, Smolowitz?
ERNIE *(Overlap)*: Let go of him. . . . Let him talk . . .

Shane continues to rough up Smolowitz.

Let *go* of him! Shane!

He slaps Shane on the back of his head. Shane reflexively punches Ernie.

SHANE: Watch it!

Ernie clutches his stomach. Shane, hyperventilating, his fist clenched, glares at Ernie. Ernie, saving face, returns to Smolowitz, hovering threateningly.

ERNIE: So how do you know?

SMOLOWITZ: That's what I heard. . . . The guy was crazy. . . . He put money all over the building. In the basement . . . in the incinerator room . . . the laundry room . . . the roof, too . . .

Ernie's considering it.

Come on. . . . It makes sense . . .

A beat.

ERNIE: If I don't find nothing . . .
SMOLOWITZ: You will.

A beat.

ERNIE *(To Shane)*: Let's go.

Ernie starts to exit to the basement, alongside the ramp. When he sees that Shane hasn't followed, he stops.

You coming or what?

A beat. Shane brandishes his fist at Smolowitz and starts to exit, not after Ernie but of his own volition, through the hole in the fence. Ernie is nonplussed for a beat. He hurries after Shane, trying to hide his humiliation from the others. They're gone. Little Earl rushes to the fence and calls.

LITTLE EARL: Ernie?, can I come?

Pause. The melee ended, all eyes turn to Joanie, lying on the pavement, shaken and crying.

MIKE *(Softly; his own face bloodied)*: Joanie?
JOANIE: No.
SMOLOWITZ: Are you all right, Joanie?

Joanie sits up but continues to hide her face with her doll. Pause.

MIKE: Melody, are you okay?
MELODY: I got four dollars. You're bleeding.
MIKE: Where?
MELODY: Your nose.
MIKE: Oh, no . . .

Little Earl starts to make his way tentatively across the yard. He looks at Joanie.

SMOLOWITZ: Stay away from her.

Little Earl looks to the others for comfort, but they're ungiving. Pause.

MELODY: Get out of here.
LITTLE EARL: Mike . . . *(He holds three dollars out to Mike)*
MIKE *(Turning away)*: No.

Little Earl, fighting back tears, drops the money and, with the others silently watching, retrieves his toy dinosaurs from the weeded area. He winds his way through the group and, when finally at the ramp, runs quickly out of the yard, home. Melody approaches Joanie, who still shields her tear-streaked face with her doll.

SCOTT: Hey, Mike?
MIKE: Leave me alone, Scott.

Melody touches Joanie

JOANIE: No!
MELODY: Are you gonna throw up?

Joanie shakes her head "no."

Mike, Joanie's gonna throw up.
JOANIE *(Starting to exit)*: No, I'm not.
MELODY: Wait. Stay. I'll take care of you. We'll play "Nurse."
JOANIE: No, Melody.
MELODY *(Following Joanie)*: You can be the nurse.
JOANIE: I'm going up.
MELODY: Don't! Please! We'll play whatever you want.
JOANIE: We can play "Mommies"?
MELODY *(Regretfully)*: I don't want to play "Mommies."
JOANIE: Then I'm going up . . . *(She continues to go)*
MELODY *(Suddenly panicked)*: Don't! Who am I going to play with? Joanie, I'm not gonna have anybody to play with!
JOANIE *(Stops for a beat)*: Tough.

Joanie turns and exits. During the above, Scott picks up the three dollar bills Little Earl had dropped. He silently offers the money to Mike who ignores the gesture. Scott contemplates what to do with the money for a beat, then nonchalantly pockets it. A beat after Joanie exits, we hear Mike and Melody's mother call from their apartment window, out of view.

MOTHER: Melody?

Smolowitz, Scott and Melody look up to the window. Mike's back is to the window, shielding his bloodied face.

MIKE: Oh, God, Melody, please please please don't tell Mommy what happened . . .

MOTHER: Melody . . .

MELODY *(Calls up to the window)*: Mommy?!

MOTHER: Melody, did you know you left your keys in the bathroom?

MELODY *(A beat)*: I did?

MOTHER: Mike . . .

MIKE: Yes?

MOTHER: Are you playing?

MIKE: YES!

MOTHER: Melody, didn't I tell you you have to get used to having your keys with you at all times?

Melody's keys, on a pink and white lanyard, come falling from the sky.

Now don't lose them ever again!

A beat. Mike goes to the lanyard, picks it up and hands it to Melody, who bursts into tears. A beat.

MELODY *(Hysterically)*: I DON'T WANT KEYS!! *(She runs up the ramp)*

MIKE *(Calls softly after her)*: Melody?

A beat.

SCOTT: Mike?

MIKE: What.

SCOTT: Too bad this had to happen.

MIKE: Yeah.

Mike is amused. He laughs and so does Smolowitz.

SCOTT: What's so funny?

MIKE: Nothing.

SMOLOWITZ: Nothing.

A beat. Mike walks away from Scott; Scott tags after him around the yard.

SCOTT: Hey, Mike? When Jay gets back?

MIKE: Yeah . . . ?

SCOTT: We could have a meeting if you want.

MIKE: Why, Scott?

SCOTT: I mean, if you want. When Jay's back, we could meet like right after supper.

MIKE *(Overlap)*: No, Scott, forget it. Tomorrow's school.

SCOTT: That's true. *(A beat)* So . . . I'll see you, I guess, in the morning.

MIKE: Yeah.

A beat.

SCOTT: Hey, we gotta have that game. How about tomorrow? We'll have Jay . . .

MIKE: I can't tomorrow. Today I could. Tomorrow I can't.

SCOTT: Well . . . see ya.

A beat.

MIKE: See ya.

Scott starts up the ramp, but stops to say goodbye to Smolowitz.

SCOTT: Bye, Jeffrey.

SMOLOWITZ *(Surprised by Scott's genuine acknowledgment)*: Bye, Scott.

Scott waves, exits. Pause. Mike is sitting in the dirt dazed, looking at the Carvel bag and holding back tears. Smolowitz approaches him, wants to comfort him but doesn't know how. He decides to leave Mike alone and heads for the ramp.

MIKE: God, I'm really bleeding, Jeffrey.

Smolowitz takes out his handkerchief and goes to Mike.

Do you think I should go to the hospital?

SMOLOWITZ: It's a nosebleed.

MIKE: Look at all this blood, oh, oh . . .

SMOLOWITZ *(Overlap)*: Put your head back. There was this kid in my class . . . ? *(He puts Mike's head back and gives Mike his handkerchief)*

MIKE: Ooo, I can taste the blood . . .

SMOLOWITZ: Just do it.

A beat. Mike checks the handkerchief for blood and sees that Smolowitz's technique is working.

MIKE: I don't want to go to school tomorrow.

SMOLOWITZ: I know . . .

MIKE: I hate first days . . .

SMOLOWITZ: Me, too . . .

MIKE: And my mother's going to work and I gotta go to Hebrew . . . and I can't go next door anymore . . .

He cries. Smolowitz gently touches Mike's head.

SMOLOWITZ: Don't cry.

MIKE: I hate line up.

SMOLOWITZ: I hate P.E.

MIKE: Oh, and what about the bird?

Smolowitz quickly shovels dirt onto the box. Mike joins him.

SMOLOWITZ: Hurry. They're gonna be back, you know.

MIKE: Why?

SMOLOWITZ: There's no more money. I just made it up.

MIKE: Yeah? You did?

SMOLOWITZ: Uh-huh.

MIKE: Very wise, Jeffrey.
SMOLOWITZ: Yeah? Thanks.

They share a laugh, like old friends.

MIKE: Come on. We'd better get out of here.

Mike hurriedly finishes the burial as Smolowitz stands and starts for the ramp. He spots his ball in the fence, where Ernie left it earlier.

SMOLOWITZ: Wow!
MIKE: What?

Smolowitz takes his ball out of the fence.

SMOLOWITZ: I don't believe it! My ball! It was here!
MIKE: Oh, yeah. They brought it back.
SMOLOWITZ: Isn't this great?

They start to go. Mike stops, puts the spoons in his pocket.

MIKE: Uh, Jeffrey . . . ?

Smolowitz looks at him. A beat.

You want to throw?
SMOLOWITZ: What?
MIKE: Throw.

A beat. Smolowitz tries to understand Mike's proposal.

SMOLOWITZ: You mean I should throw to you and then you'll throw to me?
MIKE: Yeah. We'll, *you* know, play catch. Okay? Throw.

Smolowitz self-consciously throws the ball to Mike, who catches it.

Not so hard.
SMOLOWITZ: Okay.

Mike starts up the ramp, throws the ball, Smolowitz misses it, goes after it.

(To himself) Oh shit . . . wait . . .

He and Mike share a laugh, then Smolowitz throws the ball and Mike catches it.

MIKE: Better. Watch.

He demonstrates his form in slow motion and throws the ball to Smolowitz, who catches it and is stunned.

Good catch, Jeffrey! Good catch!

Smolowitz, heading up the ramp, imitates Mike's slow-motion form and throws the ball. Lights begin to fade. Mike, now out of view, returns the ball to Smolowitz and he triumphantly catches it. As Smolowitz exits up the ramp and out of the yard—lights fade completely.

WHAT'S WRONG WITH THIS PICTURE?

□ □ □

"In this our life there are no beginnings but only
departures entitled beginnings . . . "

DELMORE SCHWARTZ,
"The World Is a Wedding"

"Hello, I must be going."

GROUCHO MARX

▢ ▢ ▢

CHARACTERS

ARTIE, 17
MORT, 40s, his father
BELLA, 70s, Mort's mother
SID, 70s, Mort's father
CEIL, 40s, Mort's sister
SHIRLEY, 40s, Artie's mother, Mort's wife

PLACE

A middle-class apartment in Brooklyn, New York.
Some years ago.

ACT ONE

At rise: a middle-class apartment in Brooklyn where shiva has taken place. As is the tradition in Jewish houses of mourning, mirrors are covered and the mourners—in this case, Artie and his father, Mort—are unshaven and in their stocking feet. Condolence cards, week-old flowers, and donation certificates are scattered about, as are paper cups, plates and platters of food; it looks as if a party has taken place—except for a memorial candle that has nearly burned out. The living room is cluttered with furniture: an older set (sofa, armchairs, lamps, etc.) and a newly delivered set, still wrapped in paper and plastic, of an entirely different style. Sid, his head bobbing back and forth, is dozing in a chair. Mort sits, despondently, on a cardboard shiva box looking at a Polaroid snapshot. His mother, Bella, is standing at the open door, saying goodbye to unseen visitors. Artie is juggling bagels.

BELLA *(To unseen people)*: Drive carefully! Wait, Artie wants to say goodbye.

ARTIE: No, I don't . . .

She drags him to the door; he resists.

BELLA: Say goodbye.

ARTIE: No . . .

BELLA *(Prodding him with gritted teeth)*: Say goodbye.

ARTIE *(Too brightly)*: Goodbye!

BELLA *(To unseen people)*: You remembered the rugelach?

ARTIE: How could they forget?

BELLA *(To unseen people)*: My pleasure. Go, go catch your elevator. We should have only *nachas*. Go, goodbye already. *(Closes
the door)* Isn't that nice? Blanche and Al? They came back after
the funeral, they didn't have to pay another call.

ARTIE: They're shiva ghouls. All they do is go from shiva call to
shiva call. They haven't paid for a meal in years.

BELLA: Is that nice? They mean well. *(She rubs a burned spot on
the coffee table)* Al's cigar I can live without.

Ceil enters from the kitchen.

CEIL: Ma, you didn't have to give them the rugelach.

BELLA: What's wrong with giving them the rugelach?

CEIL: It's Morty and Artie's rugelach.

ARTIE: It's my rugelach.

BELLA: What are they gonna do with all that rugelach? It'll go
bad.

CEIL: So?

ARTIE: My mother would've wanted us to have all the rugelach
we wanted. *(Fakes breaking down; he laughs; a beat)*

BELLA: Very funny. Look at your father. Look how miserable he
is. Why can't you be like your father?

MORT: What?

BELLA: Nothing, darling. Shiva's over now, dear. Blanche and Al
left. The last to go. They were so torn up about Shirley, I gave
them a little something to take home.

ARTIE: Our rugelach.

*Ceil, on her way to the kitchen with food, bangs her leg on a piece of
furniture and winces.*

BELLA: What did you do?

CEIL: I banged my leg, Morty, that's how crowded.

BELLA: This is normal?

CEIL: I'm black and blue.

BELLA: Your sister banged her leg.

CEIL: You want to see? *(She exits to the kitchen)*

BELLA: This is not normal.

ARTIE: You shouldn't've let them deliver this stuff, there's no room to walk.

BELLA: Blanche looks at me like what's going on here, what do I say?

ARTIE *(Over "what do I say?")*: Either we send back the new stuff or we get rid of the old stuff.

MORT: No!

ARTIE: Dad, you can't hold on to everything.

BELLA: Morty, Shirley may she rest in peace, I'm sure she didn't want you bumping into things.

MORT: The stuff stays.

ARTIE: Then let's move all the old stuff into the hall. Come on, you and me.

MORT: What the hell you trying to do, Artie?! This is your mother's furniture! She sat in this sofa your mother, Artie, we watched TV here.

ARTIE: You've got to make up your mind. You can't keep all the furniture.

BELLA: You're not thinking straight, Morty, you need a vacation.

CEIL: Ma, I gotta drop you and Pop off . . .

MORT: Shirley couldn't wait to redecorate.

CEIL: . . . I gotta go home, feed the girls . . .

MORT: She ordered this stuff months ago.

CEIL: . . . and I gotta change. *(She returns to the kitchen)*

MORT: What was I supposed to do?, tell them, No, I don't want it?

ARTIE: Great. So we've got all this furniture but there's no room for people.

MORT: That's right! This is the way I want it, so shut your mouth! *(A beat)* Did you look for that laundry ticket I asked you to look for?

BELLA: Look for it, darling, he's out of clean shirts.

ARTIE *(Still on the furniture; a new idea)*: Dad, I'll call Macy's, tell them to pick it up . . .

MORT: Don't you dare.

BELLA: Artie, darling, look for that ticket. Your father says your mother may she rest in peace took a whole batch to the laundry, they should've been ready days ago. What's your father gonna do?

MORT: I have no wife . . .

ARTIE: I'm sure if we told them what happened . . .

MORT: . . . I have no shirts . . .

BELLA: You don't know, darling. Be a good boy, look in the closet. Maybe her pockets.

ARTIE: People lose laundry tickets all the time.

BELLA *(A beat)*: I'm not leaving till we find that ticket.

Artie eagerly clambers over the sofa to get to the hall closet where he begins rummaging through coat pockets; Ceil returns from the kitchen.

CEIL: Morty, where did Shirley may she rest in peace keep her Tupperware?

Mort shrugs.

ARTIE: In the cabinet under the sink. I'll get it.

CEIL: Never mind. Stay. *(Exits to the kitchen)*

Pause.

BELLA: Morty, you need to go away. Forget a little.

CEIL *(Off)*: Ma . . .

BELLA: I'm telling you, Morty: a change of scenery. They have trips for singles.

CEIL *(Off)*: Ma, Morty's not interested.

BELLA: Hawaii, Mort.

MORT: Hawaii!

BELLA: You and Shirley may she rest in peace, you always talked about going to Hawaii.

MORT: I never took her to Hawaii. Next year, always next year . . .

BELLA: So, go! Life is short. If you want to do, do! What are you waiting for?

Ceil returns for more platters of food.

CEIL: Ma, when Morty wants to do, he'll do.

BELLA: There's a whole world out there! Europe, Mort! Africa!

CEIL: Ma, do me a favor, please, wake up Pop, I gotta get going. *(Exits to kitchen)*

BELLA: Go to Israel. See how our trees are doing.

ARTIE: Grandma, you missed your calling. You should've been a travel agent.

BELLA: Artie, you too.

ARTIE: What.

BELLA: Go away. Sightsee. Take a day trip. Go away with your friend. That girl. The one you were with the night your mother—

CEIL *(Off)*: Ma!

BELLA *(A beat)*: Any luck, Artie? *(Meaning in his search for the ticket)*

ARTIE *(Misconstruing her question; panic-stricken)*: What do you mean?

BELLA: You find the ticket?

ARTIE: Oh. No. No ticket. Thought maybe I'd find surprise messages or secret bankbooks. Here's a tissue.

Mort looks up.

She pressed her mouth to this.

MORT: Let me see.

Artie gives it to him.

ARTIE: Hold on to that. It's a relic. *(Resumes rummaging)* A couple of pennies . . . an M&M. Orange. *(He eats it)* A petrified gob of Juicy Fruit. Hold on to that, too, Dad. *(Hands it to Mort, continues)* Lots of lint. Big on lint. *(Finds a matchbook, reads it)* Oh, and a matchbook. Dad, when were you and Mommy at the Holiday Inn in Freehold, New Jersey?

MORT: No, the Poconos. I took her to the Poconos.

ARTIE: Ever stop over in Freehold?

MORT: Freehold? That's where bosses take their secretaries for a lunch hour shtup. No, your mother was a real lady. I took her to the Poconos. We watched dirty movies in a heart-shaped tub.

Artie pockets the matchbook.

BELLA: You're out of shirts, too, Artie?

ARTIE: I have shirts.

CEIL: Ma . . .

BELLA: T-shirts at shiva?

CEIL: Leave him.

BELLA: I'm not saying a tie . . .

CEIL *(Exiting)*: It's his way.

BELLA *(To Artie)*: What would your mother say?

ARTIE: Right now, not much.

BELLA *(Perturbed; changes the subject)*: Morty, what are we gonna do about your shirts?

ARTIE: Why don't you go home, if I find the ticket, I'll call you.

BELLA: What, you don't need me anymore? You don't need anybody? You're all grown up? Wait.

Ceil returns.

CEIL: Ma, I told you to wake up Pop. God, Ma! *(Exits)*

Artie goes to Sid, gently shakes him.

ARTIE: Pop? Pop?

Sid stirs, awakens.

SID: Bella?

Artie points to Bella.

BELLA: I'm here, Sid.

SID: Bella, I was stuck in traffic on the Williamsburg Bridge. A couple of guys tried washing my windshield but my windshield wasn't dirty.

BELLA: You want something, Sid?

ARTIE: Pop, let me get you a drink. *(He starts for the kitchen)*

SID: Uncarbonated.

ARTIE: I know. *(Exits)*

Mort is lost in reverie over the tissue.

BELLA *(To Mort)*: Ever since The Heart Attack, he hasn't had a drop of soda.

SID: Soda makes me *greps*. Every time I gave a *greps*, I thought I was having a heart attack.

Artie returns, hands Sid a glass of water.

Thanks, son. No bubbles?

Artie nods; Sid sips the water.

Okay.

ARTIE: I'm glad, Pop. You're tired, hm?

Sid shrugs.

Grandma, Pop's tired. You should take him home.

BELLA: He's always tired. Nothing new.

MORT *(Obsessing aloud)*: I wanted to go to the deli. No, she had to try this new Chinese restaurant.

BELLA: Morty's at it again, Ceil.

Sid, also fed up with Mort's tirade, exits to the kitchen; Bella flips through a magazine.

MORT: That was Shirley . . .

CEIL *(Off)*: Ma, let him talk it out.

MORT: . . . always trying new things.

CEIL *(Off)*: He's got to get it out of his system.

MORT: We stood in line twenty minutes so Shirley could choke to death on a thing called "moo shu pork."

BELLA: Again with the moo shu!

Sid returns from the kitchen eating a plum.

SID: Artie?

ARTIE: Yeah, Pop.

SID: There's a woman in the kitchen washing plastic forks with steel wool.

ARTIE: That's no woman, Pop. That's your daughter.

Sid draws a blank.

(Helpfully) Ceil: Whose divorce shook a nation? That Ceil.

SID: Oh. Oh.

MORT: Leave it to Shirley . . .

BELLA: What are you eating, Sid? Ceil has to go.

SID: A plum.

MORT: . . . the most exotic thing on the menu she has to order.

During the above, Artie begins to wrap food as Ceil returns from the kitchen.

CEIL: What are you doing, Artie?

ARTIE: I just thought I'd wrap some of this—

CEIL *(Stopping him)*: No, darling, I'm doing it.

ARTIE: You said you were in a hurry. I don't mind. Really.

CEIL *(Over "Really")*: That's very sweet of you darling, but you're the one who's supposed to be "sitting," so sit. *(She presses him down onto the box)*

MORT *(Continuing his tirade)*: "You never try anything new," she says to me.

BELLA *(Meaning, "Here he goes again!")*: Uh!

MORT: "The hell with new," I says to her. "Gimme a shrimp and lobster sauce combination plate any day." I was afraid of heartburn . . .

MORT AND ARTIE: . . . Look what I wound up with!

They look at one another for a beat; Artie exits to the bedroom.

MORT: Artie . . .

BELLA *(Quietly outraged)*: This is how a boy behaves his mother passes away?

Mort shrugs helplessly.

A boy yells out "liar" to the rabbi? In the middle of the funeral? I wanted to bury myself. You're his father, talk to him.

MORT: What do I say? Shirley did the talking. You talk to him.

BELLA: If I talk to him, I'll say something. This isn't normal, Morty, I'm telling you.

MORT: Ma, what do you want from me?!

CEIL *(Intervening, while wrapping food)*: Morty, watch: I'm wrapping up all the food. You and Artie got food for a couple of days.

BELLA: You hear that, Morty? Ceil's wrapping up some lovely cold cuts. If I could bend my fingers . . . I used to be such a good wrapper.

CEIL: I'm doing just fine, Ma.

BELLA: You're a *balebusteh* just like your mother. Remember when I was the *balebusteh*, Morty? Now it's your sister Ceil. What you got there, Ceil?

CEIL: A little bit of roast beef, a little whitefish, a little smoked sturgeon . . .

BELLA: You hear that, Morty?

CEIL: Some turkey breast . . .

BELLA: You hear that, Morty? Turkey breast. Slap together some rye bread, smear a little Russian dressing, you got yourself a tasty sandwich.

Artie returns.

MORT: Artie'll make me sandwiches, right, Artie?

ARTIE: Yeah.

BELLA: That's right . . .

MORT: Artie'll take care of me, right, Artie?

BELLA: Of course he will.

ARTIE: You want something now?

BELLA: Isn't that funny, I was just gonna ask you the same thing. Are you hungry, Morty?

ARTIE: What do you want?

BELLA: Tell me.

ARTIE: I'll make you a sandwich.

BELLA: You want Momma to make you a sandwich?

Mort shakes his head. Artie exits.

You sure? You promise to tell me if you want something?

Mort nods, takes out the Polaroid snapshot from his pocket and looks at it. Ceil exits. A beat.

What are you looking at, darling? A picture?

Mort nods.

What kind of picture?

Mort hands her the snapshot.

Wait, darling, let me get my glasses . . .

Bella goes into her handbag; Ceil returns with a Tupperware container.

CEIL: Tell Morty the cole slaw's in the orange Tupperware.
BELLA: Morty, just so you know, Ceil is putting the cole slaw in the orange Tupperware. My arthritis is so bad, I couldn't even burp the lid.

Ceil "burps" the lid.

MORT *(Barely audible)*: Shirley used to put leftovers in there.
CEIL *(Whispers to Bella)*: What he say?
BELLA *(Shrugs)*: Mortele, what did you say, darling?, we couldn't hear you.
MORT *(Still softly)*: Shirley used to put leftovers in there.
BELLA *(To Ceil, for corroboration)*: Shirley used to put leftovers in there?

Mort nods sadly; Ceil returns to the kitchen.

Aw, poor Morty. So many memories. *(Now wearing her glasses, she looks at the photo in puzzlement, then disbelief)* What am I looking at, Morty? Oh, my God, Morty . . .
CEIL *(Off)*: What?
BELLA: Get over here, Ceil, I can't believe this . . .

Ceil enters; Bella hands her the photo.

CEIL *(Looking at the picture)*: Morty! Oh, my God, I'm nauseous... *(She returns it to Bella, then takes it back for another look)*

MORT: You ever see such a face?

Artie returns.

CEIL: Where the hell did you get this?

ARTIE: Cousin Murray took it.

BELLA: Your retarded Cousin Murray?!

ARTIE: He takes his Polaroid everywhere.

BELLA: How'd he get away with bringing it into the chapel?

CEIL: Who would stop him, Ma? He's simple. He's got the mental age of an eight-year-old.

ARTIE: A pretty smart eight-year-old: My father had to give him ten bucks for that picture.

CEIL: Morty, you're kidding.

MORT: What a face!

Bella snatches the photo from Ceil, who exits.

BELLA: What are you talking about, Morty, it doesn't even look like Shirley. *(To Artie)* Does this look like your mother to you?

ARTIE: Never saw that corpse before in my life.

BELLA: Shirley did all kinds of crazy things to her hair but she never wore it like that. They brushed her all out! And that makeup! Since when did Shirley wear apricot lipstick?

MORT: That's how I want to remember Shirley.

BELLA *(Returns the photo to Mort)*: Then, good. You hold on to it. *(A beat)* I think it was barbaric putting Shirley in an open coffin like that in the first place.

MORT *(Mostly to himself)*: So many people hadn't seen her for so long...

BELLA: And that box!

MORT: ... It was always so hard making plans...

ARTIE *(To Bella)*: You mean The Supersaver?

BELLA: So plain, Artie, so flimsy. Those things are supposed to last.

MORT: Artie, when I go, I want you to bury me in the same kind of box you picked out for your mother. Nothing fancy.

ARTIE: Don't worry, Dad, when you die I'm gonna leave you on the F train.

Artie laughs. Mort gestures to Sid as if to say, "What a mouth on that kid." Bella, meanwhile, has begun to uncover the mirror.

MORT: Leave it, Ma, I don't want you doing that.

BELLA: I can do it, I'm alright.

MORT: No. I don't want it off. Put it back.

BELLA: Shiva's over, Morty, time to take it off.

ARTIE: Grandma, why don't you let me do that later.

BELLA: How you gonna shave with the mirrors covered?

MORT: When I want to look at myself in the mirror . . .

BELLA: What, you growing a beard? Ceil, your brother's letting his beard grow.

CEIL *(Off)*: Ma, if Morty doesn't feel like shaving . . .

BELLA *(To Artie)*: Shave, darling, set an example for your father. I didn't realize you had such a little beard. *(Meaning it's more substantial than she thought)*

ARTIE: I'll shave, we'll both shave.

BELLA: *Oy Gut*, Ceil, I got this feeling Morty and Artie are gonna be living like the Collyer brothers.

ARTIE: Aunt Ceil, what time's your date?

CEIL *(Off)*: Ma, I'm gonna be late!

BELLA: You gonna sit like this forever? Shiva's over, kids. Nobody else is gonna pay you a shiva call. There are things you've got to do: uncover the mirrors, shave. Go for a walk around the block. Take care of the clothes.

ARTIE: Grandma, we don't want to do that right now.

BELLA: Alright, sit. *(A beat)* You know you're supposed to burn the shoes.

ARTIE: Shoes?

BELLA: Don't look at me like I'm a witch, Artie, this is tradition. Jews have been burning dead people's shoes for millions of years.

ARTIE: Why?

BELLA: Look, when the Jews were in the desert, that's what they did. How'm I supposed to know?

MORT: Ma, if you burn one shoe . . .

BELLA: You gonna keep her shoes forever? Shirley doesn't need them anymore, Morty, where she is they run around barefoot.

CEIL *(Off)*: Ma!

Artie laughs in appreciation of Bella's joke.

BELLA: You gonna save all her things? All those lovely clothes . . . you gonna leave them in the closet? There are people who would flip over getting some of those clothes.

MORT: Who?, strangers on welfare? That's all Shirley would need: her beautiful garments on a rack in some thrift store.

BELLA *(To Artie)*: Come, darling, we're gonna get rid of your mother's clothes and burn her shoes.

ARTIE *(Restraining her)*: No, we are not!

BELLA: Who's gonna do it if not me? It would give me pleasure.

ARTIE: Stop!

Ceil enters.

CEIL: Doesn't anybody around here care I got an important date tonight?!

ARTIE: I care! I care!

SID *(Looking out the window)*: Artie?

ARTIE *(Goes to Sid)*: Yeah, Pop.

SID: Look at that: right across the street: a perfect park. Nobody can say your grandpa doesn't have a nose for parking spaces.

ARTIE: You're the best, Pop.

SID: Oh, you should've seen me at the wheel. I pulled into that space like in a glove. Smooth as ice!

BELLA *(To Ceil)*: What do you know about this fella tonight?

CEIL: Spoke to him once on the phone.

BELLA: And?

CEIL: Speaks English.

BELLA: And?

CEIL: Ma!

SID *(To Artie)*: When you gonna let me take you for a ride in the cab?

ARTIE: Soon, Pop. Whenever you want.

BELLA *(To Mort)*: Maybe your sister's gonna bring home a new brother-in-law for you, Morty. Would you like that?

CEIL: Ma . . .

BELLA: I'm only pulling your leg, Ceil. So sensitive . . .

SID *(To Artie)*: Tell your grandma how I worked rush-hour traffic.

ARTIE: Like a genius.

SID: You hear that, Bella? He says like a genius.

BELLA: Very nice, Sid.

SID *(Excitedly)*: I overtook that Greyhound one-two-three. Remember, Artie?

ARTIE: Uh-huh.

SID: It was breathtaking. *(A beat)* Bella, my nitroglycerine.

BELLA: You're not getting a heart attack.

SID: How do you know?!

BELLA: Your lips aren't blue.

SID: I feel burning!

BELLA: I'm not giving you your nitroglycerine unless you promise to let it melt under your tongue like you're supposed to! *(To Artie)* He chews them!

SID: Where is it?

BELLA: In my bag. Help yourself.

ARTIE: Pop, I'll get it for you.

BELLA: Let him. He needs the exercise. You've been running around all week.

Sid exits.

CEIL *(Calls to Sid as he goes)*: Daddy, get our coats while you're at it. We gotta get out of here, Ma. *(She exits to kitchen)*

BELLA: What do you want from me?! Everybody's jumping down my throat. *(A beat)* Artie, Artie, Artie. . . . Friends you can have plenty of, but a mother? One in a lifetime. *(Pause. She examines the fabric on the new furniture)* Your mother picked a very impractical fabric, darling. She had lots of opinions, your mother may she rest in peace. Maybe if she bothered to cook a little more often, she'd be alive today. Cleaning, that she could do. You couldn't put down a glass of water without Shirley pulling out a coaster. That's the kind of woman your mother was, Artie, may she rest in peace: a very particular person.

CEIL *(Off)*: Alright, Ma, enough with Shirley already!

BELLA: What did I say? "A very particular person"! I can't say "a very particular person"?

Sid returns.

SID: What was I looking for?

BELLA: Where did you go? You wanted your nitroglycerine! I said it's in my bag! My bag is right here! Maybe if you paid attention, Sid, you wouldn't forget. *(Takes a bottle from her handbag and gives one pill to Sid)* And don't chew it. Leave it under your tongue.

Ceil returns.

CEIL: Pop, what you do with our coats?

SID: What coats?

CEIL: I asked you to bring in the coats!

SID *(Chewing the tablet)*: I didn't hear nothing about coats!

BELLA: Sidney, are you chewing?

CEIL: God!

ARTIE: I'll get the coats. *(He exits)*

CEIL *(Exiting to kitchen)*: Oy, is that an Artie . . .

Bella exits to the bedroom. Sid and Mort, left alone, sit for a moment in silence.

SID: Mort?

MORT: Yeah, Pop?

Pause.

SID: Mort . . . *(A beat)* You never could park.

A beat. Artie returns with the coats.

ARTIE: Here's your coat, Pop.

Bella enters with an armful of Shirley's clothing on hangers and lays it out on the sofa.

MORT: Ma, what the hell are you doing?!

BELLA: Years from now you'll thank me, Morty. *(She begins to fold clothing)*

ARTIE: Grandma, who asked you to do that?!

BELLA: Somebody's got to do this, sweetheart . . .

MORT: Ma, no!

CEIL *(Over "sweetheart . . . ")*: Ma, what are you starting?!

BELLA: There are things that have to be done . . .

CEIL: I told you I got to go!

BELLA: . . . and I'm the one that has to do them.

MORT: You want to fold up a whole lifetime and put it in a shopping bag?!

BELLA: This is gonna take more than one shopping bag, my son.

ARTIE: You can do this some other time!

CEIL: Artie's right, Ma . . .

MORT: You're killing me, Ma . . . !

CEIL: . . . It doesn't have to be done right this minute!

MORT: . . . Is that what you want? You want to kill me?!

BELLA: All of a sudden I'm your enemy, Morty? I want to help you!

MORT: THIS ISN'T HELPING ME!

BELLA *(Throws down the clothes)*: Save the clothes! I don't care. They're not gonna bring Shirley back!

CEIL: Ma, enough! Can't you see you're upsetting Morty?

BELLA: I'm concerned.

ARTIE: Don't be concerned.

CEIL: Ma, come. *(Spots a garment of interest; a beat)* Is that Shirley's fur jacket?

BELLA: Try it on. Be my guest.

Ceil is considering it.

MORT: NO!

CEIL: Alright, alright. Not now.

BELLA *(To Mort)*: Pull yourself together! My God!

CEIL *(Still eyeing the jacket)*: Don't worry, Morty, we'll stop by tomorrow. We'll take care of everything. *(Helping Sid into his coat)* Gimme your arm, Pop.

SID: Where we going?

CEIL: Home.

SID: What about our shiva call? We had a shiva call.

BELLA *(Putting on her coat)*: This is the shiva call, Sid. We're sitting with Morty, remember? We've been here every day this week, remember? Shirley passed away.

SID: Shirley?! I don't believe it!

BELLA: In a restaurant, a Chinese restaurant.

SID: Shirley was a young woman . . .

CEIL: Let's go home, Daddy.

Bella sneaks a peek at herself in the mirror.

BELLA: Well, Morty? Artie? Look at my two little bachelors . . . *(Goes to Mort)* We must go on living, Mortele. Come, walk me to the elevator.

MORT: My life is over, Ma. This is it, this is the end.

BELLA: Oh, Morty, don't say that . . .

CEIL *(Over "don't say that . . . ")*: How can you talk like that, Morty . . . ?

ARTIE *(Over "talk like that, Morty . . . ?")*: Would you stop with that already?! You've got a good twenty-five, maybe thirty years left.

MORT *(A beat; worried)*: That's all?

BELLA: Sid?

CEIL: I'm getting him, Ma. Oh, Morty, before I forget: your thank-you notes. *(Hands Mort a box)*

ARTIE: I'll take them.

Mort passes the box to Artie.

CEIL: Morty, all you have to do is sign your name. The note is printed nice, like a wedding invitation.

ARTIE: He's not gonna do it, I'll do it.

CEIL: Look, Morty: the address book. I checked off the names of the people who came in black Magic Marker.

Ceil passes the book to Mort, who gives it to Artie.

BELLA: I would sign them for you, sweetheart, you know that, but my knuckles won't let me.

CEIL: Morty, are you listening?

ARTIE: I'll take care of it.

CEIL: This is important, Artie.

ARTIE: Okay.

CEIL: People have to get thanked.

ARTIE: Alright.

CEIL: You have to acknowledge.

ARTIE: I know.

CEIL: Very important. People go out of their way, you have to thank them. I'm gonna remind you.

ARTIE: I'll remember.

BELLA *(Hugging Artie)*: Oh Artie . . . my little Artie . . . such *tsuris*.

They kiss.

Try to find that ticket, darling, I'm gonna be up the whole night. *(Leading Mort out the door)* Come, Mort. Be careful with your father, Ceil. There's a coffee table here I didn't even see.

CEIL *(As Bella and Mort exit)*: No, I'm gonna let him walk into it and kill himself. God, Ma! *(Goes to Artie, gives him her cheek to kiss)* Be strong, Artie.

He kisses her cheek.

ARTIE *(Handing her a thank-you note)*: Thank you.

Ceil snatches the note from him.

SID: Artie?

ARTIE: Yeah, Pop.

SID: I lost my mother, Artie, I was fifty-seven years old.

ARTIE: Yeah.

SID: Not a kid like you. Fifty-seven years old but I cried like a baby. I just didn't have the strength. Better this should happen when you're young and you got the strength. It's a gift, Artie, believe me.

He kisses Artie; Artie hugs him.

CEIL: Pop, come on, Mom's holding the elevator.

ARTIE: Goodbye, Pop.

SID: Where did I park, Ceil?

CEIL: You didn't park, Daddy. I did. I drove.

SID: I parked like a dream.

CEIL: I drove, Pop. I parked. They took away your license, remember?

SID *(A beat; as they exit)*: Ah, fuck 'em. Fuck the State.

They're gone. Artie, alone, silently surveys the room. In a few beats, Mort returns, shuffling despondently with his hands in his pockets. They eye one another uncomfortably. Silence.

ARTIE *(Sings)*: "Quarter to three . . . there's no one in the place . . . 'cept you and me . . . "

Mort is not amused. Pause.

Dad? *(Pause)* Some week, huh? *(Pause)* Went fast. *(Pause)* Soon I'll be as old as Pop talking about what happened when I was seventeen.

MORT: What am I gonna do with all that closet space?

ARTIE: We keep moving but Mommy's stuck somewhere. It's like I'm watching her in the waves at Coney Island, getting smaller and smaller. This game she played with me in the waves.

MORT: Your mother was funny. *(Begins laughing to himself)*

ARTIE: She makes believe she's drowning and I cry hysterically.

MORT: She always made me laugh, your mother.

ARTIE: Yeah. See, I'm a little-little boy, maybe four, and she swims away, does a backstroke, way out, where the water's too deep, she won't let me go out that far, but I see her face—

MORT: What a face!

ARTIE: That young-Mommy face? Wet and shiny?, smiling at me?, rising away on a wave. . . . And she calls to me . . .

MORT *(Interrupting)*: What a sense of humor! We were in the supermarket once, must've been Waldbaum's, in the aisle with all the cereals . . .

ARTIE: Dad, listen: She calls to me . . .

MORT: . . . and I was pushing the cart . . . and your mother said . . . *(He can't remember)*

ARTIE: "Goodbyyeee forevverr!"

MORT *(Still trying to remember)*: She said something . . .

ARTIE: Dad . . . ?

MORT: Something funny. Something so funny, it cracked me up.

ARTIE: Then she swims back and tells me everything's okay, it was only a game.

MORT: You could be sure if it was coming out of her mouth, it was funny. She had a real talent with words. She could put together sentences of all kinds, your mother. I wish I could remember some of the stuff she said. I should've written it down.

During the above, Artie abandons his attempt to tell his story and tries to clear away some furniture by himself.

ARTIE: Dad, we really should do something about the house.

MORT: What's wrong with it?

ARTIE *(Struggling with a chair)*: Help me with this? Dad? Help me.

MORT *(Regarding the clothing)*: What class your mother had! What flair! The way she filled these things out with that body of hers! God, she was something else in the love department your mother, Artie.

ARTIE: That's great news, Dad, thanks for telling me.

MORT *(Holding up a dress)*: Oh, your mother got pizza juice on this. Made me open up the store on a Sunday morning to dry clean it. You see a stain?

ARTIE: Nope.

MORT: Of course not. I'm a professional. *(He comes across a red sequined dress)* Oh! Remember this? I bet you don't remember when your mother—

ARTIE: She wore that to my bar mitzvah.

MORT: That's right! I'll never forget how she looked that night: chandelier earrings . . . high-heeled shoes . . . her hair in a French flip. God, she was a vision. I watched her on the dance floor doing the "Alley Cat." She shimmered! Like fire she was! *(Hums a few bars of the "Alley Cat" song while holding the dress against his chest. A beat)* You can't give something like this away.

ARTIE: You can't save souvenirs either.

MORT: Never mind, you. You're too young. You don't know what love is. You know how much this thing cost? Cost me a fortune. Whatever your mother wanted she got: this dress, shoes that had to be dyed to match perfect, a beaded bag she hocked me a *chinik* for, I doubt she used it more than once. *(Examining the dress)* Look at this construction. Look how it's stitched. Even dry cleaning couldn't hurt it. Let's see how it held up. Try it on.

ARTIE: What?

MORT: Just slip it over your head a minute.

ARTIE: Why?

MORT: I'm curious.

ARTIE: You want me to wear this?

MORT: What are you getting so touchy? Who's asking you to wear it? Just try it on.

Artie takes the dress from Mort, holds it up.

ARTIE: Here, how does it look?

MORT: No, no, not like that. That's no way to see how something looks, how well it hangs. That's the trouble with beading of any kind: The garment loses shape.

ARTIE: So you put it on.

MORT: Me? You gotta be kidding. I couldn't fit into this, I'm too broad. Believe me, if I could, I would. You're lucky: You it would fit.

ARTIE: What are you talking about?!

MORT *(Angry)*: When do I ever ask you for a goddamn thing? Hm? I ask you one simple thing . . .

ARTIE: I'm not gonna put on my mother's dress just because you want me to!

MORT: It would give your dad such pleasure, Artie, such a kick.

ARTIE: To see me in a dress?!

MORT: Not just any dress, your mother's spitfire dress! She wore this to your bar mitzvah, Artie, to your bar mitzvah! We're not talking *schmatte* here, we're talking something I would give my eyeteeth to see shimmering again. Your mother wore this dress, Artie. On her body. She danced in this dress. She shook and shimmered in it. She sweated in this dress. This dress was your mother, Artie.

He lays the dress across Artie's lap; Artie considers it for a moment, then stands to put it on.

Atta boy.

ARTIE: For one minute.

MORT: That's all I'm asking.

Artie begins to step into the dress.

ARTIE: It's not gonna fit.

MORT: So, I'll have it taken in.

ARTIE: I don't know, Dad . . . *(Adjusting the dress)* Well? How does it look?

MORT *(Enthralled)*: Fabulous!

ARTIE: You're just saying that.

MORT: Sweetheart, you look exquisite!

ARTIE: Zip me up?

Mort does.

MORT: Turn around. *(Meaning in a circle)*

ARTIE: Do I have to?

MORT: Come on . . .

Artie turns.

Oh, yes! Beautiful! Again!

Artie, beginning to revel in the dress, spins around again and again; he and Mort are giddy.

Shimmer! That's right, shimmer!

Mort puts his hands on Artie's hips and sings the "Alley Cat" song as he and Artie do the dance steps. Their singing and dancing become increasingly frenetic as they wind their way through the living room. They collapse, laughing, on the sofa.

ARTIE: This thing is heavy. It pulls a little bit in the shoulders.
MORT: I can let that out. Whatever you want.

Mort puts his arm around Artie and turns on the television. Artie prepares to stand.

Sit with me a minute.

A beat.

ARTIE: Okay.

He settles back into the sofa. Mort, his arm around Artie, rests his head on Artie's shoulder. Mort laughs at something on TV. Pause. Artie gets up.

MORT: Where you going? We're just getting comfortable.
ARTIE: I thought I'd make us something to eat.
MORT: Now there's an idea!

Artie, still wearing the dress, exits to the kitchen. Mort, humming, takes off his trousers and folds them over the back of a chair. Artie returns with a tray of food and utensils.

Wow! Look at all that stuff!

Artie sets the food down on the table. Mort stands sampling the food with his fingers.

Mmm . . . ! Cole slaw . . . potato salad . . . macaroni salad . . . !
ARTIE: Use a fork.
MORT: . . . pickled herring in cream sauce . . . mmm . . . !
ARTIE: Come on, sit down, use a fork. Here's a plate. Here's a napkin. Help yourself. *(He sniffs a container of cottage cheese for freshness, makes a terrible face and sets it aside)*
MORT: Your mother always did that. What a nose on her! Never

failed. One whiff, she could tell you whether or not the thing was sour.

Artie pours two cups of Tab; Mort eyes the soda can nostalgically.

Tab . . .

A beat.

I don't know what to have. What should I eat? How about you?

ARTIE: I'm gonna have whitefish on a bagel. *(Begins to slice a bagel)*

MORT: No, don't do that. You'll cut yourself. *(Takes the bagel and knife from Artie)*

ARTIE: I can do it.

MORT *(Slicing the bagel)*: I don't want you to cut yourself; your mother was always cutting herself.

Returns the sliced bagel to Artie, who prepares a sandwich as Mort watches.

What do you do? You just smear the fish on the bagel?

ARTIE: That's right.

MORT: What about the bones?

ARTIE: You pick out the bones.

MORT: One by one?

ARTIE: That's right.

MORT: They're so tiny. Hey, you do that good.

ARTIE *(Passes the fish and a bagel to Mort)*: Here. Help yourself.

MORT: Isn't that funny? I never knew what happened to the bones. You see how good she was to me? *(Smearing fish on the bagel)* Now I have to smear on the fish and pick out the bones. Right?

ARTIE: Uh-huh.

MORT: Boy, she was some cook, wasn't she.

ARTIE: Yeah.

MORT: What an imagination on her. How about that meat loaf?

ARTIE: Yeah!

MORT: She'd throw in things you'd never in a million years expect to taste good together and they'd come out spectacular. Like a can of peas she'd throw in. Who would've thought of that? That's a talent, isn't it?, to throw things together and have them come out like a gourmet meal? Remember she'd throw together all those different things and put it in the oven?

ARTIE: Yeah . . .

MORT: Remember those casseroles she made?

ARTIE: Yeah.

MORT: What did she call them?

ARTIE: The casseroles?

MORT: Yeah, she had a name for them.

ARTIE: "Casseroles."

MORT: Right, what did she call them?

ARTIE: She called the casseroles "casseroles."

A beat. Mort is annoyed.

MORT: Always the wiseguy.

ARTIE: What's the matter?

MORT: Always with the smart answers.

ARTIE: That's what she called her casseroles: "casseroles"!

MORT *(Enraged; overlap)*: You talk to your teachers like this? Hm? Is this how you talk to your teachers, or just to your father you talk like this?

ARTIE: She called them "casseroles"!

MORT: Never mind, you little bastard. I ask you a simple question, I don't want any of that wiseguy shit.

ARTIE: I answered your question!

MORT: Look, you've been blasé about this whole thing—

ARTIE: What?!

MORT: . . . from the very beginning.

ARTIE: What are you talking about?!

MORT: The little jokes, the comments. Making a scene at the funeral?!

ARTIE: Who made a scene?! You almost jumped in the hole with her!

MORT: Never mind about me!

ARTIE: I could've been a lucky orphan: two birds with one stone!

Mort pushes his bagel into Artie's face.

Hey!

MORT: You don't stop! You don't give a damn what happened!

ARTIE: How can you say that?

MORT: I can and I do. *(Hands Artie a napkin)* Wipe your face; you've got fish.

ARTIE *(Wiping his face)*: I was the one who made the phone calls, who picked out the box—

MORT: I haven't seen you cry once all week.

ARTIE: Is that what you want? Well, I haven't gotten around to that yet. I'm new at this, okay?!

MORT: If somebody's hungry, they eat. If they're sad, they cry.

ARTIE: You're saying I'm not sad?

MORT: Starting up with the rabbi?! That's sad?!

ARTIE: He never even met her! He's making up all these lies about her!

MORT: It was a funeral! You're supposed to say nice things!

ARTIE: And everybody's sitting there listening to this garbage, nodding their heads, saying, "Yeah that was Shirley alright!" And I'm saying, "No! No! That's not who she was!"

The doorbell rings.

MORT: Then who was she?, hm, wiseguy?

Doorbell.

(Calls) Coming! *(To Artie)* Get the door.

ARTIE: Why don't you?

MORT: I'm wearing underwear.

ARTIE: So what? I'm wearing a dress.

Doorbell.

MORT: You're closer.

Doorbell again and again.

ARTIE *(Approaching the door)*: Okay, okay . . .

Artie opens the door. Standing there is his dead mother, Shirley, her face and hair caked with dirt, her shroud tattered, encrusted with mud and stained with grass.

Ma!

MORT: Shirley!

Shirley speaks as she makes her way, on sore feet, through the living room to the bathroom.

SHIRLEY: Look . . . I don't even want to talk about it. . . . I've just gotta jump in the shower . . . *(As she enters the bathroom)* Oh, the furniture came! Good!

She closes the door behind her. In a moment, while Mort and Artie remain incredulous, the shower is turned on.

MORT *(Very frightened)*: Artie? What the hell is going on, Artie?

Artie, giggling nervously, shakes his head.

See, I just saw your mother . . . *(Points to the front door, then to the bathroom)*

ARTIE: Uh-huh.

MORT: You, too?

ARTIE *(Nods)*: Daddy, what should we do?

Shirley, in the shower, is singing "Send in the Clowns."

MORT: Shhh. . . . Now I think I hear her singing "Send in the Clowns."

ARTIE: She is.

MORT *(Trying to make sense of what he hears)*: You know, she loved that song, your mother. I never understood what the words meant, but whenever she heard Sinatra sing it, she'd get all choked up. Listen to that: She's in tune and everything.

ARTIE: Uh-huh.

MORT: Artie, you think your mother's gonna haunt us by coming over and taking showers?

Artie shrugs. The shower is turned off.

SHIRLEY *(Off)*: Boys?

MORT: Shhh . . .

SHIRLEY *(Off)*: Boys? Did I get any mail?

MORT: Your mother wants to know if she got any mail.

ARTIE *(A beat; calls)*: Uh, yeah. Bills, mostly. Oh, and the new *People* came.

SHIRLEY *(Off)*: Oh, good . . . *(Enters, drying her hair with a towel)* There is nothing worse than walking around with dirty hair. I feel like a new person. Ah! Now you can kiss me.

Artie tentatively approaches, Mort restrains him.

No kiss? This is the kind of welcome I get? *(A beat; insulted)* Well, don't think I haven't noticed the dress, Artie.

ARTIE: Oh, this . . .

SHIRLEY: Yeah, "this." You let him walk around like that, Morty?

MORT: He has wild ideas.

ARTIE: It was your idea! Ma, Daddy made me put it on!

MORT *(Cutting him off)*: Ah, what the hell: You got to admit, he carries it well.

He laughs; Shirley does, too. The utter naturalness of their sharing a laugh causes him to pause.

Shirley, is that really you?

SHIRLEY: Yeah, Mort, it's me.

MORT: Now, what do you mean by "you"?

SHIRLEY: I mean, me.

MORT: Did you come to take me with you?

SHIRLEY: Take you where, Mort?, nobody's going anywhere.

MORT: Shirley! I don't believe it! You're here talking to me!

SHIRLEY: Yes, Mort.

MORT: Artie, your mother's home!

ARTIE: Yeah! I know!

Mort pulls Artie into a three-way embrace.

MORT: Oh, Shirley, Shirley, Shirley . . . !

SHIRLEY: This is more like it!

MORT: I knew you'd get it straightened out sooner or later. Leave it to your mother, hm, Artie?

ARTIE: Yeah! *(Suddenly chilled, he recoils)*

SHIRLEY: What.

ARTIE: You're cold.

MORT *(He, too, recoils)*: Boy, you are cold.

SHIRLEY *(Self-conscious)*: I am?

MORT: Here, put something on . . . *(Meaning her clothes on the sofa)*

SHIRLEY *(Seeing the clothes)*: My clothes! What are my clothes doing out here?! Look at this! Everything's gonna get wrinkled! *(She starts to put things back on hangers)*

MORT: I told them you wouldn't like it. Shirley, let me look at you! You look great!

SHIRLEY: How could I?

MORT: Artie, doesn't your mother look beautiful?

ARTIE: Actually, she looks a little pale.

MORT: What does a kid know? To me you look wonderful.

SHIRLEY: To you, you're prejudiced.

MORT: Maybe a little. *(He takes her hand, is struck again by its peculiar coldness and warms it by rubbing it between his hands)*

ARTIE: So, Ma, how'd you get here?

SHIRLEY: Don't ask.

MORT: Yeah, Shirley, what'd you do? Walk?

SHIRLEY: Yeah, I walked.

MORT: On foot?

SHIRLEY: Yeah, on foot.

MORT: From all the way out on the Island?

SHIRLEY: Uh-huh.

MORT: What'd you do?, take the B.Q.E.?

SHIRLEY: The B.Q.E., the L.I.E., the Belt, the Van Wyck . . .

MORT: Why didn't you call me?! I could've picked you up!

SHIRLEY: Morty . . .

MORT: Since when do you stand on ceremony with me, Shirley?

SHIRLEY: I didn't have a cent!

MORT: Oh, my poor baby . . .

SHIRLEY: God, look at this place! The dust! *(Tidying up)* What moron burned a hole in my finish?, it's ruined.

MORT: Shirley, you'd've gotten a kick out of all the fancy baskets that came. *(Picks up a jam jar)* Want some "Gooseberry Preserves"?

SHIRLEY: Throw that out, we're never gonna eat that shit.

Artie laughs. She takes dying flowers from a vase.

Who sent these?

ARTIE: Your boss.

SHIRLEY: *Goyim.* All they know is flowers.

She hands them to Mort to get rid of; he hands them to Artie.

I can't believe this mess! I was counting on you, Morty!

MORT: What!

SHIRLEY: I work my whole life to make a nice home, I'm gone a couple of days and you let the house fall apart! *(She starts for the hall closet)*

MORT *(Thinking she's leaving)*: No, don't go! We'll fix it up!

She takes the vacuum cleaner out of the closet.

What are you shlepping! Character! *(To Artie)* Help your mother.

He does.

SHIRLEY *(Unveiling mirrors, etc.)*: I don't know how the two of you can breathe in here! The dust, the furniture . . .

ARTIE *(To Mort)*: See? *(To Shirley)* That's what I told him, Ma, I told him we can't keep all the old stuff, he wouldn't listen to me.

MORT *(Over, ". . . he wouldn't listen to me")*: Alright, alright . . . we'll get rid of it.

SHIRLEY: Into the hall. Let the super deal with it. *(To Mort)* And I want you to shave. I don't like you looking so scruffy.

MORT: That'll make you happy?

SHIRLEY: Yes, Mort, very happy.

MORT: Whatever makes you happy. Boy, this business gave us a real scare, didn't it?

ARTIE: It sure did.

MORT: The house feels like a home again! *(He snuggles up to her and recoils from her coldness again)* You sure you don't want a sweater?

SHIRLEY: I'm fine.

MORT: Artie, get your mother a sweater.

Artie goes.

(To Shirley) Don't go away.

SHIRLEY: I won't.

Mort goes to the bathroom. Shirley sits alone for a beat contemplating the gravity of her situation. Mort is shaving while humming the "Alley Cat" song. Soon, Artie returns with a sweater and drapes it over his mother's shoulders.

ARTIE: So, Ma, what's going on?

SHIRLEY: What do you mean?

ARTIE: Come on, you can tell me. Is this a visitation?

SHIRLEY: A "visitation"? Who's visiting? I'm home.

ARTIE: But, Ma . . . .You're dead.

SHIRLEY: So? Aren't you glad to see me?

ARTIE: Of course I'm glad to see you.

SHIRLEY: Then leave it at that. Don't make waves.

ARTIE: I'd almost forgotten what you looked like, you know that? And your voice? I tried for hours last night to conjure it up in my head? I fell asleep without even coming close.

SHIRLEY: Oh, sweetheart . . .

ARTIE: Ma, all week long, ever since this happened, it's been so crazy . . .

SHIRLEY: I'm so sorry, honey, just when you needed me the most and I wasn't here to be with you.

ARTIE: I kept hoping you'd come home and make everything right again.

SHIRLEY *(Simply):* And now I'm here. Mommy's home, Artie. Everything's gonna be okay.

ARTIE: I missed you so much.

SHIRLEY: Well, you don't have to miss me anymore.

Mort, still shaving, pops in from the bathroom.

MORT: Shirley?

SHIRLEY: Yeah, Mort?

MORT: How about you cook for me that meat loaf thing?

SHIRLEY: My casserole? Sure.

More vindication for Artie. Mort returns to the bathroom. Artie follows Shirley around the room as she continues to clean it up.

ARTIE: So . . . Ma . . . *(A beat)* What are your plans?

SHIRLEY: Well, I've got this house to put together. First, we get rid of all the old furniture . . .

ARTIE: Uh-huh.

SHIRLEY: Then, I'm gonna dust, polish, vacuum, do the floors, take apart the kitchen, arrange the new stuff. I promise you, sweetheart, when I get done with this place . . . everything's gonna be perfect! *(She blows out the memorial candle)*

A recording of the "Alley Cat" song takes us into the blackout.

ACT TWO

Sinatra's rendition of "Send in the Clowns" is heard in the black.

At rise: early the next day. Most of the old furniture has been moved out of the living room; what remains is a motley arrangement of the new furniture, still in its wrapping, and a few favorite pieces from the former set. Shirley and Artie have begun to unwrap a new chair but she has stopped to scrutinize something he has shown her: the Polaroid snapshot of her dead self. Artie stands nearby, drinking coffee, taking delight in her reaction. Mort is contentedly dozing on the sofa. After a beat:

SHIRLEY: Who took this?, your Cousin Murray?

ARTIE: Yup.

SHIRLEY *(She shakes her head, "It figures")*: What they did to my hair . . . unforgivable.

She hands it back to Artie and resumes unwrapping a chair, etc. He helps her.

And that shroud! Like for an old lady. That's not how I wanted to go at all.

ARTIE: What do I know about shrouds? It was the first time I had to shop for one.

SHIRLEY: You? Where was your father?

ARTIE: Oh, he wouldn't come into the room. You know, The Chamber of Horrors in the basement of the funeral chapel? Where they have the coffins and everything? I hope you're not offended, I picked the one on sale.

SHIRLEY: A box is a box.

ARTIE: That's what I said.

SHIRLEY: Your father let you do all that awful stuff by yourself?

ARTIE: Somebody had to; he was in no shape to do anything. I even had to make the phone calls. "Hi, this is Shirley and Morty's kid, Artie? Remember my mother? Well, uh, guess what?" I lose my mother and end up telling two hundred and fifty people how sorry I am to have to break it to them.

SHIRLEY: That's not right. You shouldn't've had to do all that. You're just a kid.

ARTIE: See, now that's what I thought. I mean, didn't all the other animals help out Bambi? Everybody's treating me like it's my fault or something.

SHIRLEY: Who is?

ARTIE: I don't know . . . Dad, Grandma. *(A beat)* See, there was this . . . minor incident.

SHIRLEY: What kind of minor incident?

ARTIE: At the service. The rabbi was one of those fill-in-the-blank kind of rabbis? He even called you "Sally" a few times.

SHIRLEY: You're kidding.

ARTIE: No, I yelled out your name, correcting him, and Grandma shushed me.

SHIRLEY *(Amused)*: Uy . . .

ARTIE: Anyway, he never even met you and he's saying all these corny things about you. You would've hated it, Ma. He made you sound like anybody's mother. Well, it was getting me mad sitting there and listening to that stuff. But I couldn't control myself.

SHIRLEY: So what did you do?

ARTIE: I called him a liar.

SHIRLEY *(Enjoying this)*: You did? What did you do, you just yelled it out?

ARTIE: Uh-huh.

SHIRLEY: So what happened?

ARTIE: He stopped the service.

SHIRLEY: Yeah?

ARTIE: "If you think you can do a better job," he said, "why don't you come up here and do it yourself?" So, I did. I mean, I got up and went to the microphone and looked out and saw the faces of everybody I ever knew in my entire life and then I looked at the box. . . . And then this funny thing happened.

SHIRLEY: What.

ARTIE: I opened my mouth to speak . . .

SHIRLEY: Yeah . . . ?

ARTIE: And nothing came out. I couldn't speak. I didn't know what to say. I just stood there. With everybody looking. And I didn't know what to say. So I ran out and waited by the car till it was over.

SHIRLEY: Oh, sweetheart . . .

ARTIE: Ma, ever since this happened. . . . You know what it's like?

Shirley shakes her head.

It's like we're in the ocean, you and me. I close my eyes and we're back in the ocean. Remember? At Coney Island?

SHIRLEY: Tell me.

ARTIE: I'm a little-little boy. And we're playing in the water, splashing around, chasing the foam, having a great time, then all of a sudden, you swim away! You tell me to stay by the shore and you swim, way out, where the water's too deep for me, you won't let me go out that far. So I do as you tell me, I stay by the shore, but I see your face, wet and shiny, smiling at me, getting smaller and smaller, rising away on a wave. And you call to me. Remember, Ma? You call to me . . .

SHIRLEY: "Goodbyyeee forevverr!"

ARTIE: Yeah! "Goodbyyeee forevverr!" And I panic. "No, Mommy!"

SHIRLEY *(Laughs affectionately)*: Oh, Artie . . .

ARTIE: That's funny?, making believe you're being washed out to sea?!

SHIRLEY: It was a game!

ARTIE: I think I'm never gonna see you again! I cry. I get hysterical. Strangers ask me if I'm lost. I can't catch my breath. The tears are so thick I can't see you anymore. I can't see anything. I think my heart is gonna stop 'cause who's gonna take care of me if you're gone? And then you come back!

SHIRLEY: See?

ARTIE: You swim back and you're laughing! You're laughing!

SHIRLEY: You're mad because I didn't drown?, what.

ARTIE: What kind of trick is that to play on a kid?

SHIRLEY: Trick? I always swam back to you, didn't I? And picked you up out of the water and told you it was just a game, everything was alright? Didn't I?

ARTIE: Yeah, but why did you do that to me?

SHIRLEY: Why? I was playing with you!

ARTIE: No, no, I think you enjoyed seeing me get hysterical.

SHIRLEY: Why would I enjoy seeing you get hysterical?

ARTIE: I don't know, to see how much I'd miss you?

They look at one another for a beat. Mort stirs, panics for a moment thinking Shirley is gone, then sees her and beams with pleasure that she's still there.

MORT: Shirley!

She smiles and waves at him. Mort wakens and stretches noisily. Artie drinks the rest of the coffee.

SHIRLEY: You're drinking too much coffee; I don't like you drinking so much coffee.

ARTIE: I want to stay up with you. If you're not gonna sleep, neither am I. What if I fall asleep and wake up and you're gone?

He exits to the kitchen to make a fresh pot.

SHIRLEY *(To herself; distressed)*: Sleep? I forgot all about it . . .

MORT *(Brightly; singsong)*: Hi-i.

SHIRLEY *(Preoccupied; resumes puttering)*: Hi.

MORT: Look at you.

SHIRLEY: What.

MORT *(Romantically)*: I can't keep my eyes open and you're all over the place. I drift in and out, I see a hundred Shirleys. Shirley polishing. Shirley vacuuming. Shirley shlepping furniture. You're everywhere.

SHIRLEY: Morty, I can't sleep.

MORT: Of course you can't sleep. You're all wired up.

SHIRLEY: No, I can't sleep.

MORT: You never knew how to sit still. Always doing something. You've gotta learn how to relax, Shirley.

He leads her to the sofa.

SHIRLEY: No sleep, no dreams. . . . No more dreams, Mort! I had such good dreams.

MORT: Shhh. . . . Listen to me: Just now, I dreamed we went to Hawaii.

SHIRLEY: Hawaii?!

MORT: I got you there, once and for all. What a relief, hm?

SHIRLEY: I always wanted to go to Hawaii.

MORT: I know! I was feeling terrible.

SHIRLEY: Ever since my first luau at Hawaii Kai. We went from *Fiddler on the Roof* to pineapple everything.

MORT: Oh, the place was paradise, Shirley. Everything we dreamed it would be.

SHIRLEY: Yeah?

MORT: Sun as big as the moon. Water like Saran Wrap. These Hawaiians, they don't know from clouds.

She laughs.

I'm telling you, we were so tan I didn't recognize us. We wore flowers 'round our necks like natives. You know what you looked like?, pink flowers and a tan? Wow.

SHIRLEY *(Wistfully)*: Oh . . . *(A dreamy pause)*

MORT: Why don't we do it?

SHIRLEY: What.

MORT: Once and for all: Hawaii.

SHIRLEY: Morty, we can't do that . . .

MORT: Why not? We'll hula till the sun sets!

She laughs.

Let's do it, Shirley! We'll take a trip! You and me!

SHIRLEY: I can't.

MORT: We'll take a cruise 'round the islands! A cruise, Shirley! It's like a floating Catskills!

SHIRLEY: You go. You do it.

MORT: What do you mean? By myself? I wouldn't dream of it. Come with me!

SHIRLEY: Things are different now, Morty. Dreams change.

MORT: All you have to do is get on a plane.

SHIRLEY: I'm not getting on any plane.

MORT: You could use a vacation. We both could. After what we've been through?!

SHIRLEY: Morty, I can't take a vacation.

MORT: Why not?

SHIRLEY: You know why not.

MORT: That? I don't give a damn about that. You're here, aren't you?

SHIRLEY: Yeah, I'm home. Where I belong. As long as you and Artie want me, I'll be here. But vacations? No, not anymore. That's over for me, Morty. Which doesn't mean it has to be over for you.

MORT: Would you think about it at least?

SHIRLEY: There's nothing to think about. I can't. I'm sorry.

MORT *(Pause)*: It was a wonderful dream, Shirley.

SHIRLEY: I bet it was.

MORT: A wonderful dream. We carried on like we did in the Poconos. Remember the Poconos? Hm?

SHIRLEY: Do I remember the Poconos!

They laugh. He embraces her. They kiss. Shirley finds it strangely unsatisfying; Mort is oblivious to her depression.

MORT: Oh, Shirley . . . I thought I was never gonna hold you like this again. You know what that was like?

SHIRLEY: I know.

She breaks the embrace and resumes puttering; Mort follows her around the room.

MORT: Let's go to bed.

SHIRLEY: What?

Mort cocks his head toward the bedroom.

You gotta be kidding.

MORT: No. Why?

SHIRLEY: Just like that? In the middle of the day? You're an animal.

MORT: I am an animal. *(He nuzzles her neck)*

SHIRLEY *(Good-naturedly evades him)*: Down, Morty.

MORT: What, you're worried about him? *(Meaning Artie)* We'll shut our door. He'll get the message.

SHIRLEY: No, no, it's not that. I can't sleep with you, Morty.

MORT: Who's talking about sleep?

SHIRLEY: I mean, I don't feel sexy anymore. Isn't that funny? Me?! I don't feel sexy.

MORT: You'll lie down, it'll come back to you. That's all I ask: Let me look at you sideways again.

SHIRLEY: No, no, Morty, trust me. It wouldn't be the same.

MORT: It's like riding a bike, like swimming. Put down the rag, stop with the dusting.

SHIRLEY: No! What have I just been saying?! Things are different now, Morty. I can't anymore. All that's over, too.

MORT: Don't say that!

SHIRLEY: It is, it's over, I said!

She eludes him as Mort playfully chases her around the room.

MORT: Oh, I get it. . . . You want to play, hm?

SHIRLEY: No . . .

MORT: Okay we'll play . . .

SHIRLEY: Come on, stop . . .

MORT: I'm gonna get you!

SHIRLEY: No, Morty . . . please . . .

MORT: I'm gonna get you, Shirley!

SHIRLEY *(Calls)*: Artie? Artie?

MORT: What are you calling him for?

ARTIE *(Off)*: What.

MORT: Shirley, please, I want us to go to bed.

SHIRLEY *(Calls)*: Tell me how your date went!

MORT: What?! What date?

SHIRLEY *(To Mort)*: Remember he had a date? You know: Pam.
    (Calls) How'd it go last week you and Pam?

ARTIE *(Off)*: Fine.

MORT: You don't want me anymore? Is that it?

SHIRLEY: Morty, stop, I didn't say that.

MORT: We'll talk. Come on. We'll go inside, lie down and talk.
    Okay? We'll take it slow. We'll see what happens.

SHIRLEY *(Shakes her head, takes his hand comfortingly. A beat.
    Calls)*: Artie, come here a minute.

MORT *(Annoyed)*: Wonderful. Call Artie.

Artie stands near the entrance to the kitchen.

ARTIE: What.

SHIRLEY: You had a nice time?

ARTIE: I had a nice time.

SHIRLEY: She came over?

ARTIE: She came over. Okay? *(Returns to the kitchen)*

MORT: This is the girl you're talking about?, the college girl?

SHIRLEY: Yeah. *(Calls)* Do anything special?

ARTIE *(Returns)*: What are all these questions?!

SHIRLEY: Nothing. I just want to know did you stay in?, did you
    go out to eat?

ARTIE: We stayed in.

SHIRLEY: Good. That's all I wanted to know.

Artie goes. She calls.

Artie?

ARTIE *(Off)*: What!

SHIRLEY: Did anything . . . happen?

ARTIE *(At the entrance)*: What do you mean?

SHIRLEY: You know.

ARTIE *(Returns to kitchen, blushing)*: Ma-a . . .

SHIRLEY: Uh-oh, I'll take that as a yes.

MORT *(Embarrassed but proud)*: You mean him and that girl?

SHIRLEY: Uh-huh. *(Calls)* Congratulations!

Artie groans in the kitchen.

Say something to him.

MORT: Yeah? Like what?

SHIRLEY: I don't know, something . . . fatherly. You've got to try talking to him, Morty.

MORT: I'm no good at that.

SHIRLEY: Try.

MORT *(Calls)*: Artie?

ARTIE *(Off; annoyed)*: What.

MORT: C'mere a minute.

A beat. Artie enters with coffee; Mort beams at him.

So! How do you like that! *(Playfully roughs up Artie)* Son of a gun. He looks different to me already. Doesn't he? Big shot, you don't say a word, hm? You don't say a word to your dad?

More roughhousing and hair mussing, which Artie enjoys.

SHIRLEY *(During the above)*: Well, good. I had a feeling.

ARTIE: You did? What do you mean?

SHIRLEY: You seemed ripe to me. Ready. I thought it would be nice if we got out of your way and let you have the place to yourself.

MORT: See what a mother you have?

SHIRLEY: Seemed like the perfect night to shlep your father out to eat.

A beat.

MORT: Wait, when was this?

SHIRLEY: Last week.

ARTIE *(A beat)*: Oh, God . . .

MORT: Wait a minute. . . . This is the night we went out for Chinks you're talking about?

ARTIE: Oh, no . . .

SHIRLEY: Uh-huh.

ARTIE: This is too much . . .

MORT: Shirley, what are you saying?!

ARTIE: I don't believe this . . .

SHIRLEY: I wanted to try that new restaurant. You know how I love grand openings.

MORT: You made me go out to eat so he could get laid?!

SHIRLEY: Shhh . . .

ARTIE: You died for my sins, Ma.

SHIRLEY: Don't be a jerk.

MORT: You mean to tell me your mother is eating her last supper and you're up here screwing some girl?!

ARTIE: She's not "some" girl!

SHIRLEY: Morty . . .

MORT: That's what was going on here?!

SHIRLEY: Don't make it worse.

ARTIE *(To Shirley)*: I wanted you out of the house but I didn't mean permanently!

SHIRLEY: Of course you didn't.

MORT: Look how you stick up for him!

ARTIE: I knew it was all my fault! I knew it! I knew it!

SHIRLEY: Artie, stop it! It's nobody's fault! It happened! You had nothing to do with it!

MORT: You're always on his side, no matter what! He comes first! Ever since he was born!

SHIRLEY: Morty, the kid hurts. Help him!

MORT: I lost you 'cause of him, Shirley, don't you see that?! It's 'cause of him we went out to eat in the first place! I wanted to go to the deli! But no!, you had to try this new Chinese restaurant!

SHIRLEY: Morty . . .

MORT: I always gave in to you! Whatever you wanted! If only I put my foot down this one time! This one time! If only I insisted! But, no! No! And look what happened! *(Starts to exit to the bedroom)*

SHIRLEY: Where are you going?

MORT: I got a headache. I want to lie down.

SHIRLEY: Morty, don't go, I need you with the furniture . . .

MORT: I want to lie down, I said!

Mort exits. Pause.

SHIRLEY: Oh, boy . . . *(A beat)* Don't do this to yourself. Come on. Stop beating yourself up. I gave you a gift, Artie. A present. *(A beat)* Was it good at least?

Artie shrugs equivocally.

It gets better, believe me.

ARTIE: He's had it in for me for years.

SHIRLEY: No, he hasn't.

ARTIE: I always felt like a foreign-exchange student around here and you were my interpreter. Without you, our words just kinda bump up against each other and make noise. Ma, you don't know what it's like here without you.

SHIRLEY: Sweetheart . . .

ARTIE: How could you do that to me?! How could you leave me alone with him?!

SHIRLEY: He's your father, he loves you!

ARTIE: He doesn't know me. We have nothing to say to each other! *(A beat)* Did he make you happy?

SHIRLEY: What?! What kind of question is that? Of course he made me happy. He's a very sweet man, your father. We were very happy.

ARTIE: You were?

SHIRLEY: Oh, yeah. We really had something.

ARTIE: What.

SHIRLEY: Something special.

ARTIE: What, what made it special?

SHIRLEY: I don't know. I can't put it in words.

ARTIE: Try.

SHIRLEY: Artie . . .

ARTIE: I need to know.

SHIRLEY *(A beat)*: It's little things.

ARTIE: Like what?

SHIRLEY: It's . . . the way people felt about us. People envied us. Friends. Are you kidding? Friends were jealous of our marriage, that's how special we were. Everybody's favorite couple, that was us.

ARTIE: Then why were you so restless all the time?

SHIRLEY: Restless? I wasn't restless.

ARTIE: Yeah, you were. You were always changing things. You were never satisfied.

SHIRLEY: I was a perfectionist.

ARTIE: You always had this thing about the furniture. Once I came home from school at three o'clock and the living room was completely rearranged. I thought I went into the wrong apartment by mistake.

SHIRLEY: That's not 'cause I was restless. That's 'cause I was always coming up with new ideas.

ARTIE: Why wouldn't you just leave things the way they were if you were really happy with them?

SHIRLEY: I don't know . . .

ARTIE: You used to change your hair color like practically every week.

SHIRLEY: Not every week. I was experimenting with tints.

ARTIE: It was very confusing when I was little. I never knew what you'd show up looking like in my dreams.

SHIRLEY: So big deal. So I dyed my hair. I liked trying new things. What's wrong with that?

ARTIE *(A beat)*: Ma, I know about the Holiday Inn.

SHIRLEY: What Holiday Inn?

ARTIE: The Holiday Inn in Freehold, New Jersey.

SHIRLEY: I don't know what you're talking about.

ARTIE: It's okay. Daddy doesn't know.

SHIRLEY *(A beat)*: Artie, your imagination is going wild.

They look at one another for a beat.

You wouldn't understand.

ARTIE: Oh, but I do. I'm saying it's okay, Ma. I understand. You were restless.

SHIRLEY: Why do you keep using that word?

ARTIE: Well, you're here, aren't you?

A beat. The front door opens and Sid pokes his head in.

SID: Hell-o-o . . .

ARTIE: Oh, shit. . . . Hi, Pop!

SHIRLEY: Sidney!

ARTIE *(To Shirley)*: I forgot to tell you . . .

SID: Ceil dropped me off. She's circling. No place to park. Bella went to pick up an Entenmann's. I gotta pee.

He heads for the kitchen; Artie grabs him and steers him in the right direction.

By the way, Shirley, I was very sorry to hear what happened. *(He exits into the bathroom)*

SHIRLEY: Oh, God . . . company's coming, I can't have the house looking like this. . . . Give me a hand . . .

They arrange furniture. Sid enters from the bathroom. He follows them from place to place which contributes to his confusion.

SID: False alarm. My prostate. Don't have the reservoir I had in my youth. Once I could hold my water hundreds of miles at a time.

SHIRLEY: How are you, Sidney?

SID: How am I? Doctor says I'm a medical miracle. Should've been dead by now. Getting another cataract, this time in my left eye, 'cause I liked the one in my right eye so much. I blink and I blink but the picture don't get sharp. *(Squinting at her)* How are you, by the way?

SHIRLEY: I'm fine, Sidney.

SID: "Sidney." Always "Sidney." Never "Pop," never "Sid." "Sidney." *(Whispers)* Artie, she was away, right? What was it?, a milk farm or something?

ARTIE: Well, no, Pop, she . . .

SID *(Without waiting for a response)*: Nice to see you, Shirley.

SHIRLEY: Thanks, Sidney, it's nice to see you.

SID: What was I gonna do? Stay home? Never should've retired. Used to have a pinochle game? Now I have solitaire. Bella hates cards. All I need is to break my hip. Kiss of death. One day my mother's making gefilte fish from scratch, the day after that. . . . My mother passed away, I was fifty-seven years old and I cried like a baby. *(To Artie)* Where was she?, in the hospital?

ARTIE: No, not the hospital, Pop.

SID: Careful, don't pop any stitches. You look good, Shirley.

SHIRLEY: You think so?

SID: We should throw a party for you now that you're back. How about that anniversary party you and Morty threw for us?

SHIRLEY: You still remember that party?

SID: Like it was this minute.

ARTIE: What party?

SID: Before you were born. Before my diabetes, before Ceil got divorced, before Bella's hysterectomy . . . *(To Shirley)* Everybody was still alive. My sister Ruth was alive, you were alive. My mother. My mother passed away . . .

SHIRLEY: So you liked that party, hm, Sidney?

SID: What a party! How come we don't have parties anymore? Anybody left to invite? Everybody's gone or going. I'm going, you're gone. Was it a surprise party?

SHIRLEY: Sure.

SID: Yeah?, were we surprised?

SHIRLEY: I think so, or at least you pretended to be.

SID: I remember the cake: everything from Ebinger's. Blackout cakes.

SHIRLEY: That's right.

SID: Streamers . . . balloons sticking to the walls . . . *(To Artie)* How is it they stick to the walls?

ARTIE: Static electricity.

SID: Is that what it is? Amazing. It was like New Year's Eve. And all our friends. How'd you get hold of all our friends?

SHIRLEY: Phone calls.

SID: Wasn't that some party? Who was there?

SHIRLEY: All your friends.

SID: Artie, it was one of those once-in-a-lifetime times, everybody you ever knew right there in one house! Then, everybody went home! A messy house, crushed pretzels in the carpet —Bella was on her hands and knees picking up crumbs— and you didn't even mind 'cause there were so many nice things to talk about while you did the dishes. And I bet she doesn't remember, but she danced with me.

ARTIE: Yeah?

SHIRLEY: I did?

SID: See? I knew it: She doesn't remember.

SHIRLEY: I danced with a lot of people.

SID *(To Artie)*: You ever dance with her?

ARTIE: I don't think so.

SHIRLEY: You don't think so? I tried to get you to dance with me at your bar mitzvah. You put up such a stink. *(To Sid)* Big shot. Too old to dance with his mother.

SID: His loss. *(To Artie)* She was some dancer. *(Becoming more urgent)* We danced together, you and me. Bunny Berigan was on the hi-fi. I held you close! You threw your head back and laughed. Your hair was auburn then. Red lipstick smudged on your teeth. Shirley, Shirley, Shirley . . . I held you close! You wore a burgundy dress with a sash. *(To Artie)* Oh, God, she doesn't remember.

SHIRLEY: Sidney, you're gonna get yourself sick.

SID: I held you so close, Shirley. You threw your head back and laughed.

ARTIE: Pop, calm down . . .

SID: She laughed! She could've slapped my face but she didn't! *(To Shirley)* Why didn't you slap my face?

SHIRLEY: What are you talking about, Sidney? Why would I slap you?

SID *(Reaching for her)*: Come here . . .

SHIRLEY: Why?

SID: I want to show you.

He tries to take Shirley's hands but she pulls away.

What's the matter?

SHIRLEY: My hands are cold.

SID *(Taking her hands)*: Don't be ridiculous. They're like toast.

Humming Vernon Duke and Ira Gershwin's "I Can't Get Started," he dances with her; she laughs.

I'm crazy about that laugh of yours. Look at those eyelashes. Look at that mouth. Oy, Morty doesn't know what he's got.

SHIRLEY: He knows.

SID: If he knows what he's got, he doesn't know what to do with it now that he's got it.

SHIRLEY: Sidney!

SID: "Sidney!"

They dance slowly for a while.

SHIRLEY *(Suddenly)*: Sidney! You were making a pass at me!

They stop dancing.

SID *(Distressed)*: Of course I was! What did you think I was doing?

SHIRLEY: In front of all those people?

SID: Nobody saw. Maybe Morty did. Yeah, I think maybe Morty gave me a look.

SHIRLEY: Sidney . . . I didn't know . . .

SID *(A beat)*: You mean . . . all these years . . . I was ashamed of something you didn't even know I did? I kept quiet. I kept my distance. I took naps. I thought you thought I was a monster.

SHIRLEY: No, I just thought you were tired.

SID: No . . . Shirley . . . it was that little dance we had, you and me, that dance, at that party, with the streamers and the balloons on the walls, and that laugh of yours with your head thrown back so gorgeously . . .

She slips back into Sid's arms and they dance slowly around the room, Artie watching them. Sid sings the last phrase of "I Can't Get Started."

(To Artie) Didn't I tell you she was some dancer?

Doorbell. Shirley goes to answer the door.

ARTIE: Wait! Let me get it. Hide.

SHIRLEY: Why?

ARTIE: Please? Get in there till I tell you to come out. This has got to be timed just right.

SHIRLEY: Artie, you're a weird kid.

ARTIE: I know.

Shirley goes into the bathroom; Artie shuts the door. Doorbell.

Do me a favor, Pop, don't tell them she's here.

SID: You mean it'll be like a surprise party?

ARTIE: Yeah, a surprise party.

SID: Oh, good . . . *(Goes to the door)* Just a second . . . *(Fumbles with the locks)*

ARTIE: Pop . . . Pop, I'll do it.

Artie unlocks the door. Bella, holding a grocery bag with an Entenmann's cake in it, enters, followed by Ceil; they're in the middle of a conversation.

BELLA: So he was a little overweight.

SID: Hell-o-o . . .

BELLA: Hello, Artie, darling. *(She kisses Artie)*

ARTIE: Hi.

CEIL: He was fat! Hiya, Artie. *(She gives Artie her cheek to kiss)*

ARTIE: Hiya.

BELLA: Maybe if you showed him a little love, he'd sign up with Weight Watchers.

CEIL: Ma-a . . . *(Takes the bag from Bella, starts for the kitchen)*

ARTIE: Notice anything different?

BELLA: I was just saying to myself. . . . Look what's going on here, Ceil.

CEIL: I see! *(Exits)*

SID: So? How's everything?

BELLA *(Looking around)*: What is it, Sid.

SID: Nothing. I just wanted to know how's everything.

BELLA: Everything is fine. Your daughter let another one get away, otherwise everything is fine. Artie, darling, you're arranging?

ARTIE: That's what it looks like.

BELLA: All by yourself?

ARTIE: Well . . .

SID: Shhh . . .

ARTIE: I had a little help.

BELLA: You mean your father?!

CEIL *(Returns; excitedly)*: Remember the stove last night, Ma, how disgusting?

Takes Bella's hand, leads her to the kitchen.

Get ready for the shock of your life. My kitchen should only look like this.

They're gone.

SID *(To Artie)*: If we had even a couple balloons . . .

BELLA *(Off)*: Oh, my God!

SID: . . . a red and a pink . . .

CEIL *(Off)*: Is that spotless or is that spotless?

SID: . . . Rub 'em against the wall . . . !

Shirley, holding Comet and a sponge, pokes her head in from the bathroom.

SHIRLEY: How long am I supposed to stay in here?

ARTIE: Not yet! Get back!

SHIRLEY: Alright, I'll do the tub.

As Artie shuts Shirley in the bathroom, Bella returns, followed by Ceil holding a cake.

BELLA *(Enters kvelling)*: I knew I'd get through to them. *(Seeing the bathroom door close, she goes to it)* Is that my Morty? Hm?

ARTIE: Uh, Grandma . . . ?

BELLA: I was up the whole night worrying.

CEIL *(Noshing on cake)*: I know.

BELLA *(At the bathroom door)*: Morty?, Momma is so proud of what you accomplished, sweetheart. Hurry so I can eat you up.

Mort enters from the bedroom; Bella is somewhat confused. Artie is enjoying this.

Oh, there you are.

MORT *(Beaming)*: Did you see?

BELLA: I certainly did.

MORT: Is that something?

BELLA: It's marvelous.

MORT: Who would believe such a thing?, right?

BELLA: Not me.

MORT: Never in a million years.

BELLA: Never. Give Momma a smooch.

They embrace.

Mazel tov, Morty. That kitchen, it's a work of art.

MORT: Tell that to the artist. Where is she?

Artie gestures to the bathroom. Mort nods. A beat.

BELLA: Mort? Is there a cleaning girl in your bathroom?

MORT: What are you talking about, Ma? I asked if you saw her.

BELLA: Who?

MORT: Shirley!

SID *(Silencing Mort)*: Shhh . . .

BELLA: What do you mean Shirley?

CEIL: Oh, God, Ma . . .

BELLA: Shirley came all the way over to clean the house?

MORT *(Laughs)*: Yes! Artie, tell them.

SID *(To Artie)*: Where was she anyway?

CEIL: What's gonna be with Morty?

MORT *(Prodding Artie)*: Tell them.

ARTIE *(Matter-of-factly)*: It's true. She came home.

SID: Shhh . . . supposed to be a surprise . . .

CEIL: Artie . . .

BELLA *(To Artie)*: Enough with the jokes!

CEIL: Why torture him?

ARTIE: She's home! My mother came home!

BELLA: Comedian!

MORT: No, she did! She rang the door! You should've seen her standing there, my poor baby, she walked all the way . . .

CEIL: You're breaking my heart, Mort.

BELLA: Look what you're doing to your sister.

MORT: The two of us, I'm telling you, we were beside ourselves. Right, Artie?

He and Artie share a laugh.

CEIL: Oh, God . . . *(Exits to bedroom)*

BELLA *(Takes Mort's hand)*: Listen to me: Grief, Mort . . .

MORT *(Smiling)*: Ma . . .

BELLA: It does things to people.

ARTIE *(Enjoying the fuss)*: She's in the bathroom, Grandma.

BELLA: When will you stop?, when we have to put him away?

ARTIE: See for yourself. Open the door! She's scrubbing the bathtub!

BELLA: A little respect for the dead, Artie.

Ceil enters, donning Shirley's fur jacket.

MORT: Oh no you don't . . .

BELLA: Good, Ceil.

MORT: Put it back!

CEIL: It's for your own good, Morty . . .

MORT: You can't just go to her closet and take things!

BELLA: Ceil is right! You gotta snap out of it, Morty!

MORT: Shirley's not gonna like this . . .

CEIL: Shirley doesn't need it anymore, she's dead, Mort . . .

SID *(To himself)*: Is that what I heard? Dead?

CEIL *(To Mort, continued)*: Dead and buried. I'm alive, let me enjoy it.

BELLA: That's right.

CEIL: Shirley would've wanted it this way.

MORT *(Calls)*: Shirley!

Bella shakes her head sadly at Mort's display.

CEIL *(Models for Sid's approval)*: Daddy?

MORT *(Calls)*: Ceil's got on your beautiful jacket!

CEIL: What do you think, Daddy, hm?

SID: Nice.

MORT *(Now struggling with Ceil)*: Alright, take it off! Take it off!

CEIL: Morty, stop! She's dead, Morty! Shirley is dead! You gotta
   let go!

Artie opens the bathroom door, revealing Shirley.

ARTIE: Ta dahhh!

SHIRLEY: Hi.

MORT: There's my Shirley!

SID: SURPRISE!

SHIRLEY: There was a ring around that bathtub you would not
   believe. Sit down, break in a chair! What can I get you?

Bella and Ceil are stunned into silence.

BELLA *(Her eyes on Shirley)*: Ceil, my glasses are in my bag.

Ceil hands it to her.

   Thank you, dear. *(Finds her glasses, puts them on, looks at
   Shirley for a beat)* Does that look like Shirley to you, Ceil?

MORT: It's Shirley.

BELLA: I'm asking Ceil. Ceil?

CEIL: Yeah, Ma.

BELLA *(A beat)*: So, Shirley? *(A beat)* Good for you.

MORT: See? What did I tell you? She was here all along!

SHIRLEY *(To Bella)*: What do you think of the place? It's getting
   there, don't you think? I'm finally getting it right. Please.
   Don't mind me. Everybody sit.

CEIL *(Taking off the jacket)*: Shirley . . . I didn't mean anything . . .

SHIRLEY: That's okay, Ceil.

CEIL: I only wanted to see how it felt.

SHIRLEY: That fur . . . always made me feel like a million bucks.

CEIL: You always had such nice things, such pretty things.

SHIRLEY: Thanks, Ceil.

CEIL: You always *kibitzed* with the men at cousin's club meetings; I helped in the kitchen. You always made the men laugh. Follow the sound of men laughing: There was Shirley. You always looked good. Everybody thought so. My father . . . *(Strokes the jacket lining)* I always loved that: "Shirley" stitched inside in fancy script. *(She puts down the jacket)*

BELLA *(To Mort)*: So did you find out about your shirts at least?

MORT: Oh, yeah, Shirley, what'd you do with the laundry ticket for all my shirts?

BELLA: He's out of clean shirts.

SHIRLEY: Oh! *(Goes to the front closet, takes a paper-wrapped Chinese laundry bundle from a shelf)* They were right here! I never got a chance to put them away!

MORT: Ha! How do you like that!

BELLA *(Unenthused)*: Leave it to Shirley to solve the big mystery.

SHIRLEY: What's the matter, Bella, aren't you glad to see me?

BELLA: Glad? Glad is not the word. *(She walks away from Shirley)*

MORT: Ma, what's the matter with you?, is that how you talk to Shirley? After all she's been through?

BELLA: What do you want me to say? "Welcome home, Shirley"? I can't. I don't approve.

SHIRLEY: You? You never approved.

BELLA: I beg your pardon? I approved more than you know. More than you know, young lady. I'm not the kind of person who shows much. I'm not like your father-in-law in that respect.

SID: Huh?

BELLA: Nothing, Sid. *(Continuing, to Shirley)* This I don't approve. I saw you laid out in the chapel, Shirley. I watched them close the lid and put you in the ground and cover you up with dirt.

MORT: Ma, why even bring that up?

BELLA: Why?! 'Cause the dead don't dust, my darling! The dead don't redecorate!

MORT: Ma, what do you want to make waves for?

BELLA: This isn't right, Morty! This is not how it's supposed to be. *(To Shirley, gently)* Look: You're in the middle of supper, the middle of redecorating, the middle of your life: It happens. Too bad about you. You don't get to keep a foot in the door. You're either in or you're out. And you, my dear Shirley, you are not in.

MORT: What kind of way is that to talk?! I'm not gonna have you talk to my wife like that!

BELLA *(To Shirley)*: You think this is helping him? You think this is helping either of them?

MORT: Never mind about me. I have a tongue. I can speak for myself.

BELLA *(To Shirley)*: And just how long do you expect to keep this up?

SHIRLEY: As long as the boys need me, I'll be here.

BELLA: Is that so? And that's okay with you, Artie?

ARTIE: What?

BELLA: It's okay with you having your dead mother around like this?

Artie doesn't know what to say.

MORT: Alright, that's it. If you don't approve . . . go! Goodbye!

SHIRLEY: Morty . . .

MORT: Leave us alone!

BELLA: Fine! Let's leave them alone with dead Shirley. Ceil? Sid? *(Gets her coat, etc.)*

SHIRLEY: Don't go, we're family!

CEIL *(Waking Sid)*: Stop dreaming, Pop, we're going home.

SID *(Waking from a dream; being helped into his coat)*: Shirley?

SHIRLEY: Come on, sit down, eat your cake. We'll talk.

MORT *(To Shirley)*: Forget about them. All they want is to keep you buried. We don't need them.

ARTIE: We don't?

MORT: We don't need anybody. The hell with them.

BELLA: You know, Shirley? Quite a number of people came to pay respects.

SHIRLEY: Yes?

BELLA: Many, many people came to the chapel.

SHIRLEY: Really?

BELLA: Oh, the place was jammed. And here, people in and out all week. Neighbors, old friends from the Year One. . . . The food they sent! The platters! So many donations, so many trees planted!

CEIL *(Anxious to leave)*: Ma-a . . .

BELLA: I'm coming. *(To Shirley)* I guess what I'm getting at, Shirley. . . . What do we tell all these people? They went to all that trouble. *(A beat. As she touches Mort's face in a gesture of farewell)* You know my number. Artie? You've got your whole life. Time heals.

Artie kisses her cheek. A beat.

Shirley, you should rest in peace.

Bella exits. Ceil, holding Sid, starts for the door.

CEIL: By the way, Shirley, in case you were wondering. . . . That was me . . . I was the one wrapped up all the leftovers.

SHIRLEY: Thank you, Ceil, I appreciate it. You did a wonderful job.

CEIL: You think so?

SHIRLEY: Ceil? *(She offers the jacket. A beat)* Take it. It's yours.

CEIL: I couldn't . . .

SHIRLEY: Please. I want you to have it. *(She puts it in Ceil's hands)* Wear it in good health.

A beat. Sid approaches Shirley.

SID: Shirley?

Ceil tugs on Sid's arm.

(To Ceil) Let go my arm.

CEIL: Say goodbye, Pop.

SID: Let go my arm. Shirley? *(To Ceil)* Don't pull on me!

CEIL: Oh, the hell with it! *(She exits)*

SID: Shirley? When I'm sleeping? Driving home? You're the one sitting next to me, Shirley, you are, the road map on your lap, reading me directions. *(He kisses Shirley's forehead)* See you soon. *(He starts to exit)*

ARTIE *(Goes to hug him)*: Bye, Pop.

Sid pats Artie on the cheek and exits.

MORT *(To Artie)*: Lock the door.

Artie's anxiety is growing; he doesn't lock the door.

SHIRLEY: But, Morty, they're your family.

MORT: This is my family, right here.

ARTIE: Dad . . .

MORT: It's like a dream come true! We're together again, Shirley! Nothing else matters.

SHIRLEY: I don't know about this, Morty . . .

MORT: All I want is to be with you. Artie and I'll keep you company. Right, Artie? Artie, lock the door.

ARTIE: Why?

MORT: We don't want anybody from out there coming in.

ARTIE: Dad, you don't mean it . . .

MORT: Just do it. *(To Shirley, as they sit down together)* Are we gonna have ourselves a ball! It'll be like a vacation, only we'll stay home.

SHIRLEY: But you're gonna have to go back to work.

MORT: The hell with work.

SHIRLEY: You're gonna have to earn a living. You've got Artie to take care of.

MORT: Why bother to leave the house when I can stay here and be with you?

SHIRLEY: I don't want you doing that for me, Morty.

MORT: Nothing out there is important anymore, Shirley. We don't have to go anywhere, we don't have to see anybody, we don't have to do a thing. Nothing would make me happier than just sitting here knowing you're next to me.

He rests his head on her shoulder. Shirley's discomfort is growing.

Artie, I told you to lock the door.

ARTIE: No.

MORT: What do you mean no? Do you love your mother or what?

ARTIE: Of course.

MORT: Then lock the door.

ARTIE: If I lock everybody out, that means I'm locking us in. I don't want to lock us in. Mommy, Grandma was right, this isn't gonna work. You shouldn't be here anymore.

MORT: Hey! If you don't like it, you can go, too!

SHIRLEY: Morty, don't say that.

MORT: He wants to get rid of you, Shirley!

ARTIE: No, I don't!

MORT: Yes you do! That's what you're doing! You want to push your mother out that door forever?, is that what you want?!

ARTIE: No! I don't want her to go! *(To Shirley)* You're tricking me again! I saw you rise away on a wave! But you're really gone this time! You can't come back.

SHIRLEY: But I haven't finished taking care of you!

MORT: Don't listen to him, don't listen to him, Shirley . . .

ARTIE: How am I gonna miss you if you won't go?!

MORT *(Pushing Artie around)*: Everything's always you! What about me this time?!

ARTIE: Daddy, you think I want this?

SHIRLEY *(Overlap)*: Morty, stop it. . . . Leave him alone!

MORT *(To Artie)*: If you don't want her around, then you should go!

SHIRLEY: But I'm the one who's dead!

MORT: No, no . . . not for me you're not. You're not dead. You'll never be dead. Shirley, I'll do anything you want . . .

SHIRLEY: Morty . . .

MORT: I'll make it easy for you here. What do you want? Tell me.

SHIRLEY: Morty, stop this . . .

MORT: You don't have to lift a finger. Tell me what to do! *(He holds Shirley to him and carries her around the room)* YOU CAN'T GO!

SHIRLEY *(Struggling)*: Mort!

MORT: I'm nothing without you!

SHIRLEY: Artie, help me!

ARTIE *(Trying to separate them)*: Dad . . . !

MORT: I could hold on to you like this forever!

SHIRLEY *(Overlap)*: No, Morty . . . stop!

ARTIE *(Furiously trying to pry them apart)*: Daddy, stop! I don't want to lose you, too!

Pause. Mort slowly releases her. A beat.

MORT *(To Artie, gently)*: Me? I'm here.

Pause.

SHIRLEY: Such a stupid death.

ARTIE: I know.

SHIRLEY: Not what I had in mind at all. Killed by a piece of pork stuck in my windpipe?! Is that stupid?!

ARTIE: It really is.

MORT: So it went down the wrong pipe. So what?, could've happened to anybody.

SHIRLEY: Oh, but those poor people who run the restaurant! It was their grand opening! And all those hungry people waiting in line?! I must've ruined their appetites!

MORT *(Comforting her)*: Shhh . . .

SHIRLEY: One minute I'm tasting plum sauce, the next thing I know, I'm on the floor, drowning.

ARTIE: Did you see your whole life passing . . . ?

SHIRLEY: No, just feet. Feet of Chinese waiters. *(A beat)* I never felt so cheated in my life.

ARTIE: I'm sorry, Ma.

SHIRLEY: Why couldn't I have gone slowly? Hm, Morty? Like in the movies. Could've had bedside scenes. Long goodbyes. Me, in pink lacy nightgowns, and perfume. We could've prepared together. I could've tidied up, nice and neat. Wouldn't I have been great, Artie? Cheerful, cynical . . .

ARTIE *(Smiling)*: Yeah . . .

SHIRLEY: . . . valiant till the end, withering away with dignity?

MORT: Shirley, all that matters is you're here and you're staying here.

SHIRLEY *(To Artie)*: I can't stay, can I?

Artie shakes his head. A beat. Shirley begins to make finishing touches. Pause.

MORT: Look. . . . Maybe we can work something out.

SHIRLEY: I don't think so.

MORT: Maybe you can stay a little while longer.

SHIRLEY: No, Morty, I can't.

MORT: A couple more days, even.

ARTIE: Dad, no.

MORT: You can spend weekends here or something.

SHIRLEY: No, Morty, I don't think that would work.

MORT: No?

She shakes her head. A beat.

What'll I do, Shirley?

SHIRLEY: You'll learn new things.

MORT: I can't.

SHIRLEY: You'll have to.

MORT: It's too late.

SHIRLEY: Of course it's not, Morty, don't be ridiculous.

Pause.

MORT: You're really going, Shirley?

SHIRLEY: Yes.

MORT: When? Soon?

SHIRLEY: A couple of minutes.

MORT: That soon, hm?

Her eyes on Artie, Shirley nods. Pause.

I just want you to know I'm not crazy about this.

SHIRLEY: I'm not either, really.

MORT: You can still change your mind.

SHIRLEY: No.

Pause.

MORT: You're always welcome here. Remember that.

SHIRLEY: I know.

MORT: I mean it.

SHIRLEY: I know, Morty, thank you.

Pause.

MORT: So. . . . How you getting back?

SHIRLEY: Same way I got here.

MORT: Oh, no you're not. I'm taking you.

SHIRLEY: You really don't have to.

MORT: You think I'm gonna let you go off by yourself? I'll drop you off.

SHIRLEY: Yeah?

MORT: How's that?

SHIRLEY: That sounds nice.

MORT: I'm just gonna have to stop for gas. Tell you what: Why don't we make a little trip out of it? I'll drive slow. We'll take our time.

SHIRLEY: Okay.

MORT: We'll take in the scenery.

SHIRLEY: Nice.

MORT: And if you get hungry, I'll take you to that seafood place. Remember how you loved their bay scallops?

SHIRLEY: Mmmm . . . yes . . . !

MORT: And if we pass any flea markets along the road?, we'll stop, I won't say a word.

SHIRLEY: Thanks.

MORT: No big deal.

SHIRLEY: Good.

MORT: No rush.

SHIRLEY: No rush. *(A beat)* I'm gonna go put on something pretty.

MORT: Good idea.

SHIRLEY: I'll be right back. *(She exits to the bedroom)*
MORT *(Calls)*: Take your time!

A long, awkward pause, like in Act One when Mort and Artie are alone for the first time.

Artie?
ARTIE: Yeah? *(A beat)*
MORT: I'm not mad at you.
ARTIE: Oh?
MORT: You're not mad at me are ya?
ARTIE: Mad? Not mad. *(A beat)*
MORT: So I guess this is just one of those things, huh?
ARTIE: I guess. *(A beat)*
MORT: Gee, I sure wish this didn't have to be.
ARTIE: Me, too. *(A beat)*
MORT: Must be rough losing your mother. I mean, I wouldn't know what that's like.

Artie looks at him. A beat.

You know I think you're a good kid, don'tcha, Artie?
ARTIE: Yeah?
MORT: Always thought so. *(A beat)* Hey, I don't suppose you'd maybe want to go away with me to Hawaii or someplace, would you?
ARTIE: No, Dad.
MORT: No, hm? Didn't think so. Not such a good idea, hm?

Artie shakes his head no.

No, I guess not. *(A beat)* Who knows? Maybe I'll go by myself. How does that grab ya?
ARTIE: Yeah, you should.
MORT: I will. I'll get a tan, I'll eat pineapple. I'll send you post-cards. How's that? Can I send you postcards?
ARTIE: Of course.
MORT *(Suddenly near tears)*: I don't know what I'm gonna do, Artie. . . . You gotta help me.

ARTIE: Daddy, I can't.

Pause. Mort nods. A beat; he sees that Artie's shoelace is untied and ties it for him.

MORT: Careful. You could hurt yourself.

Shirley enters wearing the red dress.

Oh!, would you get a load of this!
SHIRLEY: You like it?
MORT: Fabulous!
SHIRLEY: It's not too loud?
MORT: If it is, the hell with them. You look beautiful. Artie, doesn't your mother look beautiful?
ARTIE: Yeah, she really does.
MORT *(To Shirley)*: Let's see you shimmer.

Shirley shakes.

Look at that!
ARTIE: Could you go now? Please?
MORT: Uh, yeah, sure . . . *(To Shirley)* You want to take anything with you?
SHIRLEY: Like what?

Artie takes the matchbook out of his pocket and looks at it.

MORT: I don't know, some pictures, maybe? Pictures of us?

He looks through the drawer of the sideboard for photos. Artie hands her the matchbook. She looks at it quizzically, then it registers.

SHIRLEY: "Holiday Inn, Freehold—"

She and Artie look at one another. She puts the matchbook in her purse as Mort hands her some photos.

No, I don't need pictures. I'll remember. *(She admires the room)* Well!
ARTIE: Nice.

Shirley is tempted to rearrange a pillow; Artie gently stops her.

Just leave it. It looks good.

SHIRLEY: Yeah? What do you think, Morty? Not bad, hm?

MORT: What are you talking about "Not bad"?: Good.

SHIRLEY *(A beat)*: "Goodbyee forevverr . . ." *(Nervous laugh)*

ARTIE *(Quietly)*: Please . . . just go?

SHIRLEY: Say goodbye?

Artie looks at her after for a moment, then turns away. A beat. She smiles.

Okay.

MORT: Artie, will I see you later?

Artie shrugs, "I guess."

How about when I come back, I take you out to eat? Hm?

ARTIE: Sure.

Shirley and Mort start to exit; she stops to admire the room.

SHIRLEY: It's amazing what a little rearranging'll do.

A beat. She exits; Mort follows her out, then sticks his head in.

MORT: Artie? Lock up.

Mort closes the door. Artie, alone, is confronted by the silence and his own grief. He walks around the room for a moment, then suddenly goes to the front door, opens it, and calls down the hall.

ARTIE: Mommy?!

A beat. He slowly shuts the door. As the lights fade, he looks like he is finally about to cry.

THE MODEL
APARTMENT

❑ ❑ ❑

LOLA, and her husband, MAX, both in their 60s, are Holocaust survivors; they speak with eastern European accents

DEBBY, late 30s, obese, unkempt, mentally disturbed, is their daughter; the actress who plays Debby wears a realistic "fat suit" which is shed when she appears as DEBORAH, her half-sister who died in infancy during the Holocaust

NEIL, 15, short and skinny, is Debby's black lover; a mildly retarded kid who lives on the streets of Manhattan

PLACE

The model apartment in a condominium development in Florida. Its large sunken living room is also used for dining and sleeping; the kitchen is fully exposed; a corridor leads to the bath and dressing rooms. Floor-to-ceiling windows and sliding doors open onto a small, enclosed sun porch, a patch of foliage, and, at street level, the edge of an asphalt driveway. Lots of glass and chrome. Indoor-outdoor carpeting. Plastic plants. Candlesticks, ashtrays, and bric-a-brac are glued to surfaces. Objects function solely as decoration; the television and appliances are state-of-the-art but hollow.

This play is performed without interruption.

Scene One

Night. The apartment is dark. We hear a car pull into the drive-
way and see its headlights through the windows. We hear Lola and
Max get out of the car and unload luggage. Soon we hear talking
and giddy laughter at the front door of the apartment; we can
see their movements through the crack of light beneath the door.
They set down bags and fumble with keys. We hear them speak;
there is a playfulness about them (particularly Max), like that of
newlyweds.

LOLA: Now which is the key?
MAX: Give me.
LOLA: He said the gold. They all look gold.
MAX: *Give* me.
LOLA: He gave us the wrong keys.
MAX: Let *me*.

Lola tries another key.

You just did that one. Lola, please . . .

LOLA *(Over "Lola, please . . . ")*: So many keys, Max, how do they expect us to know which is which?

MAX *(Over ". . . which is which?")*: Will you let *me*?!

LOLA: Take. I have no patience for this.

Max tries a key; no luck.

Ha!

MAX: Shhh.

The next key proves successful.

Uh! What did I tell you?

He opens the door; they're silhouetted in the doorway. Lola sighs deeply.

MAX: If you *gave* me . . .

LOLA: They could've at least left a light . . .

MAX: . . . we would've been in by now.

LOLA: You could kill yourself walking into a strange room.

MAX: I'll carry you.

LOLA *(Pretending she thinks it's a silly idea)*: Max . . .

MAX: I'll *car*ry you. Why?, you think I'll pull something?

LOLA: Max, we have no light.

MAX: Across the threshold, no?

LOLA: No fooling around, it's dark.

Max, laughing, continues to joke around with Lola.

It's *dark*.

MAX *(Groping in the dark for a switch or lamp)*: I'm afraid I'll knock something over.

LOLA: Break something. I don't care. I'm sick from this, Max. What we went through . . . the way they shlep us around . . .

Max turns on a lamp. A beat; Lola takes in the room; she's impressed.

Nice.

MAX *(Beaming)*: See that?

LOLA: Oh, Max . . .

MAX: See? And you were worried.

LOLA: I wasn't worried, I didn't know . . .

MAX: Would I let you suffer?

LOLA: I like the effect with the lamp.

MAX: Uh-huh. See?

LOLA: Isn't that an unusual effect?

MAX: I'm telling you: these furnishings: tops.

LOLA *(Taking inventory)*: Hi-*fi*, T*V*, *dish*washer, *ice* maker . . .

MAX: The man *said* luxury.

LOLA: This is like ours?

MAX: Ours is bigger, the one bedroom.

LOLA: There's no bedroom?

MAX: No. This condo is cheaper with the one room.

LOLA: Who wants to live in one room? Not me. Not after what I left.

MAX: Some people . . . *(Shrugs)*

LOLA: You don't go from five and a half rooms to one room.

MAX: Some people don't care.

LOLA: What we left, Max! You'd have to carry me out of here. We'd be on top of each other, no room to breathe.

MAX: You got all of Florida to breathe! Who stays home in Florida?!

LOLA: So where do you sleep?, on the couch?

MAX: It opens up. *(He investigates the couch)* See?

LOLA: Oh, I *see*.

MAX: It opens up. I was right.

LOLA: How good could that be for your back every night?

MAX: Some people don't mind . . .

LOLA: I like a little support.

MAX: For one or two nights this is gonna kill you?

LOLA: How do *you* know one or two nights?

MAX: That's what the man said.

LOLA: And you believe him?

MAX: Why?

LOLA: You saw what our place looks like. They still have to *paint*, they still have to lay the indoor-outdoor carpeting.

MAX: So?

LOLA: All I'm saying, one or two nights, it's a conservative esti-
mate, I don't believe him, he's lying. If he thinks they can
finish up tomorrow. . . . They won't finish.

MAX: So the day after.

LOLA *(A beat: she casually tries to move an ashtray but discovers it's
glued down)*: Uh! Look at this! They glued it down!

Max shrugs.

I should never've let you talk me into this. You *had* to run . . .

MAX: Lola . . .

LOLA: Give them a little extra time I said, to make sure.

MAX: Alright . . .

LOLA: This is not why I came to Florida.

MAX: It's only for the time being! *Listen* to you! You make it
sound like torture.

LOLA: They promise you a certain date . . .

MAX: Alright, okay!

LOLA: You plan, you ship furniture, you drive down, and what
happens? You get there and you can't live there with the bare
walls and the bare floors and a *toilet*, ucchh . . .

MAX *(Losing patience)*: It's only for the time *being*!

LOLA: You put every cent you got into a condo and they treat you
like animals.

MAX: Think how it's gonna be!

LOLA: I know, I know . . .

MAX: This is even better than I pictured in my head. No?

LOLA: Why we had to come all this way for *this*, to be treated like
this . . .

MAX: We're here, there's nothing we can do. What can we do?
You want to eat your *kishkas* out?, fine.

LOLA *(Over "fine")*: All I'm saying: We could've stayed home, in
our own house. It isn't fair we should have to go through this.

MAX *(Over "we should have to go . . . ")*: Fair? What is fair? Lola,
please, trust me. Wait till the morning and the sun is out and
we'll stroll.

Lola nods.

Think about Florida. Forget about everything else. We're in Florida now. We made it. In one piece.

He laughs; Lola does, too.

The hell with everything else.

LOLA: Yeah? Forget? Ha.

MAX: Look. Look where we are, you and me: You ever see such luxury in your life? Look at that TV. Top of the line. Maybe they got cable. Hm? Maybe they got a sexy picture.

He turns the TV on; it fails to go on.

LOLA *(Examining the kitchen floor)*: What do you think of the rust?

MAX *(Investigating the set)*: What's the matter with this thing?

LOLA: I wonder since they didn't lay the floor yet . . .

MAX *(Clicks the set on and off, smacks it, etc.)*: Hm . . .

LOLA: Max? What do you think of the rust as opposed to the avocado?

MAX *(Still on the set)*: What the hell's going on here? It's busted.

LOLA: For all they put us through . . .

MAX *(Checks the rear of the set and sees that there's no picture tube)*: Uh! How do you like that.

LOLA: The least they could do is let me have the rust. Don't you think?

MAX: You see this? Hm? You paying attention what's going on here? It's just for show!

LOLA: What.

MAX: The TV! It's empty!

LOLA: Good. TV is always empty.

MAX: Those bastards.

LOLA: You'll survive, Max, listen: The rust is warmer, no? The rust would bring out the rust in my dishes.

MAX *(Still focused on the TV)*: You should've thought of that before.

LOLA: It didn't occur to me, alright? In the morning I want you to call the man—

MAX: Some luxury!

LOLA: —tell him the least he can do is let me have the rust, cancel the avocado.

MAX: *Goniff.*

LOLA: You'll call the man. You saw how embarrassed he was.

MAX: That wasn't embarrassed.

LOLA: It's embarrassing to have to move people around like this in the middle of the night.

MAX: What people? *Us.* Who else has to go through this? Everybody else's condo is done. Painted, carpeted. Just us. The story of my life.

LOLA: Call the man. He said anything he can do.

MAX: Wait, that was tonight. When it's *day*light . . .

LOLA: You'll call him. You'll say, "Yes, as a matter of fact there *are* some things you can do for us."

MAX *(Finds the stereo doesn't work either)*: Liars . . .

LOLA: Why should we pay for our inconvenience, no? He said anything he can do, don't hesitate, remember? Well? Tell him we want to change the floor. We're entitled, no? what else? I'll make a list. *(Looks in her bag, finds an envelope, writes on it)* What else? Maybe he'll let us have a window treatment like that.

MAX: You like that?

LOLA: Well . . . it's nice.

Max shrugs.

No? Alright, forget the window.

MAX: I'm a drape man. I like drapes.

LOLA: Not in a hundred-degree heat do you want drapes on your windows.

MAX: No?

LOLA: You don't do drapes in the tropics, you do bamboo.

MAX: Whatever you want. What do I know?

Pause.

LOLA: You're disappointed.

MAX: Who's disappointed?

LOLA: You want to go.

MAX: Go where? No.

LOLA: We can go back; it's okay by me.

MAX: No.

LOLA: You're unhappy: the TV.

MAX: No no no.

Pause.

LOLA: I'm only trying to . . .

MAX: I know.

Lola thinks of something she wants from a particular suitcase.

LOLA: Where's the valise? We left the valise in the car.

MAX: I know. I brought the overnight.

LOLA: You're not gonna leave the valise on the backseat.

MAX: Why?, who's gonna take it.

LOLA: Max, I need it.

MAX: There's nobody here, this whole side of the development.

LOLA: You want *me* to shlep it in?

MAX: Just leave it. We're only gonna be here one or two nights, why bother shlepping it back and forth?, we *got* the overnight bags.

LOLA: You don't leave things in the car for people to look inside and steal.

MAX: There's nobody out there.

LOLA: Even worse. Go, Max. You never know. Cubans, I understand, all over Florida.

MAX: You're being ridiculous.

LOLA: *I'm* being ridiculous? *Who* had to run to Florida to a condo that isn't ready? Better safe than sorry. Please, Max, before you sit down and take off your shoes and your feet swell: the valise.

MAX: Alright, alright, alright . . .

He goes; she remembers the grocery bag they entered with, takes it to the kitchen area, opens the refrigerator, and puts milk and other groceries inside. She realizes that the bulb is out.

LOLA *(To herself)*: What's with the bulb? *(She reaches inside; the refrigerator isn't cold; she opens the freezer, touches it, and realizes*

that it isn't on) What? *(She pokes around the back of the refrigerator looking for the plug; she finds its cord but the plug has been
snipped off)* Oh, my God . . .

Max returns struggling with a valise.

The fridge, Max! Look! *(Shows him the cut cord)*

Max laughs.

Very funny, our milk is gonna turn!

Max's laughter grows.

I bought all this food for breakfast . . .
MAX: So it doesn't work . . .
LOLA: A nice breakfast in our new place.
MAX: And I was gonna watch TV. So what? So *what?*
LOLA: Perishables. Everything's wasted.
MAX: So the man is a bastard. The fridge is a fake. So?
LOLA *(Tragically)*: Milk . . .

Max puts his arms around Lola, reassuringly. Blackout.

Scene Two

*Lola is seated on the sofa eating out of a plastic bowl; Max, stand-
ing, eats off the top of the TV. Silence.*

LOLA: So?

Max shrugs. Pause.

Good?

Max nods equivocally.

No good?
MAX: It's good, it's good.

LOLA: Better we should eat breakfast tonight. Waste not . . .

Pause.

Are you gonna sit?

MAX: I don't want to sit.

LOLA: You sure?

MAX: I'm sure.

Pause.

LOLA: I did something wrong?

MAX: You didn't do anything wrong, I feel like standing. So many hours driving . . .

LOLA: Stand. *(Shrugs)*

Long pause.

I wonder what she's doing.

No response; Max is suddenly depressed. Pause.

Don't you wonder?

Max shakes his head no; shrugs; pause.

MAX: No. No, I don't wonder.

Pause.

LOLA: Uh, *now* I did something wrong. *(Sighs; long pause)* What did you give her?

MAX: I gave her.

LOLA: How much?

MAX: I don't know, three hundred, five hundred.

LOLA: Which.

MAX: Five hundred I think.

LOLA: No. Yes?

MAX: Four something.

LOLA: That much?

Max shrugs. Pause.

I gave her a check.

MAX: Besides what I gave?

LOLA: So?

MAX: I gave her close to five hundred!

LOLA: So I gave her a little more. What is five hundred gonna do. How far is *that* gonna go?

MAX: So what'd you give?

LOLA: A check.

MAX: Yeah, I know, how much?

Pause.

LOLA: Twenty-five hundred.

MAX: Twenty-five *hun*dred?!

LOLA: Shhh. I *knew* it . . .

MAX: Why twenty-five hundred?! I gave her *five* hundred.

LOLA: *Four*-something you said.

MAX: You know what she's gonna do with it?! Huh?!

LOLA: Better to give her a nice lump all at once . . .

Max grumbles.

She'll leave us alone. Right? Isn't that what you want? If she don't need nothing—anything—if she doesn't need anything . . .

MAX: That's not how we worked it!

LOLA: Max! *(Meaning "quiet")*

MAX: The more you give, the faster it goes! Don't you know that by now?!

LOLA: But we were going away. For good. It's not the same.

MAX: Oh, God . . . it doesn't stop. It doesn't stop . . .

LOLA *(Over "It doesn't stop . . . ")*: It's not the same, Max. We left. So I gave her something to tide her over a little.

Max sighs, grumbles.

I couldn't give her nothing. She'll leave us alone.

Long pause. Lola goes to her valise, opens it, takes out a paper bag and a package of plastic cups. Max gestures "What's that?"

I thought a celebration. *(Takes a bottle of wine out of the bag)*

Blackout.

Scene Three

Max's Walkman is set up on the table, playing opera. Lola is clothed but barefoot; Max, wearing a T-shirt, is also barefoot and his belt is undone. They have been drinking. They move slowly, close together, rhythmically, almost dancing, for a long time. Max hums while gently kissing her face and neck. He unbuttons Lola's blouse and nestles his head in her breast.

Blackout.

Scene Four

Debby, grossly obese and unkempt, moves around the room inspecting it; she's like a blimp, the Hindenburg, slowly floating, winding through the apartment, from object to object, while Lola buttons her blouse and Max puts on his shoes.

DEBBY: Fancy. *(Pause; admires plastic plant)* Pretty flowers.
MAX: How did you come?
DEBBY: I followed the sun.
MAX: How did you *come.*
DEBBY: I *was* gonna skydive in but I remembered your heart condition.

Lola sighs deeply.

I thought the sight of *me* floating down from the sky might scare you to death so I drove.
MAX: Drove what? What did you drive?
DEBBY: I *have* a car.
MAX: You have a car?

DEBBY: I *have* a car.

MAX: How do you have a car?

LOLA: Max . . .

DEBBY: I have a car because I have a car, Daddy. I was *given* a car.

MAX: Who gave you a car?

DEBBY: Don't look at me like that, Daddy, I don't like you looking at me like that.

MAX: How am I looking?

DEBBY: Stop.

MAX: Alright, I'm not looking . . .

LOLA: There's no food.

DEBBY: I like it here.

LOLA: Did you hear what I said?

DEBBY: Such luxury.

LOLA: There's no food: The fridge is a fake.

DEBBY: Oh, Mommy, this is comfy.

LOLA: I have nothing to offer you.

DEBBY: I like it here. Where do you sleep?

LOLA: Who.

DEBBY: Where do you *sleep*.

LOLA: We sleep here. There is no bedroom. This is it. It's very
small.

DEBBY: It's perfect.

LOLA: For the time being. There's no room. This is it. The sofa
opens up.

DEBBY *(Sings)*: "Castro Convertible."

MAX: So you drove in a car.

DEBBY: I followed the sun.

LOLA: I wish I had something to offer you.

DEBBY: I went where the boys are. Isn't this where the boys are?

Max looks quizzical.

Connie here?

MAX: Connie?

DEBBY: Connie Francis here?

MAX: I can't talk to you when you're like this.

DEBBY: Like what?

MAX *(To Lola)*: This is what I'm paying them for?, so she can run away to Florida?

Lola shakes her head; she doesn't know.

DEBBY *(Plops herself into a chair)*: Ooo, this is the *life!*

MAX: They're supposed to keep an eye on her. This is how they keep an eye on her? They don't even call to tell us!

LOLA: How they gonna call us, Max?, we have no phone . . .

DEBBY: Excuse me . . .

MAX: She wasn't ready for the residence . . .

DEBBY: Excuse me, you got a pool here?

LOLA: A pool? A swimming pool?

DEBBY: There's got to be a pool here.

Lola shrugs.

There must be. Oh, come on, there's gotta be. I packed a suit. Two-piece bikini. Hot pink. Two sizes too small, so I'll have to lose weight. What I need, Daddy, I need to sit in the sun, relax a little. Rub on some oil, sleep in a chair, and bake. Last time I was tan, I looked West Indian. Haitian or something. I'm so pale I could die. I'll roll down my straps, get tan all over. Brown shoulders, brown everything.

MAX: How did you find us?

DEBBY: I told you, I followed the sun.

MAX: We're not where we're supposed to be. How did you find us?

DEBBY: I used my noodle. I *have* a brain.

LOLA *(To Max)*: I'm trying to tell her we have no food.

MAX: No. No food.

LOLA: I have nothing to offer you.

DEBBY: I ate on the road. Howard Johnson's. All the fried clams you can eat I ate. You got to watch out at Howard Johnson's. Ask Connie Francis. It's a front for the Nazis.

Lola sighs deeply.

She got raped by a Nazi dressed like a bellboy. I had a close call myself. This Nazi? He was sitting at the counter eating a pistachio sundae. Had a scar on his eye like somebody tried to scratch it out. But very handsome. Like Pat Boone. I memorized his face so I could tell it to the police and they could send sketches to the highway patrol. Very smart, no?

Max shakes his head in frustration.

He was gonna sterilize me. I saw shiny tools in his jeep. I got in my car. He followed me. I was gonna double-cross him and pull over and let him screw me in the backseat and kill him with one of his own scalpels just at the point of orgasm and save mankind, but I lost him in traffic.

Max looks to Lola for corroboration; she shrugs and sighs deeply.

You gotta watch out at Howard Johnson's. Poor Connie. What she went through! Some comeback, though, hm? Wow, what a triumphant return, hm? Sometimes I wish *I* could go away just so I could come back. Judy Garland. Every *day* for her was a comeback. I would love a comeback. Who would I come back *as? (A beat)* Deb-or-ah.

Max reacts, looks away.

No more of this "Debby" shit: "Deborah," tan all the time, ribs showing. Hanging out with surfers. Some of my best friends are surfers. Don't look so *close!*

MAX: Nobody's looking!

DEBBY: My chin, I'm all broken out. I don't know why, over and over, always the same place. Maybe food that drips? Pizza grease maybe?, the red stuff that comes out of the cheese? Neil says I drool in my sleep. Maybe my drool runs down my chin, makes me break out always the same place?

MAX: Who?

LOLA *(At the refrigerator)*: Completely empty. Just for show.

MAX *(To Lola)*: Shhh! *(To Debby) Who* says?

DEBBY: Huh?

MAX: Who did you *say?*

Pause.

DEBBY: I have a new boyfriend.

A beat.

His name is Neil. He loves me.

LOLA: You're seeing a *boy?*

DEBBY: You wouldn't believe how much he loves me, Daddy. Can't keep his hands off me.

LOLA: She's seeing a boy.

DEBBY: I have to tell him to cut it out in public, it embarrasses me. I slap his hands. I blush. I love when people see.

MAX: I'm tired.

DEBBY: The boy can't keep his hands off me, Daddy.

MAX: Good. Lola . . . ?

DEBBY: He squeezes me. Holds me tight. Strokes my hair.

MAX: Lola, I'm tired.

LOLA: What do you want from *me?*

Max opens the sofa and makes the bed during the following.

DEBBY: He's got big arms, Neil. Muscles you would not believe. Like a strong man. He lifts weights. Lifts me off the ground, I laugh, I shake, carries me 'round like a bag of air. A balloon. Cotton candy. Melts in your mouth not in your hands. He loves my cooking, Mommy.

LOLA: Yes?

DEBBY: He takes me to the movies, Neil. I don't care what. I loovvve the dark. We go to Times Square?, work our way down the block?, movie to movie?, night after night? Triple features sometimes. Kung fu. Neil loves kung fu. He's a black belt world champion himself. And horror. I love horror. I love horror so much. I love to scream. Neil makes believe it bothers him. He puts his hand over my mouth? I make believe I stop. Then he takes it off? I scream again. We do that a lot. He buys me popcorn. Butter. Lets me eat all I want. He doesn't care if

I'm chunky. Says he likes a girl he can sink his teeth into. Says he likes a girl with hips he can grab on to.

MAX: I'm tired.

DEBBY: When we fuck?, says it's like fucking all the oceans of the world.

Lola sighs deeply. Max shakes his head and clicks his tongue in shame.

This boy is nuts about your Debby, Daddy.

MAX: Very good.

DEBBY: Aren't you happy for me? Hm? Hm, Daddy?

MAX: Very happy.

DEBBY: He would do anything for me. Anything. He wants me to be happy.

MAX: Good.

LOLA: Max . . .

DEBBY: If there's something I want, he gets it for me. I liked this car I saw on the street? Stole it for me just like that. *(Snaps her fingers)*

Lola sighs deeply.

MAX: I'm too tired. *(He gets into bed)*

DEBBY: My face lit up. You should've seen me. I could cry right now just thinking about it. Nobody's ever done anything like that for me before.

MAX: Good night.

DEBBY: What a car. Great mileage.

LOLA: Debby. Dear.

DEBBY *(Concerned)*: What's the matter, Mommy?

LOLA: What are we going to do with you?

DEBBY: Don't worry, I can take care of myself.

LOLA: I wish I had something to offer you. I have no food.

DEBBY: I know. You said. I ate clams I told you.

LOLA: Where are we going to put you? There's no room.

DEBBY: I'll stay on the floor.

LOLA: No . . .

DEBBY: I'll sleep on the floor, I don't care. I like sleeping on the floor. Like in the camps.

LOLA: Dear, I won't have you sleeping on the floor.

DEBBY *(Lying on the floor)*: Ooo, comfy.

LOLA: Debby, get up.

DEBBY: Just like in the camps.

LOLA: Debby . . .

DEBBY: Mommy, lie down next to me, you'll see.

LOLA: Get up, you can't sleep on the floor. Max?

DEBBY: Mommy, lie down, I'll hold you. Don't be afraid.

LOLA: Oh, God, Max. Max.

DEBBY: It's not so bad. Mommy?

LOLA: Max, she's on the floor.

MAX: Debby, get off the floor.

DEBBY: I like it.

MAX: Debby, get up off the *floor*!

Lola sighs deeply.

DEBBY: Don't look at me so funny, Daddy.

MAX: Who's *look*ing at you?

DEBBY: What, I got something hanging out my nose? Look the other way. Look the other *way*. I got enough problems without you looking at me queer.

MAX: Debby, I'm tired. What we went through today.

LOLA: Yes. It's true.

DEBBY *(Over "Yes. It's true")*: What you went through! Always what you went through! What about me?! What about what *I* went through?!

LOLA: Shhh . . .

DEBBY *(Over "Shhh . . . ")*: You think I have it easy?!

LOLA: Nobody said . . .

DEBBY: My own parents! My own mother and father!

MAX *(Guiltily; playing dumb)*: What.

DEBBY: "What." What do you think? Come on. Skipping out on me! Running out! *Aband*oning me! Ring a bell?!!

LOLA: No. Who.

DEBBY: I went home to see you! For a visit! I rang the door. I rang and rang. I hollered. Fay from next door came out 'cause I was hollering. In her *bath*robe. "Didn't you know, Debby," she says. "Didn't you know? They went to *Flor*ida," she says. "They re*tired*." "Retired?! What do you mean retired? People don't just pick up and re*tire* just like that."

LOLA: Don't you remember, sweetheart?

DEBBY *(Over "... sweetheart?")*: "My own parents! My own parents don't just pick up and retire." It's a good thing Fay heard me holler. She gave me your address.

MAX *(To Lola)*: *Who* did?

LOLA *(To Max)*: Fay from next door.

Max shakes his head.

You don't remember we mentioned it?

DEBBY: *Men*tioned it?!

LOLA: You don't remember we talked about Florida?

DEBBY: I remember we *talk*ed about it ...

LOLA: You don't remember we told you we were going away?

DEBBY: Not *yet*! You weren't supposed to go *yet*!

LOLA: Yes, darling.

MAX: Yes.

LOLA: Your medication.

DEBBY: *Fuck* my medication!

LOLA: You lose track of time

DEBBY: You're gaslighting me! You're making me crazy!

LOLA: Nobody's making you crazy!

DEBBY: *Next* week! You were supposed to leave *next* week! That's what you said! *Next* week!

A beat.

LOLA: So? We decided to get an early start.

DEBBY: By running away in the middle of the night?! Tear ass out of Brooklyn at four in the morning? Fay told me: four in the morning. No notes, no last goodbyes. Just a final *shtup* of *gelt* and on your way.

Lola sighs deeply.

Boy. On the road again you two. Always on the road. Always running away from *some*thing. Load up the car, fill the tank, turn the key. Keep an eye on the rearview mirror, Daddy. You never know when that VW van'll turn on its siren and come and get you. Run, Daddy. Go. Get on the road at four in the morning, before the sun comes up. Make up a name when you check in at Howard Johnson's. You're on the road. You can be anybody on the road. Who knows a Jew from a goy on the road in West Virginia? Don't sweat too much. Don't let your hand shake when you sign in. They're trained to pick up stuff like that. Don't give yourself away. Florida's just across the border. Don't blow your cover. You're almost there. You're almost free! *(Giggles mischievously; a beat; girlishly)* You can't run away from me, Daddy.

Lola opens the kitchen cabinet, revealing a box of corn flakes and milk.

LOLA   *(Lightly, with feigned surprise)*: Oh! Look what *I* found!

Max puffs up his pillow disgustedly and rolls to his side to sleep. Blackout.

Scene Five

Max is asleep and Lola is fixing a makeshift bed out of cushions for Debby, who is in the bathroom.

LOLA   *(Hums for a while, then talks to Debby)*: I'm making you a lovely bed. It'll do you fine. We'll figure things out in the morning, after we're rested. You'll eat a little something, you'll sleep. Who can think straight, all those hours on the road, those lights coming at you. Who can *see* straight? The bed I'm putting together for you, is gonna be so cute and so comfortable . . . *(She accidentally brushes into Max's foot, thinking she's disturbed him)* Ooo.

Max snorts, in his sleep, undisturbed; a beat.

(To Max) Sleep, Max. That's right, you sleep. The world is coming to an end. Sleep, darling. *(A beat)* What a talent you got for escape. How'd you get so lucky? *(A beat)* How come sleep doesn't trick you? It tricks me. It's no friend to *me*. How did sleep ever get to be your friend? It's so simple with you. You shut your eyes and you're gone. Safe. *(A beat)* Where, where do you go? What goes on in there? You got some chippie in there with you, Max? That's what I think: Sleep is your mistress. With her you can be safe. She'll tell you all the time how big and strong you are. I don't tell you, right? No, *she* tells you. With her, you can talk. With *me* . . . no talk. No talk at all. What do *I* get? *(A beat. She looks at him)* Silence.

Max snorts again.

Silence and snoring.

DEBBY *(Opens bathroom door a crack)*: Mommy, no toilet paper. *(Shuts the door)*

LOLA: Oh, my . . . no toil—wait. *(Looks around, thinking)* Don't do anything *yet* . . . oh, God . . . don't worry. Just sit tight.

DEBBY *(Off)*: Mommy, what am I gonna—

LOLA *(Over "what am I gonna—")*: Just sit tight, I told you. *(Remembers she has tissues in her handbag and gets them)* Okay . . . *(Knocks on bathroom door)* Open up.

DEBBY *(Off)*: What.

LOLA: I got.

DEBBY: Don't look.

LOLA: I won't look, open up. I'm your mother.

Debby opens the door a crack, snatches the tissues from Lola's hand, shuts the door.

MAX *(Calls softly, in his sleep)*: Deborah?

Lola turns suddenly to look at Max, her eyes filling with tears. Blackout.

Scene Six

Max is alone. The apartment is in darkness except for the occasional lights of cars passing in the night.

MAX: Deborah? *Dvoyreh?*

We become aware of the presence of a figure, a lithe young woman, Deborah, who drifts elusively around the furniture. Max senses her presence, sits up and listens for a moment before speaking to her as if she were a little girl.

Darling . . .

She giggles softly.

(Playfully) I hear you! Please . . . *Neshomeh mayneh* . . . I need to see that face. *Loz mikh zen dayn shayn peniml!* [Let me see that pretty face!]

He waits; she still lurks in the dark.

Don't tease me! You're always slipping away from me! *Dvoyreh, hartzenyu mayns* . . . [My sweetheart.]

A beat. Deborah comes out of the darkness for a moment; then, giggling, she recedes into the shadows again. Max smiles.

Uh! Okay. *Ot doh biztu. Bizt doh, tokhter mayneh.* There you are! *Oy, mayn lebm! Zis kind.* [My sweet child.] I knew you'd be back. You tease me, you do, but *du koomst alehmol tzurik! Sar'a nakhess bizt du! Bizt mayn nakhess. Mayn teyer kind!* [. . . you always come back! What a pleasure you are! My darling child!]

Deborah smiles shyly.

A zah shmeykhl! A zah lieb shmeykhl! [Such a pretty smile!]

DEBORAH: *Tateh* . . .

MAX: Shhh . . . *zitz mit mir.* Sit. *Mer bet ich nisht.* [Sit with me; that's all I ask.]

He waits a beat; she sits.

That's my girl! *Mayn zis meydeleh.* [My sweet little girl.] Let me just look at you. Look what a beauty you turned out! So pretty! So polite! So respectful! *Oy,* what a girl! My angel!

DEBORAH: *Tateh . . .*

MAX: I love how you say "Tateh."

DEBORAH: *Tateh.*

MAX *(Gently; he doesn't want her to speak)*: Shhh.

Long pause; they look at one another. Max begins singing a Yiddish lullaby to her in a sweet voice. After a while, Deborah gets up and drifts into the shadows again but he is too enraptured by his nostalgic song to notice. He stops singing only when he realizes that she is gone. A beat.

(Suddenly frightened) Deborah?

Blackout.

Scene Seven

Lola and Max, as they were at the end of Scene Five: she, standing, looking at him; he, sleeping. Debby, in the bathroom, opens the door a crack and passes through something ripped out of a newspaper. Lola, perplexed, takes it and looks at it as Debby closes the door.

LOLA *(Meaning, "What are you doing?")*: What.

DEBBY *(Off)*: Coupons.

LOLA: Coupons?

DEBBY *(Off)*: Q-pons.

The toilet flushes and Debby emerges from the bathroom fixing her clothing and carrying a newspaper.

Cottonelle bathroom tissue. Cottony soft. Thirty cents off. You need toilet paper. Never hurts to have extra, right? No such thing as too much toilet paper. Stock up. You never know. *(Tears more coupons from the paper and hands them to Lola)* Here: "Save twenty-five cents on new Sara Lee Bagel Time Bagels." Thirty cents on 7-Up. Hershey's Syrup, "Twenty cents off."

LOLA *(Over "Hershey's Syrup . . . ")*: What do I need this? No . . . take, take . . . I don't need Hershey's . . . I don't need 7-Up . . .

DEBBY *(During the above; tearing more coupons)*: 'Tato Skins! 'Tato Skins! Made from the skin of dead potatoes! Minute Maid, Mommy, you like Minute Maid.

LOLA: Well . . .

DEBBY: Take. No expiration date. That's *good*. That's the best. You got plenty of time. Save it. You never know. Tropicana! Ooo. Twenty-five cents off.

LOLA: I already got Minute Maid.

DEBBY: Take both. Ooo, Bumble Bee, Mommy! Bumble Bee! *(Sings the "Bumble Bee" theme song)* "Bum-Bum-Bumble Bee, Bumble Bee Tu-u-na . . . "

LOLA *(Over Debby's singing)*: Enough with the coupons. You want food?, yes or no. *(Takes the paper away from Debby)* Yes or no?

DEBBY: Yes.

Lola sets down the box of cereal and milk in front of Debby. Pause.

(As if she's remembered something) I didn't *tell* you!

LOLA *(Eagerly)*: What?

DEBBY: The last time I visited the concentration camp, they turned it into a bungalow colony.

Lola sighs deeply, gets ready for bed; Debby eats out of the cereal box and guzzles milk.

They put chintzy drapes on the barbed wire. Raisin cookies were in the ovens. The food, Mommy! Such portions! I was stuffed! None of that stale bread and soup shit. All the salad bar you can eat! Shrimp! Like at Beefsteak Charlie's.

Lola sees the mess Debby is making; utters a disapproving sound.

Hugh Downs was Colonel Klink, the concentration camp counselor. And the Nazis' uniforms were in storage. In mothballs. They put on Bermuda shorts and V-neck T-shirts. They looked like Jewish fathers with numbers on their arms.

LOLA: Debby...

DEBBY: It was tricky picking out the Nazis from the Jewish fathers, but I could pick 'em out right away. It's a good thing I took those courses. You never know what's gonna save your life. I was the lifeguard. I guarded the pool.

LOLA: Debby... watch...

DEBBY: I yelled at the children running barefoot where the ground was wet. That's a great way to slip and fall and crack your skull open. I know; I've done it.

LOLA: Watch with the milk. Sweetheart... look at yourself...

DEBBY: I got a Red Cross lifesaving thing stitched to my bathing suit. I had to pass a test. I loved guarding life, in the sun, swimming, saving children. Best job in the whole camp. I wore a whistle 'round my neck and I didn't hesitate to use it.

LOLA *(Trying to wipe Debby's face with a tissue)*: Come, dear...

DEBBY: The Nazis thought I had spunk.

LOLA *(Wiping Debby's chin; sighs)*: The Nazis, the Nazis...

DEBBY *(Overlap)*: They decorated me with the most adorable pink swastikas.

LOLA *(Gasps at Debby's milk-soaked blouse)*: Look at you, young lady... come on, off...

During the following, Lola struggles to get the blouse off Debby.

DEBBY *(Overlap)*: I wore a sash across my bathing suit. I was Miss America. Bess Myerson was Eva Braun. What a tour de force for Bess! She was positively adorable. We played bingo together, me and Bess. We won prizes. She won the coveted Oscar and I won the most adorable handbag made of Jewish hair.

Lola has gotten the blouse off and exits with it to the bathroom;

Debby stays put. Silence. Max is snoring; Debby speaks softly, in a whisper, in time to his snoring.

Every night there was singing . . . by the campfire. We sang by the flames. Wood crackled. Sparks flew . . . like fireflies. We were in tune . . . all of us. Stars twinkled in time to the crickets. We all breathed together . . . in and out . . . and in and out and in and out . . . that was my favorite time: singing by the flames.

Lola returns with a towel.

LOLA *(While wrapping the towel around Debby)*: That blouse is absolutely filthy. I'm soaking it. I don't remember that blouse. I didn't get you that blouse.

DEBBY: Mommy, I love dreams, don't you?

LOLA *(Pouring cereal and milk into a bowl)*: Let's try this again.

DEBBY: This is a dream.

Lola settles in next to Debby and feeds her cereal with a plastic spoon.

I was trying on a dress at A&S? In one of those rooms?

LOLA: Shhh . . . not while you're eating . . .

Debby takes a few spoonfuls in silence.

Good girl . . .

DEBBY: I took off my pants, and my shirt, and my shoes. And I looked at myself in the mirror only it was *your* face and you told me to get ready for the gas chamber.

Lola sighs deeply while shaking her head.

So I took off my bra and my panties and I screamed, "The gas shower's starting," and I ran out, and the lady who gives out the numbers when you walk in yelled after me and I ran past stacks of coats and skirts and a black security guard grabbed me and put one of the coats on me, took it right off the rack, something I never in a million years would've picked—glen plaid—and took me to the manager's office. *(Getting sleepy, she rests her head on Lola)* Everybody was watching.

LOLA *(Lulling her)*: Shhh . . .

DEBBY *(Softly)*: Everybody was watching, Mommy. I fell asleep in the manager's office. *(A beat; even more softly)* Woke up all wrinkled.

Debby begins falling asleep while Lola rocks her for a long beat.

(A sleepy whisper) Mommy, I love dreams, don't you?

Lola continues to rock Debby gently to sleep. Blackout.

Scene Eight

A bedside lamp illuminates the room. Debby is asleep on cushions on the floor. Lola, distressed, has awakened from a bad dream.

LOLA *(A small, frightened voice)*: I didn't look. I was afraid to look.

MAX *(Whispers; weary but sympathetic)*: What good is it?

LOLA: If I looked . . . if I looked, they'd've seen me looking.

MAX: Shhh . . . go to sleep . . .

LOLA: They'd've made the connection. They'd've sent me *with* her . . .

Max nods, "I know."

You don't want to call attention to yourself.

MAX: I know. *(Changing the subject)* Tomorrow . . .

LOLA: They'd've sent me, too.

MAX: Tomorrow you'll put on a hat . . .

Lola smiles, nods.

We'll walk around, get to know the place.

Lola smiles. Max kisses her good night, turns over to sleep. Pause.

LOLA *(A voice haunts her; far away)*: "Lo-la . . . Lo*la*! Look at me!"

MAX *(With his back to her)*: What good is it?

LOLA: I didn't look. She called me, her voice was torn up from screaming, but I walked, I kept on walking. I didn't look back.

Lights, and Lola's voice, begin to fade.

Like my own mother was a stranger. I didn't look . . . I didn't look . . .

Fade to black.

Scene Nine

Max and Lola are sleeping. Debby is asleep on the floor. Glass shatters. Someone, unseen, is heard entering the apartment through the bathroom window. Max is jolted awake. Terribly frightened, he nudges Lola.

LOLA: Hm?

Max gestures for Lola to be quiet.

What, Max, what?

Debby turns, makes stirring sounds.

MAX *(Whispers)*: Listen. Someone.

DEBBY *(Singsong)*: What'sa matter?

MAX: Shhh . . .

LOLA *(Whispers to Debby)*: Somebody's here he says.

DEBBY *(Soothingly)*: Don't worry, Daddy, it's America.

A stranger enters the dark room; he's a short, wiry, black teenager who is mildly retarded. He freezes when he sees the three of them. Lola gasps. A beat.

STRANGER: Debby?

Debby stands; a beat.

DEBBY: Neil? *(She steps forward to get a better look)* I don't believe it . . . oh, my God . . .

Her hand over her mouth in shock, like a contestant on "The Price is Right," Debby bounds toward Neil, bursting into tears of joy and hysteria; we can't understand everything she says through her blathering. Her language is foul but the mood is conciliatory.

You little fuck . . .

NEIL: Debby, I'm sorry . . .

DEBBY: You know how worried I was about you? Huh?

NEIL *(Embracing her; breaking down, too)*: Sorry . . . I'm sorry . . .

DEBBY: Where did you go?, where did you *go*?

NEIL: I came *down* here.

DEBBY: No, no, be*fore*. Where'd you go when you went? *(Teeth gritted, she punches him)* You fuckin' piece of shit, how could you walk out on me like that?

NEIL: No I din't . . . no I *din't*.

DEBBY: I wake up and you're gone. What am I supposed to think?, huh? What am I supposed to think?

NEIL *(Over ". . . huh? . . . ")*: I din't walk out, I had to go.

DEBBY: You lie to me, Neilly, you lie to me all the time . . .

NEIL: I *swear* . . . went back to the shtreet . . .

DEBBY: Oh, God . . .

NEIL: No, I came back to your house . . . you were gone!

DEBBY: I love you too much! It's no good for me how much I love you!

NEIL: I'm sorry . . .

DEBBY: You're not sorry, you're not sorry . . .

NEIL *(Bawling and shrieking)*: I am! Debby, I *am*! Come down looking for you! To Florida?! I ain't sorry?!

DEBBY *(Over "I am!"; kissing him)*: I know . . . I know you are, sweetie pie . . . I know you are, lover boy . . . I know . . .

NEIL: Don't run away no more . . .

DEBBY: I won't . . . I won't . . . I go crazy, Neil, I go nuts . . . *(Still crying)*

Their kisses become more passionate and they feverishly grope one another.

(Whispery and girlish) Oh, God, Neil . . . I love you too much . . . I can't help it. . . . You make me crazy . . . I can't help it . . . Oh, God, Neil . . .

They fumble with clothing and in an instant they're having intercourse. Lola and Max, still in the darkness in the midst of all this, are appalled but too fascinated to do or say anything; Lola averts her eyes but Max cannot avert his.

Oh, God, oh, Neil . . . oh, God, oh, Neil . . . don't take it out, don't take it out . . . oh, God, oh, Neil . . . Oh, God, oh, Neil . . .

Lights begin to fade.

. . . don't take it out, don't take it out . . . oh, God, oh, Neil . . . don't . . . don't . . . good . . . good . . . good . . .

Lola shakes her head and clicks her tongue. Fade to black.

Scene Ten

The lights are on. Debby stands beaming beside Neil, her arm laced through his.

DEBBY: Mommy? Daddy? I'd like you to meet Neil.

Neil tries to pick up an ashtray but it's glued to the table; he laughs.

Neil?

Neil laughs while making a show of trying to lift up the ashtray.

This is my mother and my father.

NEIL *(Still working at the ashtray)*: Oh, man . . .

MAX: What is he doing?

DEBBY: Neil?, honey, stop.

NEIL: Stuck.

MAX: Tell him to leave it.

DEBBY: Neilly?, stop.

Neil succeeds in tearing the ashtray off the tabletop.

MAX: Hey! What the hell you think you're doing?!

DEBBY: Wow. I told you he was strong.

Neil hands Lola the ashtray.

MAX: You want to get us all in trouble?

DEBBY: Make a muscle.

Lola takes the ashtray from Neil; she smiles, nods her thanks. Max snatches the ashtray from Lola.

Make a muscle. He's a muscleman, I'm telling you. *(Stroking Neil's arm)* Make a muscle.

Neil yanks his arm away from her.

MAX *(Trying to replace the ashtray)*: He broke it. Look at that, he broke it.

LOLA: Shhh . . .

DEBBY *(Over "Shhh"; cradles Neil's head; like a little girl talking about her dolly)*: Isn't he sweet? He's my baby.

Neil enjoys the tenderness but, embarrassed, he pulls away from Debby to explore the room.

MAX *(Still fiddling with the ashtray)*: They'll make us pay. Supposed to leave it the way we found it and look what he *does*.

NEIL: Man, this place . . .

DEBBY *(To Neil)*: Sit, honey.

NEIL: Rich.

MAX: *Now* what is he doing?

DEBBY: What.

Max gestures toward Neil with incredulity.

You never liked my friends. *(To Neil)* Honey, sit.

Neil does, and seems to relish sitting in a comfortable chair; he pulls off his sneakers.

MAX: Who said to make himself at home?

LOLA *(To Neil)*: I have no food. *(Shrugs apologetically)*

Max glares at Lola. Neil remembers something; reaches for a paper bag in his jacket pocket, gives it to Lola. Lola looks at him quizzically.

DEBBY: Isn't that nice? Neil brought a present. *(Makes a spiteful face at Max)*

LOLA: I don't want a present . . .

Neil gestures for her to take it.

DEBBY: Mommy you gotta.

MAX *(To Lola)*: You don't want anything from him.

Lola hesitates, then reaches for the bag.

NEIL *(Sees the tattooed numbers on Lola's forearm and pulls up his sleeve)*: Hey. I got one, too. *(Reveals a tattoo on his arm)*

DEBBY: Isn't that cute?

LOLA *(Smiles uncomfortably as she self-consciously covers her arm and pulls a plastic-wrapped package from the bag)*: Bagels?

NEIL: Sara Lee.

DEBBY: Sara Lee Bagel Time Bagels?! Oh, Neil, you shouldn't have . . .

Debby hugs and kisses him all over his face. Neil, embarrassed, wriggles out of her hold. Debby, giggling, continues to make kissing sounds and gestures toward Neil.

NEIL *(Angily pulls away from her)*: Stop!

DEBBY *(Wounded, repentant)*: I'm sorry. I'm sorry, honey . . .

MAX *(To Debby)*: What does he want?

DEBBY: Daddy, be nice.

MAX: What's he doing here?

LOLA: Max . . .

DEBBY: He loves me. He came after me.

MAX *(To Neil)*: This isn't a hotel, I'm very sorry.
LOLA *(Softly; to Debby)*: He came from New York?
DEBBY: *Ask* him.

Lola shrugs, at a loss.

Talk to him. I want you should get to know him.

Neil laughs as he snaps a glued candlestick off the dining room table.

MAX: *Uy! Now* what?!

Max yanks the candlestick away from Neil and tries to replace it. Neil looks at Max for a beat, then snaps off the other candlestick.

Uy Gut . . .
DEBBY: What are you so scared of?
MAX: They'll make us pay!
DEBBY: So what?

Neil hands Max the second candlestick and giggles.

MAX: He can't *do* what he pleases. We don't live here, we're guests here! They'll bill us!
LOLA *(Over "They'll bill us!")*: Shhh . . .
DEBBY: Oh, Daddy . . .
MAX: We promised the man: leave it the way we found it.
LOLA *(Smiles compassionately)*: It was an accident.
DEBBY: Yeah.
MAX *(Over "Yeah")*: What are you *talk*ing "an accident"?! You saw: He—
LOLA: Oh . . . *(Gestures, "Don't make such a big deal")*
MAX *(To Neil)*: How would you like it if somebody came into *your* home?

Neil looks at Max with genuine innocence.

LOLA: He doesn't understand.
MAX: Huh?
LOLA: He wanted to pick it up.

NEIL *(Shrugs)*: Wanted to pick it up.

LOLA: Yes. *(To Max)* See?

MAX: They didn't *want* you to move it, that's why they glued it down.

NEIL: Why?

MAX: Why? How do *I* know why? This is their place, this is how they want it. Who are we to judge?

DEBBY *(Opens the bag of bagels, begins eating)*: Such a coward. My own father, I don't believe it.

MAX *(To Debby; over "I don't believe it")*: You shut up.

LOLA: He doesn't understand, Max.

MAX *(To Neil)*: These are the rules. You go by the rule. You don't like them?: too bad.

DEBBY: Don't Make Waves: the story of his life.

LOLA: He doesn't understand.

MAX *(Over "He doesn't understand")*: You come here, out of nowhere, you rip the place apart . . .

LOLA: He's not ripping the place apart, Max, he's only . . .

DEBBY *(Over "Max, he's only . . . ")*: Such a scaredy cat. I swear. Everybody's a Nazi to you.

MAX: Don't start with your Nazis!

DEBBY: Hotsy totsy, a new-born Nazi. What did Hitler say when Eva Braun had a baby?

NEIL: What?

DEBBY: "Hotsy totsy, a new-born Nazi." *(Laughs hysterically)*

LOLA *(Through the laughter)*: Neil? *(A beat)* Neil? You came from New York?

DEBBY: Neil?, talk to Mommy, she wants to talk to you.

NEIL: Yeah? *(Meaning "What is it?")*

LOLA *(A beat)*: You came from New York?

NEIL: Uh-huh.

LOLA *(Nods: "That's nice"; a beat)*: How's the weather?

NEIL: Cold. *(Shrugs)* Freezing.

LOLA: Is that so? *(Clicks her tongue)* We got here just in time, Max, they're freezing in New York.

MAX *(Whispers to Lola)*: What is the matter with you?

LOLA: What.

MAX: Making conver*sation* with him?

DEBBY *(Girlishly)*: What are you whispering?

LOLA *(Overlap; whispers to Max)*: What *should* I do? I'm trying to make the best of it . . .

NEIL: The cops come load everybody up off the shtreet.

The three look at Neil; a beat.

MAX: Huh?

NEIL: It's freezing they make you. Y'understand? Debby lets me stay her place.

Max looks at Debby, who shrugs.

MAX: You pick strangers up off the *street*?!—

DEBBY: I *knew* you were gonna say that . . .

MAX: —let them stay in your *home*? Debby Debby Debby, you *sleep* with this boy?

DEBBY: Oh, Daddy . . .

MAX *(Over "Oh, Daddy . . . ")*: Who knows where he's been? Don't you hear what's going on with people like this?

DEBBY: What, you never slept in the dirt?

LOLA *(To Neil)*: You have family?

Neil looks to Debby for support.

DEBBY: Well?

NEIL *(After a beat)*: My grandma.

LOLA: Your grandma?

NEIL: My grandma she died.

LOLA: Oh.

NEIL: She look after me.

LOLA: Yes.

NEIL: Cook and stuff.

LOLA: Yes.

NEIL: Like a mother.

LOLA: Aw . . . Max, *d'hairst*? [You hear?]

Max gestures to leave him out of it.

NEIL: Burned up.

LOLA *(Gasps)*: A fire?

NEIL *(Nods)*: Uh-huh.

LOLA: What a shame. . . . A fire, Max.

MAX *(His compassion awakened in spite of himself)*: Yeah, yeah.

NEIL: Got too much smoke when the building caught fire's what they say.

LOLA: Ah yes.

NEIL: Took her out, tried to y'know make her breathe?

LOLA: Yes?

NEIL: Took her shirt off, tried to make her breathe right there on the shtreet, everybody watching, but no, got too much smoke.

Lola sighs.

Yeah. She look after me. So . . . then I go to the shtreet. Y'understand?

LOLA: Yes. *(Sighs)* All alone in the world.

NEIL: Eighth Avenue.

DEBBY: That's where I found him, all dirty . . .

NEIL: Debby she come up, talk to me. Ax me stuff. Took me to Olympic for hot cocoa. She was nice. *(Shrugs; a beat)* Took me to *her* house. *(Shrugs)* Wash my clothes. Give me a bath. Soap. *(Shrugs)* Fucked in the bathtub.

Max shakes his head in disbelief.

LOLA *(Calming Max)*: Alright, alright . . .

NEIL *(Overlap)*: Man, there was water going fast. Floor. Man. Never fucked a woman so fat. Like the ocean. She was nice to me. *(Shrugs)* Let me sleep in her bed. Sheets and stuff. *(Shrugs; a beat)* She was nice. *(Shrugs)* I guess she's like my girlfriend.

DEBBY: Aw, he is sooo sweet . . . *(Kisses Neil's head)*

LOLA *(To Neil)*: Your mother?, where is *she*?

NEIL: Jail? Dead? Brooklyn? *(Shrugs)*

LOLA: Brooklyn? You're from Brooklyn? Where in Brooklyn?

NEIL: Beverley Road?

LOLA: Isn't that something?! Beverley Road! *We* used to live on Beverley Road! You hear this, Max?: Beverley Road.

MAX: Very nice.

LOLA *(To Neil)*: What number?

NEIL: 619? *(Shrugs)*

LOLA: 619? We were 630! How do you like that? We were neighbors! Small world. You hear this, Max?: practically next-door neighbors! Across the street from each other. I don't remember you. Isn't that funny? We lived there eleven years. Must've just missed each other. The neighborhood . . . changed . . . *you* know. Beverley Road, I can't get over it. What a coincidence. Of all the streets in the world . . . yes, Beverley Road, that's where we lived, our first apartment. Yes. Right after the war.

MAX: I'm looking at my watch and I don't believe it. *(Gets into bed)*

LOLA: Neil will get a kick out of this.

DEBBY *(Knows where this is headed; groans)*: No he won't.

LOLA: Neil?

MAX: Lola, what are you starting?

LOLA: Neil, you'll get a kick out of this.

DEBBY *(Stomps around the room)*: Mommmmyyy . . .

MAX: Debby, shhh! Lola . . .

LOLA: Neil?

NEIL: Yeah?

LOLA: During the war?

DEBBY *(To Neil; she lays his head on her lap)*: A bedtime story. One of Mommy's bedtime stories.

LOLA *(Brightly launches into her story, which she's told dozens of times before)*: There was this girl I knew there, in Belsen.

DEBBY *(Starting a limerick)*: There was a young girl from Belsen . . .

LOLA: A young girl, younger than me.

Debby hums the second line of the limerick.

With the blackest eyes. Like shiny marbles. Eyes you just *had* to look into, you couldn't look away, that's the kind of eyes this girl had. Anna her name was.

DEBBY: Anne Frank, Anna Frank.

LOLA *(Over "Anna Frank")*: Anna Frank from Amsterdam. Yes. The same.

MAX: Lola, *must* you?!

LOLA: And we were friends there, the two of us.

DEBBY: Like sisters.

LOLA *(Simultaneously)*: Like sisters—

MAX: Lola, enough. Look at the time!

LOLA: —like she was my baby sister, that's how we were. I was all of eighteen, remember, and already buried *(Sighs)* my mother *and* my father, and my sisters and I thought my brother was dead, too, only it turned out that he survived the war but went crazy after, I lost him *that* way.

DEBBY *(Over "I lost him that way")*: Mommy, just tell it. God . . .

LOLA: And Max, I didn't meet Max till after. And *he*, he just came out of hiding, in the woods—

MAX: Lola!

LOLA: —and when he came out—

MAX *(Trying to stop her)*: Hey hey hey.

LOLA: —when he came out, he found out his bride and a little baby girl, a little girl named Deborah—

MAX: Wait wait wait . . . what are you doing?!

LOLA: —a little girl named Deborah he was crazy about—

MAX: What are you *do*ing?

LOLA: —and when he came out, they were dead—

MAX: This is mine to tell!

LOLA: —they died, while he was hiding, in the woods.

MAX: Shut up with that! Who *asked* you?! That's *my* life! When I want to discuss *my*—

LOLA *(To Max)*: What am I saying? I'm saying fact.

MAX: Yes, and when I want to discuss—

LOLA: When do you ever discuss? You never!

MAX: I'm talked out! No more!

LOLA: So *I* should shut up?, because *you*—

MAX: Yes! What does the boy care?

LOLA *(Over "care?")*: It's interesting! *(To Neil)* Isn't this interesting?

NEIL: Uh-huh.

LOLA: See? You never let me talk.

DEBBY: I wish we had popcorn.

MAX: What good is it, Lola? What good is it, over and over—

LOLA: Go to sleep! Sleep! Like you always do!

Max covers his head with a pillow.

Good! Perfect! Sleep! *(A beat; tries to remember where she left off)* So . . . there was this girl I knew there, in Belsen.

DEBBY *(Over "in Belsen")*: No, no, you did that already.

LOLA: Oh.

DEBBY: Later, much later. "Alone in the world."

LOLA: Yes? *(Shrugs; resumes)* So, I was alone. All alone in the world—

NEIL: Like me.

LOLA: Yes. Like you. —I was alone. All alone in the world and this girl she was my friend. In the camp. Two people couldn't be closer. We helped each other get through each day and each night. Every morning we woke up was a triumph. We filled the time with talk, me and my little friend Anna. We told each other stories about what *was* and what *will* be.

DEBBY: What stories she told!

LOLA: What stories she told! You know the expression "like an artist"? She painted pictures with words.

DEBBY: Pictures with words.

LOLA: You had a perfect picture in your head of everything she described. You knew what all the faces looked like, every member of her family, her cat, the boy she wanted to marry, Peter. "Anna, you tell such wonderful stories," I told her.

DEBBY: "You should be a writer."

LOLA *(Simultaneously)*: "You should be a writer." And she told me,

DEBBY: "I *am* a writer."

LOLA *(Simultaneously)*: "I *am* a writer. As a matter of fact, I've written a whole book." "What kind of book," I asked, "does such a young girl write?" And she told me, "A book of ideas and observations, ideas about life. A kind of a diary," she said. "And where *is* this diary of yours," I asked my young friend. And she smiled. "You'll see, one day you'll see." And I didn't think anything of it except her black eyes twinkled in such a way I can seen them right now. And then I said to her, "Well, why don't you keep a book *here*, here in the camp?" And she said,

DEBBY: "Lola, what a good idea, I can't thank you enough."

LOLA *(Simultaneously)*: "Lola, what a good idea, I can't thank you enough." So, thanks to me, all the time we were at Belsen, she secretly kept a book. A diary, another diary. Where she found the paper to write on I'll never know. Whatever she could get her hands on. Little scraps, rags. She wrote things down all the time. Whenever you saw her, she was jotting something down. All day long. She'd be too weak to eat, but there was Anna, writing. In plain sight, writing. Finally I had to say something. "Anna, what's with all the writing? The guards are gonna find out and murder you." And do you know what she said to me?

Pause.

DEBBY *(Prompting Lola)*: "I don't care *what* . . ."

LOLA: "I don't care *what* happens to me," she said. "I may not survive the war but I must write down everything, everything I see and everything I feel. All I care about is people should see what I write and know the truth and remember. I want people to remember." She kept on writing, right till the end. Sometimes she was too starved to keep her head up but I held it up for her so she could write. When she got too sick—typhus she had—too sick to hold even a matchstick to write with, *I* wrote for her, I took dictation from Anna Frank. *(A beat)* As you would imagine, I was a big character in this book. I was the hero—

DEBBY *(Correcting her)*: Heroine.

LOLA: The heroine. Well, it was *her* book, true, but I was there, on every single page. "Lola did *this*," or "Lola said *this* today." "Lola gives me the strength to go on." "Lola has such courage." Can you imagine? *Me*, Lola, I gave Anna Frank the will to live may she rest in peace.

A beat.

DEBBY: When she died in my arms.

LOLA: When she died in my arms, and I'll never forget it as long as I live, she made me promise: "Hide my book, Lola." Her voice was weak, I had to bend my ear close. "Don't let them take it," she said. "Make sure people read what I wrote, people should know. Promise me, Lola, promise me." I promised. And little Anna Frank smiled, and closed her eyes and she was gone, right in my arms. *(Becoming choked up)* I did the best I could. I tried to save it. It was my story. I promised Anna. I kept it hidden. Every day I lived in fear. I trusted no one. If only the Nazis didn't find it and piss all over it . . .

DEBBY: That's new.

LOLA: If only that book lasted through the war. . . . I'm telling you, I was the heroine, it was my story. She wrote about *me*! I could've given people hope. But my story, *Lola*'s story, told by Anne Frank, went up in flames with her at Belsen. The Belsen diary. The *other* diary. The diary nobody knows about. The diary *I* told her to keep.

DEBBY: She's so fulla shit.

LOLA *(To Neil)*: Believe me, I was there.

DEBBY: And I was at Woodstock.

LOLA: There was another diary. I know; I was in it. On every page.

DEBBY *(Over "On every page")*: Who's gonna say no? Huh? Who's around to say no?

LOLA: On every single page: my name. "Lola this and Lola that . . . "

DEBBY: Mommy, you don't know what's what anymore. You *think* you knew Anne Frank.

LOLA: I DID! I DID! But who knew this little girl, the young friend I gave my crumbs to, my little sister, who *I* inspired, who knew what she would become?, this girl with black eyes writing, writing all the time. Who knew what she would mean to the world? Just a girl, but a magical girl. Her name was Anna. Anna Frank from Amsterdam. Yes. The same. *(A beat)* Years go by. Our boat comes into New York in fog so thick, I never got to see the Statue of Liberty. Then. One day, in Brooklyn, in my kitchen, on Beverley Road, I see in *Life* magazine a story about a diary found in Amsterdam, and a picture, a picture of a girl with eyes like black marbles and I say, Anna! You said to me, "One day you'll see!" Anna, my little friend! *(A beat)* And that, Neil, is the story of me and Anne Frank.

Long pause.

NEIL: Who?

Blackout.

Scene Eleven

Max, alone in the dark room.

MAX *(Dreaming; urgently, agitated)*: Deborah? Where did you go now? Please . . . *Tokhter mayneh* . . . come back. I can't see you. —Dvoyrehleh? *(He waits anxiously for a moment, approaches where he thinks he sees her) Koom, ich muz redn mit dir.* [Talk to me.] Listen . . . help me . . . all my life, I'm homesick . . . .This hole in *mayn hartz* . . . it doesn't stop . . .

Deborah appears, winds through the shadows; Max tries to follow her.

Hello, darling . . . forgive me . . . I never sat shiva for you. This ache . . . it doesn't go away . . . it gets worse with time. Not better, worse. Tell me, sweetheart . . . tell me: When does it end?

DEBORAH: *Es nemt keynmol nisht keim soff.* [It never ends.]
MAX: No, don't say that!

Deborah shakes her head no as she recedes into the shadows.

It must end! It must! *(Looking around for her)* Deborah?

Blackout.

Scene Twelve

Max awakens with a start at the sound of Debby and Neil laughing in the bathroom. Water is running; Debby is giving Neil a bath. Max reorients himself and sees that he and Lola are alone. Suddenly, he gets out of bed and urgently gathers his things.

LOLA: What. *(Meaning, "What are you doing?")*
MAX: Come, we're going.
LOLA: What?
MAX: We're getting out of here.
LOLA: Max . . .
MAX: We can escape.
LOLA: What are you talking "escape"?
MAX: We have to do something, Lola, this'll never end.
LOLA *(Scared, she watches him pack for a beat)*: Where?, where would we go?
MAX: A motel, we find a motel for the night.
LOLA: Why?, when we're here?
MAX: Are you listening to me or what?
LOLA *(Over "or what?")*: Max, no, you don't mean it. Just leave her here?
MAX: She'll survive. She always does. She'll survive.
LOLA *(Over "She'll survive")*: Not again, Max. We tried that before. We left her in Brooklyn. It didn't work, she followed us all this way. She needs us.
MAX: She doesn't need us. She needs to *torture* us.

LOLA: So what if they sleep on the floor, it's the middle of the night.

MAX: No.

LOLA: It's comfortable here.

Debby and Neil are heard laughing wildly in the bathroom.

MAX: "Comfortable." Ha. Get your things, we're going right now.

LOLA: I don't like traveling in the dark for no reason.

MAX: What "no reason"?! Listen what's going on here! This is a nut house!

LOLA: *I don't want to travel in the dark!*

A beat.

I don't want to leave all this.

MAX: What?, what are you leaving?

LOLA: I like it here. Everything we could want, Max. It's nice.

MAX: *Lis*ten to you! Stay! Stay like your mother stayed!

Lola winces.

She didn't want to leave her beautiful home and her, her *furniture*, so she stayed! She could've gotten out—

LOLA: Sha! *(Meaning "shut up")*

Pause.

MAX: Lola, Lola . . . they won't find us. I promise. We'll get in the car and go.

LOLA: I don't want to run, Max, please. No more running.

MAX *(Stuffing her things into suitcases)*: We'll find a motel. A TV that works. A hard mattress. A *mattress*. A decent night's sleep—

Suddenly, the bathroom door opens and Debby, in a bright mood, her face a mask of red lipstick, bursts in singing; Neil follows, laughing. Max shakes his head in frustration.

DEBBY: " . . . I feel pretty and shitty and gay! And I pity—"

LOLA *(To Debby, as she goes to her)*: What did you do?

MAX *(To Lola)*: Just leave her.

DEBBY: "—any girl who isn't me today!"

LOLA: My lipstick . . .

NEIL: I helped.

LOLA: You certainly did. *(Moistens a tissue with her saliva and cleans Debby's face)*

DEBBY: "—See the pretty girl in that mirror there?—"

NEIL *(Laughing)*: She's funny.

LOLA: Very funny.

MAX *(Overlap; to Lola)*: Leave her! Just leave her!

LOLA *(Overlap; to Debby)*: I can't turn my back on you for two minutes . . .

DEBBY: "—(What mirror, where?)—"

LOLA *(Sighs while wiping her face)*: Debby Debby Debby . . .

DEBBY: "—Who can that attractive girl be-e?—"

MAX *(To Debby)*: All right, listen.

DEBBY: "Such a pretty face, such a pretty face—"

MAX *(Overlap; to Lola)*: You see?

DEBBY: "—such a pretty face, such a pretty face, such a pretty MEEE!!"

MAX: *LISTEN!*

DEBBY: WHAT!

MAX: Enough. This has to stop.

DEBBY: We're having a pajama party. Don't be a poop.

MAX: *Listen* to me . . .

DEBBY: Party poop. Such a party poop.

MAX: Your mother and I had a talk.

DEBBY: A talk? What kind of talk? *(To Lola)* Mommy?

LOLA *(Shrugs)*: Your father . . .

DEBBY: You never let me have fun. Such a killjoy. Such a poop.

MAX: This isn't gonna work. You shouldn't've come.

DEBBY: Why? I'm *here.*

MAX: It's no good. You follow us, why do you follow us?

DEBBY *(Trying to embrace him)*: 'Cause I wuv you, Daddy.

MAX *(Taking her arms off him)*: We're getting out of here.

DEBBY: We are?

MAX: Not you. Your mother and me, we're gonna go.

DEBBY: *Now?* Mommy . . . what do you mean "go"?

NEIL *(To Debby)*: Where they going?

LOLA *(To Debby)*: Your father . . . I don't know . . . a motel . . .

DEBBY: It's like three o'clock in the morning . . .

MAX: We can't all stay here together.

DEBBY: But we *are* . . . we *are* all together.

NEIL *(To Debby)*: They're going away?

LOLA: We *are* managing, Max.

NEIL: Debby?

MAX: This is managing?

DEBBY *(Overlap)*: What do you want? You want us to be quiet?, we'll be quiet. Neil, shut up. *(Punches Neil's arm)*

NEIL: Ow . . .

DEBBY: No noise, I said . . . *(To Max)* Here. . . . You want room?, we'll make room . . . *(Pushes furniture)*

LOLA: Debby . . .

DEBBY: I'm making room . . . Neil . . . ?

Neil also moves furniture.

MAX: Stop it! Leave the place the way we found it!

DEBBY *(Continues disrupting the room)*: I'm making room . . . I'm making room . . .

MAX *(Overlap)*: Hey . . . hey . . . *(To Lola)* They'll tear the place apart. *(To Debby)* Look—stop that!—look . . . *(Takes money from his wallet)* Here, the two of you find a motel.

DEBBY: Motel?!

MAX: Better you should go.

DEBBY: I don't *wanna* go . . .

LOLA: Max . . .

DEBBY: . . . I wanna stay with *you* . . .

MAX *(Handing Neil money)*: Here . . .

DEBBY: Don't, Neil . . .

NEIL *(Taking the money from Max)*: If you want to give me money, give me money.

MAX: More? *(Gives him more from his wallet)* Take more.

NEIL: You want to give me money?, I'll *take* your money . . .

Debby slaps his hand.

(To Debby) If he wants . . .

DEBBY *(Snatches money from Neil)*: You don't want his money.

MAX: That's it. That's all. My pockets are empty. No more.

LOLA *(Over the above; to Max)*: Where they gonna go, what they gonna do?

MAX: There are motels we passed, right off the highway.

DEBBY: I'm unforgettable. You can't forget me. I'm unforgettable. Nat King Cole sang that song about me. I'm Mona Lisa.

Max shakes his head; he's had it.

NEIL: Mister. Please? Just a place to sleep.

DEBBY *(Sings)*: "Unforgettable, that's what I am . . . " *(Etc.)*

MAX *(Over Debby's singing)*: Come on, get your stuff . . .

LOLA: Max . . .

NEIL: Got no place to go. Please, mister.

MAX *(Over "Please, mister")*: The both of you. Whatever you've got . . .

LOLA: You can't just—

NEIL: I'll be quiet

MAX: I walked out of the woods. For what? For *this*?

DEBBY *(Sings)*: "Call me unforgettable . . . call me . . . unreliable . . . "

MAX *(To Neil)*: The last Jew in Europe. Sure. What kind of last Jew? What do I got to show for it? Hm? A condo in Florida? A daughter? Some daughter.

DEBBY *(To Max)*: You don't like me, huh?

Max looks as if that's the biggest understatement yet.

LOLA: Don't talk like that. . . . Of course he likes you. He loves you. We both love you.

DEBBY *(Stalking Max around the room)*: What, I'm not svelte enough? Not pretty enough? Not smart enough?

LOLA: You're very smart . . .

DEBBY: I won a scholarship award in fourth grade. Just me and Carol Ann Wiener. She was my best friend. What do you want me to do, Daddy? Rip off my rolls? Tear off my skin?

MAX: Lola, I will not—

DEBBY: Starve myself to death? Would that make you happy? Huh? How could I possibly be as pretty as Deborah? Skin and bones. Stick my finger down my throat. Vomit rots your teeth. Mengele was my dentist. He was Mister Wizard. He put my teeth in Coca-Cola. They burned like acid. Mengele taught you brain surgery.

MAX: What Hitler didn't do to me, *you* are doing . . . !

Debby gasps in mock horror.

LOLA: Max!

MAX: It's true! What *he* didn't do . . .

DEBBY: You made me, Daddy-O. You and Mengele and Frank-enstein.

MAX: Uh! *Franken*stein now!

DEBBY: All the brain surgery you did on me! Night after night! Anne Frank was in the next bed. You rewired my brain! Took out my memory! That's why my head always aches!

LOLA: What should we have done? Not told you anything . . . ?

DEBBY: Mommy?

LOLA: Yes, dear, what?

DEBBY: They're all inside me. All of them. Anne Frank. The Six Million. Bubbie and Zaydie and Hitler and Deborah. When my stomach talks, it's *them* talking. Telling me they're hungry. I eat for them so they won't be hungry. Sometimes I don't know what I'm saying 'cause it's *them* talking . . .

LOLA *(Over "talking . . . "; to Max)*: See? She doesn't know . . .

DEBBY *(Over "she doesn't know . . . ")*: Deborah talks to me. She tells me to do things. It all started with her, you know. You thought it was me. It's her fault. She was the life of the party but the party died before I got here. I can sing! I can pass out pigs in the blanket! I can be a lampshade! I'M ALIVE! I CAN'T HELP IT I WASN'T EXTERMINATED!

MAX *(Singsong)*: I'm not listening . . .

NEIL: Don't be sick, Debby . . . please . . .

DEBBY: I was in the woods with you, Daddy. Covered with leaves. I remember things I never saw. I was gonna save you. Hiding from the Nazis . . . night after night . . . waiting for the Nazis to come. And you always had that picture . . . that picture you carried in your shoe all through the war. This little doll. This little broken doll. This little Deborah made you cry and cry. I NEVER HAD A CHANCE! YOU EVEN GAVE ME HER NAME! HOW COULD YOU GIVE ME HER NAME?!

MAX: *Dos nemt nisht kim soff!* [This never ends!]

LOLA: *Zee ken sich nisht helfen.* [She can't help it.]

MAX: *Vos sie vil rayst zee dir orois!* [What she wants, she rips out of you!]

DEBBY: SPEAK ENGLISH! I hate when you do that! You're in America now! We speak English! This isn't the U.N.! This isn't *Judgment at Nuremberg* with Maximilian Schell!! Speak English! I'm sick of all the whispering in Yiddish and German! I could never understand what the doctors were saying but I knew they were talking about me, sticking things in me, cutting me open and stuffing all these dead people inside me. Millions and millions of dead people inside me. It's so crowded and noisy in here, I can't hear myself *think* anymore! This is not my heart. My heart never sounded like *this*. Where is *me*? What happened to *me*? How was I supposed to *sleep* with Nazi doctors screwing around with me all night? AND YOU LET THEM! *(She attacks Max)*

MAX: NO!

DEBBY: YOU LET THEM DO WHAT THEY WANTED!

MAX: STOP IT!!

DEBBY *(Overlap)*: I should've been dreaming sweet dreams like other little girls—YOU LET THEM IN THE HOUSE! YOU LET THEM IN MY ROOM!

Debby begins strangling Max.

MAX *(Struggling to free himself of Debby; screaming)*: Help me!
She's killing me!

*Debby is out of control; Lola and Neil try to get her away from
Max. Blackout.*

Scene Thirteen

Debby is tied up and gagged. Max strokes her hair and speaks gently, reasonably. Lola waits at the window; Neil is crying.

MAX: Debby. *(Shrugs)* I pour everything I *got* into you. Nothing
works. Special schools, special doctors. Hospitals. "Residences." In-patient, out-patient. My head spins from you. *(A
small chuckle)* You're amazing! I never knew a person like you.
You don't give up. You come after us no matter what. You're
amazing! We don't sleep at night, worried what you might do.
We live our *lives* worried what you might do. We gotta face the
facts: You gotta help yourself. I can't make you get well. Your
mother can't make you get well. You gotta get well your*self*. *(A
beat)* It's time we go our separate ways I think.

*Debby struggles to speak in protest under her gag. Max soothingly
touches her hair.*

Shh shh shh. You think I en*joy* this? The way we have to live?
Yelling and carrying on? No good. How many good years we
got left, your mother and me? Think about it. *(Shrugs: "What
am I supposed to do?")* I'm a simple man, nothing special. I
walked out of the woods. For what? So I could come to
America? Sell sportswear in Flatbush? For this I walked out of
the woods? Where are the children? Where are the grandchildren? *(A beat)* Look, darling . . . all I want . . . I want to clip on
my clip-on sunglasses, put up my feet, sit in the Florida sun,
read my *Wall Street Journal*, see how my stocks are doing. *(A
beat)* Sweetheart . . . *(Pause)* Debby . . . *(A very deep sigh)*

Why can't we just shake hands, wish each other luck. Hm? Is that so terrible? Shake hands, *zy'gesunt.*

Debby just looks at him.

Am I so bad? I'm such a bad person? Such a bad father?

An ambulance siren is heard approaching. A beat; Max shrugs.

All I want is a little peace. Is that so terrible?

Blackout.

Scene Fourteen

Lola stands by the open front door. Max faces away from her. The ambulance's red light spins off the walls of the apartment. Silence.

LOLA: You won't ride with her?

Silence.

You don't have to. I will. You can follow in the car.

Silence.

I can't turn my back. Maybe you can, I can't turn my back.
MAX *(A realization):* Uh! You're glad she came.
LOLA: What?
MAX: You're glad she came.
LOLA: I'm glad she's safe now, yes. I was worried.
MAX *(Over "yes. I was worried"):* You're glad she *came.* You need her.
LOLA: She *is* my child.
MAX: You *need* her. You need her *mishagas.*
LOLA: You don't understand a mother.
MAX: Oh, no?
LOLA: No, you don't.
MAX: She is hopeless, Lola. Let her go. Stay with me.

Pause.

LOLA: I'm responsible. Who's responsible if not me?

MAX: A trick of fate. I'm not responsible.

LOLA: Max, I'm responsible and you're responsible, too.

MAX: Madmen are born the same way as sane men. A trick. Why am I alive today: It's all a trick.

LOLA: She's our daughter, Max. You don't turn your back on your own child.

MAX: "Child." You make her sound like an infant. An infant needs taking care of. An infant you keep clean and fed. This is no child. She can *crush* me, Lola! She can kill me and she will! If this keeps up . . . *(A beat. Softly)* Let her go.

Lola shakes her head no. Pause.

MAX: Then why did we come?

Pause.

LOLA: You wanted it.

MAX *(Nods, hurt; pause)*: And you?

LOLA *(With uncertainty)*: I wanted it, too. For you.

MAX: Ah.

LOLA *(With more conviction)*: You wanted it and I wanted it, too.

Pause.

MAX: We talked about coming down here . . .

LOLA: Yes.

MAX: For years and years: Florida. Was it gonna be something!: Florida.

LOLA: Yes.

MAX: We'll buy our place in the sun and we'll enjoy.

LOLA: Yes.

MAX: Once and for all: you and me, just us. Florida.

Long pause.

LOLA: I can't deny her, Max. She exists. What am I supposed to do?, shut my eyes and ears?

MAX: Yes.

LOLA: You don't mean it.

MAX: *I shut my eyes and ears.*

LOLA: And what do you see?

MAX: What I *wish* to see.

LOLA: And what you do *not* wish to see?

Long pause; they look at one another.

(Sadly; her eyes filling) My darling Max . . .

Blackout.

The Last Scene

*Lights up, very brightly. The next morning. Max, wearing a ca-
bana suit, is asleep on a chaise lounge on the sun deck. The* Wall
Street Journal *has fallen to the ground. We hear the tape of an
opera he's listening to on his Walkman. Deborah enters. Silence.*

DEBORAH: I miss you at *Pesach, Tateh.* Everyone is there but
you. We always talk about you. We do. We haven't forgotten.
We wonder how you survived. Everyone is very old now, but
healthy. Smashed bones are mended, muscles are restored.
Hair has grown in nicely. Thick, shiny hair. And we've all put
back the weight we lost, some of us *too* much. Everyone is
dressed in their best, their fanciest clothes reserved for holy
days. You should see. We look like ourselves again. A very
handsome family. I'm still the youngest, so I get to ask the *feir
kashas.* I let the boy cousins compete for the *afikoman.* I won't
play with them. They're wild. They tease me and run around
the living room. They're restless, I know. I am, too. But I like
to stay with the men. Zaydie Duvid and Zaydie Schmuel con-
duct the seder together and argue about everything. The seder
goes on into the night. I'm hungry, so hungry, but I can hardly
keep my eyes open. The boys shriek and tug on my hair.

Mameh and Bubbie Sura and Bubbie Bessie and Aunt Chaya and Aunt Rifke and Aunt Freyda—all the women—they all worry about the food, keeping the food fresh and warm. There is so much food! The kitchen is noisy with women. The dining room is cloudy with smoke and opinions. It's like it used to be when we were all together. No, it's noisier, there are more of us together now than there were before, so many of us.

Lights begin to fade slowly.

It's *Pesach* all the time, *Tateh.* I can't remember when it wasn't *Pesach.* I miss you all the time. The men are always arguing. And a feast is always awaiting us in the kitchen. And I'm always hungry, always hungry. And the boys are always running wild. And the arguing in the dining room goes on and on, into the night. And I can't keep my eyes open, I've sipped too much wine, and I don't want to go to sleep hungry, but my eyes are closing, they're closing, and I don't want to fall asleep and miss the feast, I don't want to miss the feast . . .

Fade to black.

THE LOMAN FAMILY PICNIC

☐ ☐ ☐

CHARACTERS

DORIS, 38

HERBIE, 40

MITCHELL, 11

STEWIE, 13

MARSHA, 23

TIME

Around 1965.

PLACE

Coney Island, Brooklyn, New York.

ACT ONE

Scene One

In the black: A Broadway overture segues into Mantovani's rendition of "Autumn Leaves."

At rise: a high-rise apartment in Coney Island, Brooklyn. Around 1965. A picture window looks out onto an identical, parallel high-rise building with dozens of picture windows. The room is decorated with Spanish Provincial furnishings: wrought-iron sconces, heavily carved wooden shelves, floor lamps, sofa, TV/hi-fi console, etc. A door in the dining area leads to a terrace overlooking the neighboring building. It's shortly after three o'clock on a late October afternoon. Doris, thirty-eight years old, wearing a housecoat over her pajamas, sits on the sofa with her wedding dress on her lap. She is cutting it to shreds with a pair of scissors.

DORIS *(To us):* On the day I was married the world showed every sign of coming to an end. It rained—no, poured. Thunder. Cracks of lightning. Big Pearl S. Buck tidal waves. You get the picture. Did I turn back? Did I cancel? Did I say never mind, no thank you? A good omen, my mother told me. There had never been such a terrifying convergence of weather post-Noah; a good omen. Hail, did I mention hail? Like my mother's matzo balls falling from the sky shouting *Don't! Don't!* each time a *knaidel* smacked the roof of the rented limo. A better omen still, my mother said, hail. What about sunshine?, Momma?, I asked, what about a sunny wedding day? Also a good omen, my mother said. *(A beat)* I began to distrust her. *(A beat)* Two seconds in my wedding dress: splattered with mud. I should've known. Look at this: ruined. From day one. *(Points to various stains)* Mud, rain, hail, locusts, boredom, moraine . . . *(Looking directly at us)* I love the way my life has turned out. I have two wonderful boys. Mitchell is my baby. He's eleven. And Stewie is gonna be bar mitzvahed next Saturday at ten in the morning, to be followed by a gala affair starring me. What boys I have! I'm very lucky, knock on Formica. Smart?! Mitchell has a reading level, goes off the charts. So smart are my boys. Their father is not at all threatened by how smart they are. They aren't showoffs. I don't like showoffs. I raised my boys to stand out but not too much, you know?, otherwise people won't like you anymore. Look what happened to the Jews in Europe. Better you should have friends and be popular, than be showy and alone. My Aunt Marsha may she rest in peace taught me that. She was very popular. *(A beat. Refers to the wedding dress)* Last night was my wedding anniversary. Eighteen years. Herbie had to work, what else is new. I love the way my life has turned out. Did I say that already? On the day I was married the world showed every sign of coming to an end . . .

Mitchell, eleven years old, enters through the front door carrying schoolbooks.

Mitchell. What are you doing home from school?

MITCHELL: School let out; the day is over; I came home. It's three-thirty.

DORIS: Oh, my God. You're home from school and I haven't been out all day? I didn't even put on any clothes? I'm not depressed.

MITCHELL: I didn't say you were depressed. What are you doing with your wedding gown?

DORIS: I got the greatest idea for a Halloween costume—you're gonna love this: the Bride of Frankenstein.

MITCHELL: You're gonna tear up your wedding gown for a costume?

DORIS: I'm not disenchanted with my marriage.

MITCHELL: I didn't say you were disenchanted with your marriage.

DORIS: I still love your father.

MITCHELL: I didn't say you didn't.

DORIS: I love my life. I love the way my life has turned out. Your father doesn't bore me. What if your father and I got a divorce?; who would you live with? Never mind, only kidding. So, how was school today?

MITCHELL: I owe Miss Schoenberg fifty cents for lunch. You forgot to put lunch in my lunchbox again.

DORIS: Did I? Oh, honey, I'm sorry. I'm not a negligent mother.

MITCHELL: I didn't say you were. I said you forgot. Anyone could forget.

DORIS: I guess I was just preoccupied with how much I love my life. Don't you love this room? Isn't it unusual? I need a job. I have to get out of the house.

MITCHELL: I have good news.

DORIS *(Voraciously)*: Ooo, what? I'd love some good news!

MITCHELL: Remember that poster I made for Brotherhood Week?

DORIS: The rabbi and the priest and the black hand shaking hands with the white hand?, yeah . . . ?

MITCHELL: Well, today Miss Schoenberg announced to the class that I was a citywide finalist.

DORIS *(Shrieks in delight)*: OH, MY GODDD!! To the class?!!

MITCHELL: Yeah, and it's gonna hang in the bank!

DORIS: The bank?!

MITCHELL: The Lincoln Savings Bank.

DORIS: The Lincoln Savings Bank?! It's gonna hang there?

MITCHELL: Uh-huh.

DORIS: With your name?!

MITCHELL: Yeah, on an index card or something, written.

DORIS: People are gonna see your name?, in the bank?

MITCHELL *(Proud)*: Yeah.

DORIS: I'm dying. Sweetheart! Oh, this is wonderful news! I'm so proud of you! The bank!, for everyone to see! You're talking finalist now, not the winner, right?

MITCHELL: Finalist, you know, like in Miss America before they choose the winner.

DORIS: So you're not the winner yet but you have a shot.

MITCHELL: Right.

DORIS: Citywide?

MITCHELL: Yeah. The winner gets to go to City Hall and meet Mayor Lindsay.

DORIS: I'm dying.

MITCHELL: The *Daily News* comes.

DORIS: Pictures?! With Mayor Lindsay?! Oh, God, what would I wear?

MITCHELL *(Reminding her)*: I'm only a finalist so far.

DORIS: That's right, you may not even win, I'm jumping the gun. Oh, sweetheart, you've made my day.

MITCHELL: Miss Schoenberg says I'm very creative, I could have quite a career as an artist.

DORIS: Well, I'm sure. Both my sons are very talented. And your father is not in the least bit threatened by you or your brother.

MITCHELL: Miss Schoenberg says I can do whatever I like when I grow up. I have so many options because I'm such a strong student. She says I shouldn't rule out the Ivy League.

DORIS: For what.

MITCHELL: For college.

DORIS: You're eleven years old.

MITCHELL: So? Miss Schoenberg says attitudes toward academic achievement are developed at a very early age. You've seen my report cards: I'm a born overachiever.

DORIS: You mean Harvard, Princeton?

MITCHELL: Yale . . .

DORIS: Tell Miss Schoenberg she can put you through college.

MITCHELL: She says there are scholarships.

DORIS: Look, sweetheart, we are not Ivy League. We are City College. We're not like those people. City College was invented for people like us. You get a perfectly decent education.

MITCHELL: Whatever happened to the immigrant ideal of education or death?

DORIS: It died in the Depression. Miss Schoenberg is a troublemaker.

MITCHELL: Don't you want me to fulfill my potential? Don't you want me to continue getting excellents?

DORIS: Of course I do. But don't let your head get too big, it's unseemly. To be excellent is one thing; to be outstanding is another. We aren't fancy people, we're hand to mouth. We are middle-middle class, smack in the middle.

MITCHELL: But, Mom—

DORIS: Do you want to kill your father completely? He's half-dead just treading water. How would we explain Ivy League to the relatives? They think we're rich already, because we live in this luxurious high-rise; then they'd really despise us. We want everyone to love us. Remember what my Aunt Marsha always said may she rest in peace: Don't go around thinking you're better than everyone else 'cause you'll be alone in the end. Dream, my son, but not too big.

Stewie, almost thirteen, stomps through the front door.

STEWIE: I've had it. Cancel the bar mitzvah.

MITCHELL: Hi, Stewie.

DORIS: What are you talking about cancel the bar mitzvah?! I can't cancel the bar mitzvah. What happened?

MITCHELL: Hi.

STEWIE: Mr. Shlosh is a cretin.

DORIS: He's a rabbi.

STEWIE: I don't care he's a rabbi, he's still a cretin. We're going over my Haftarah . . .

DORIS: Yeah . . .

STEWIE: I know almost all of it by heart.

DORIS: Thank God.

STEWIE: And I'm really singing it this time. Like Jerry Vale. Soft and sweet? It's so beautiful I'm embarrassing myself, I feel my cheeks getting hot. And I get through the whole thing perfectly, I sound just like the record, and he doesn't even compliment me!

DORIS: Alright, so he's not gushy.

STEWIE: He's not human.

Mitchell laughs.

I decided to have a conversation with him?

MITCHELL: Yeah . . . ?

STEWIE: Big mistake. I mean, I've been sitting in this room with this guy with bad breath for years, reading the same stuff over and over, preparing me for the big day, right?, and he never even talked to me! I don't mean Talmudic dialogue, I mean your basic chat.

DORIS: What do you want from him?! He's an old man!

STEWIE: I gave up my boyhood to him, Ma! Hundreds of afternoons I'll never get back! I missed years of watching *You Don't Say* after school! That's irreplaceable, Ma.

DORIS: Oh, stop.

STEWIE: So I thought I was entitled to ask a question at least. I said to Shlosh, "Okay, so finally I can read all these little symbols right to left. Great. Now tell me what it means." Well, the guy looks like he's gonna go berserk. *(To Mitchell)* Like Ray Milland in *X—the Man with the X-Ray Eyes* right before he plucks his eyes out?

Mitchell giggles.

"Tell me what I'm reading," I said, "tell me what the words mean." He looks at me like I'm not speaking any known language. "What does it mean?!," I said, "what am I saying?!" "What does it matter?," he says, "you can read it." "Yeah, but what does it mean?!" "It means you will be bar mitzvah!," he says. "But the words don't mean anything to me, they're just these funny, *chuchy* little sounds." "Those funny sounds," he says, "are what make a boy different from a Jew!" "So?! You taught me how to read but you didn't teach me how to understand! What kind of Jew is that?!" This does not go over big. His lips are turning blue. I think he's gonna have an angina attack. *(Beat)* All he cares about is rolling out bar mitzvah boys to repopulate the earth. We look the part and we can sing, but we don't know what we're saying! I have had it!

DORIS: You have to go through with your bar mitzvah, Stewie.

STEWIE: You don't know what it's like, Ma, day after day of this. I'm being brainwashed.

DORIS: You're just getting cold feet. You'll be fine.

STEWIE: I can't do it, Ma.

DORIS: Yes you can. Just like Sammy Davis, Jr. Say it: Yes I can.

STEWIE: Ma . . .

DORIS: He lost an eye and everything. And that man is a Jew. Yes I can, yes I can . . .

STEWIE: But I don't want to.

DORIS *(Infuriated, through gritted teeth)*: How dare you do this to me!

STEWIE *(Also through gritted teeth)*: What?, what am I doing to you?!

DORIS: You know how hard I've been working to make you a beautiful party?!

STEWIE: Me? It's not for me. Make your beautiful party! I just won't be there. Tell everybody I got the runs!

DORIS: Don't do this to me, Stewie! Don't make me cancel! We'll lose all our deposits! Is that what you want?! Hm?! Your father's blood money down the drain?! The hall, the band, the flowers?! The caterers?! I already bought my dress, what do you want me to do with it?, hock it? I've spent days laying out response cards like solitaire and clipping tables together! This is no time to be a prima donna, Stewie. One more week. That's all I ask. Give me the *nachas*, then you can do whatever the hell you want. You want to renounce Judaism?, renounce Judaism. Become a monk, I don't care.

A beat.

STEWIE *(Teeth gritted again)*: Remember, Ma, I'm doing this for you. I'll go through with it, and sing nice, and make you proud, and make the relatives cry, but once I'm bar mitzvahed, that's it, Ma, I'm never stepping foot in that place. Never again.

DORIS: Thank you, darling, thank you.

Doris kisses and tickles Stewie; he squeals with delight.

MITCHELL *(During the above)*: Stewie? Hey, Stewie.

STEWIE *(Annoyed)*: What.

MITCHELL: You know the poster I made?

STEWIE: Yeah . . .

MITCHELL: I'm a finalist.

STEWIE *(Unenthused)*: Wow.

DORIS *(To us)*: Isn't it wonderful how my boys get along?

Blackout.

Scene Two

Around midnight. Some lights are still on in the windows across the way. Doris, Stewie and Mitchell have all fallen asleep in front of the TV. Stewie is lying flat on his back with his accordion strapped on. We hear a key in the front door and in a moment Herbie, a burly forty-year-old, enters wearily, a shopping bag in each hand and newspapers tucked under his arm.

HERBIE: Daddy's home! The provider is here! *(He waits, expecting to be greeted ceremoniously, but his sleeping family doesn't budge. Facetiously)* Gee, it's good to be back in my family's waiting arms! In the bosom of my family! Don't all of you jump up and kiss me at once! *(A beat)* Daddy's home! Another day, another dollar! *(A beat)* The warrior is back! I'm black and blue but I'm back in one piece! From a whole day of busting my balls for you! Gee, I can't wait to get up at six a.m. so they can be pounded to bits all over again! Oh!, but look what Daddy brought! Wow! What a guy! What a dad! *(Unloads as he speaks)* Milk, orange juice, half a dozen bagels: poppy, salt, cinnamon-raisin, pumpernickel, plain, garlic; one of each! Plus, for the boys: half gallon of their favorite, fudge swirl! Wow! Gee, thanks, Dad! Aw, you're welcome, son! *(A beat; still no reaction)* What a day! The place was a madhouse! Customers on the phone, at the counter! They were all over me! The cash register didn't stop! I still hear ringing in my ears! I was so busy, I didn't even have time to pee! A whole day! I wouldn't be surprised if my bladder just exploded one of these days, pshhhoo!, like a water balloon! *(Takes off his shoes)* Phew! Can you believe a stink like that comes out of a man?! *(Massages his feet)*

DORIS *(Stirs, sniffs his aroma)*: Herbie? When'd you get home?

HERBIE: Hours ago.

DORIS: You did not. . . . Boys? Boys, wake up.

Mitchell yawns, rubs his eyes, etc. Stewie remains asleep.

MITCHELL: What time is it?

DORIS: Daddy's home; you're on.

MITCHELL: I have to get up for school soon. I need nine or ten hours in order to function properly.

DORIS: Just say hello to your father.

MITCHELL: Hi, Dad.

DORIS: Kiss him.

Mitchell sleepily gets up, kisses him.

Stewie, play him that piece on the accordion. Stewie!

Stewie, still lying on his back, plays "Lady of Spain" on the accordion. Banging is heard from downstairs as Stewie rushes through the piece.

Isn't it wonderful how your son serenades you? You're not

threatened by Stewie's musical abilities, are you, Herbie? Of course not. *(Nudging Mitchell)* Tell your father what happened in school today.

MITCHELL: What.

DORIS: You know, the big news. The bank, Mayor Lindsay.

MITCHELL: Oh, do I have to?

DORIS: Yes you have to. *(To Herbie)* I'll go get your supper. *(As she goes off to the kitchen)* Wait till you hear this . . .

Pause.

HERBIE: Well?

MITCHELL: It's nothing. Can I please go to bed?

DORIS *(Off)*: No. Tell him!

MITCHELL *(Sighs, then wearily)*: Remember that poster I made?

HERBIE: Poster?

MITCHELL: I made a poster.

Herbie shrugs.

Remember she made me show it to you one night when you came home?

Herbie thinks, shrugs.

The rabbi?, the priest?, the black hand shaking hands with the white hand?

HERBIE: Oh, yeah. That was a poster?

MITCHELL: Yes.

HERBIE: Oh, okay. So?

MITCHELL: Today I found out I'm a finalist for the citywide Brotherhood Week poster competition.

A beat.

HERBIE: A what?

DORIS *(Off)*: A finalist. Citywide. A contest.

HERBIE: Finalist?

DORIS *(Off)*: It means it was one of the best. In the whole city.

HERBIE: Is that good?

DORIS *(Off)*: Yes, it's very good.

HERBIE: Oh. Well, good.

DORIS *(Off)*: Tell him about Mayor Lindsay.

HERBIE: What about Mayor Lindsay?

MITCHELL *(Dully, while yawning)*: If I win, I get to meet Mayor Lindsay.

HERBIE: Oh. *(A beat)* I didn't vote for him.

Mitchell and Herbie look at one another.

DORIS *(Enters with a plate of food)*: Isn't it wonderful how your father takes pride in your achievements? Most fathers don't do that. Most fathers only know how to compete with their sons and are threatened by everything they do. You're very lucky. *(To Herbie)* Here, I made you a dietetic dinner. Three-and-a-half-ounce can of tuna packed in water with one table-spoon of low-calorie Miracle Whip in lieu of mayo. One scoop of low-fat cottage cheese on a bed of lettuce. I weighed and measured everything very carefully, according to Jean Nidetch. *(Sits down at the table with Herbie)*

Silence.

So? How was your day?

Herbie shrugs. Pause.

Business?

HERBIE *(Shrugs, then)*: Good.

DORIS: Uh-huh. *(Pause)* Everybody?

HERBIE *(Shrugs, then)*: Same.

DORIS: Uh-huh.

She sighs; her boredom and despair are palpable but she continues to sit in silence, struggling to stay awake while watching him eat. There's a shift in the lighting and they're now convivially relating to one another, as old friends, stories they've never before shared, each telling how the other died.

HERBIE: It was around eleven one night.

DORIS: Yeah . . . ?

HERBIE: We were in bed, watching the news. You got up to go to the john; I dozed off; you came back. The toilet was still running. And then you shook, like.

DORIS: Hm.

HERBIE: The kind of shake you do when you're in a dream, falling?

DORIS: Uh-huh . . . ?

HERBIE: Well, your shake woke me up and I looked at you and you looked funny to me.

DORIS: Uh-oh.

HERBIE: Very white; and I touched you and you felt funny.

DORIS: Uy.

HERBIE: I shook you: Doris, Doris. It was like you passed out, only worse.

DORIS: Uy uy uy.

HERBIE: 9–1–1 I called. I held your cold foot and told you, we're gonna get you some oxygen, Doris, everything's gonna be okay. And the sirens came soon, red lights flashed 'round the windows, and the buzzer buzzed and I buzzed 'em in. They're on their way up, Doris, don't worry, any minute. . . . The bell. I let 'em in, I was still in my shorts and didn't even care, didn't even think to put on my pants. And they came in, noisy with oxygen, stretcher; they *zetzed* some furniture on the way in.

DORIS: Not my furniture . . .

HERBIE: Easy, I said, and led 'em to the bedroom, and I sat up in bed watching them work on you. Boy, they hit you hard.

DORIS: They did?

HERBIE: Don't hurt her, you got to do that so hard? They pumped on you, your pajama top was open, and I wasn't even embarrassed 'cause these guys are professionals, I thought, they do this all the time. Remember the time the car died on that bad part of Ocean Avenue and the Triple-A guys started her right up?

DORIS: Yeah . . . ?

HERBIE: That's what I thought: Come on, guys, start her up.

DORIS *(Laughs affectionately)*: Oh, Herbie . . .

HERBIE: Let's go. One more press, two more, come on Doris, three more, come on, okay this time, this time, come on baby. You were gonna snap out of it like when you think in the movies somebody drowned but they cough up water and they're fine. Cough, Doris. Come on, cough. And then you were gonna sit up and turn pink again and say what the hell happened, Herbie?

DORIS: Of course.

HERBIE: I waited. *(A beat)* What the hell happened you were supposed to say.

Pause; Doris is shaking her head.

DORIS *(After a beat)*: Well, you. You took forever.

HERBIE: Yeah . . . ?

DORIS: Talk about milking it: longest deathbed scene in history.

HERBIE: You're kidding.

DORIS: The waiting. The drama. The boredom. What a character; couldn't let go.

Herbie laughs.

I thought I myself would die of exposure to weeks of fluorescent lighting and hospital food.

HERBIE: You're funny.

DORIS: Every day was something else. Good news one minute, talk about safe-deposit boxes the next. You did not know what hit you, my darling.

HERBIE: Is that so.

DORIS: You looked at me with a look: What is going on? Your lungs went, then your kidneys conked out and the whites of your eyes went yellow and you blew up like Buddha.

HERBIE: Geez . . .

DORIS: You were all tubes and bags of plasma and shit, *bubeleh*, and your big belly trembled with the air the machine fed you. Do you want to die?, I asked you on Day Twelve, and you shook your head yes.

HERBIE: I did?

DORIS: Yes, and then something remarkable happened to your face.

HERBIE: What.

DORIS: It lost all the tensed-up lines in your forehead and 'round your mouth. And your features looked young and smooth, like when you were a G.I. You were Claude Rains turning visible again, for the last time, before my very eyes. The old Herbie came back, the *young* Herbie, the Herbie before everything, *my* Herbie, smooth of brow and cute of nose. . . . The face of my oldest of friends came into focus out of the fog of machines and sour odors. . . . I got you back for a second, Herbie, so letting you go wasn't so bad.

Herbie holds her hand. They look at one another for a beat. He remembers something.

HERBIE: Oh, and the part I thought you'd love:

DORIS: What.

HERBIE: While they were pumping away at you?

DORIS: Uh-huh . . . ?

HERBIE: The doorbell rang. The schmuck from downstairs.

DORIS: Friedberg?

HERBIE: The schmuck, right?

DORIS: Yeah. What did he want?

HERBIE: Wait. "What the hell kind of racket's going on up here," he says, "you know what time it is?!!" Look, I said, my wife just passed away.

DORIS *(Amused)*: Uy vey.

HERBIE: "Oh yeah?," the schmuck says, "Oh yeah? Well you should hear what it sounds like downstairs!"

Doris and Herbie laugh hysterically. Pause. The lights shift back to present reality. Doris yawns.

DORIS: I give up. Mitchell, do me a favor: Keep your father company while he eats, I can't keep my eyes open.

Mitchell takes her place at the table.

HERBIE *(To Mitchell; looking at his dinner with distaste)*: You want this?

DORIS: You see how much he loves you? Good night, boys.

She taps Stewie as she exits to her bedroom. Stewie groggily gets up off the floor, the accordion bellows sounding, and goes to his room. Silence. Mitchell yawns, taps his foot, while looking through the newspaper.

HERBIE: You want to go out, throw a football around?

MITCHELL: Now?

HERBIE: That was a joke.

MITCHELL: We've never thrown a football around in our lives.

HERBIE: I know; that's the funny part.

MITCHELL *(After a pause, he steps away from the table and speaks to us)*: For school, Miss Schoenberg made us read this play that Arthur Miller wrote a long time ago, before I was born, about this salesman with two sons who lives in Brooklyn? Sound familiar? I know; I read it like three times 'cause I couldn't believe it either. There are all these similarities. Except Willy Loman, the guy in the play?, the salesman?, doesn't sell lighting fixtures. *(A beat)* Anyway, in the play he goes insane and kills himself by smashing up his car so his family can collect his insurance money, even though I thought you can't collect if you commit suicide, which is what I said in class but Miss Schoenberg said not necessarily. *(A beat)* Arthur Miller himself grew up in this very same spot practically. Many years ago. He walked the same streets I walk every day. He played in our schoolyard probably. I heard that his family's house was one of the houses they wrecked so they could build our middle-income luxury building here in Coney Island. At least that's what Miss Schoenberg said. *(A beat)* Anyway, we have to get up in front of the class and do like oral book reports?, but instead of doing the usual if-you-want-to-know-how-he-kills-himself-you-have-to-read-the-play kind of thing, I decided I'm gonna do something else, something different. *(A beat)* So, I'm writing this musical-comedy version of *Death of a*

Salesman called *Willy!* With an exclamation point. You know, like *Fiorello!? Oklahoma!? Oliver!?* So far I've come up with a couple of songs. Like, when Biff and Happy are up in their room and they hear Willy downstairs talking to himself?, they sing this song called "Dad's a Little Weird" which goes: *(Sings)* "Dad's a little weird, he's in a daze. Could it be he's going nuts, or is it just a phase?" *(A beat)* Well, it's a start. What do you think?

Blackout.

Scene Three

The middle of the night. The apartment is dark. Most of the windows in the building across the way are dark, too. Doris has insomnia; she wanders into the living room smoking a cigarette. We hear, off in the bedroom, Herbie snoring.

DORIS *(Through gritted teeth, to herself)*: That snoring . . . if he doesn't stop that snoring . . . it rips at my *kishkas* every time he breathes. Every time he breathes is one more tear in my life. I love my life I love my life I love my— *(To us)* We have to stay together, at least till after the bar mitzvah. What would be the point? I have to have my day of glory. We have to be intact. Otherwise it's bittersweet forced-smiles brave-front stuff. "This is Mrs. Norman Maine." Destroys me every time. When it was on the Million Dollar Movie three times a day for a week, W.O.R. Channel 9, I turned on the TV the last five minutes for a guaranteed cry. "Hello, everybody. . . . This is . . . Mrs . . . Norman . . . Maine." I'm getting misty just thinking about it. And she'd bring the house down. Everybody'd jump to their feet for a standing ovation, clapping till their hands hurt. Fifteen times a week I bawled in front of the TV. The boys'd come in from school, take one look at me pink-faced and teary and say "Uh-oh; *Star is Born*," and go off to their room. *(A beat)* Now, if Herbie walked into the waves at Coney Island. . . . If he walked into the ocean à la James Mason and made me a widow, there's no question I'd go through with the bar mitzvah. I'd wear black sequins and clutch my boys to me with my head held high like Jackie Kennedy in the rotunda. Then I'd go through with it solo. But a divorce?

During the above, a woman is seen climbing down onto the terrace from the one above. She is dressed in '40s attire, a brunette beauty with her hair in a pageboy. Her name is Marsha and she's twenty-three years old. She looks in the picture window, opens the terrace door and steps inside.

MARSHA: There you are, Doll.

DORIS: Aunt Marsha.

MARSHA: I been looking all over for you. All these apartments look alike. I almost dropped in on the Glucksterns by mistake.

DORIS: Come in. What do you think of my life? What do you think of little Doris now? Hm?

Marsha explores the room.

What you had to say always meant so much to me. What do you think? Does it look the way you once imagined my life would look when you held me in your arms, like a big sister at a pajama party, and we dreamed out loud together? Hm, Aunt Marsha?

MARSHA *(After a beat)*: Spanish, Doll?

DORIS: No? It's so unusual, don't you think? I go for Spanish. I don't know what it is about Spanish. Maybe it has something to do with the Inquisition. It's a taste I cultivated on my own. You don't like it.

MARSHA: Who said?

DORIS: I always thought you'd approve; isn't that funny? You're always looking over my shoulder whenever I go shopping. To this very day: What would Aunt Marsha think? I see you nod or make that face.

Marsha jokingly makes a disapproving face.

Yeah, that's it. You never liked it when I went too fancy. Not too fancy, you don't want to be too fancy. You taught me that.

MARSHA: You funny kid.

DORIS: Kid? I'm thirty-eight years old, Marsh. You'd've hated thirty-eight. Sometimes I think you had the right idea.

MARSHA: What, checking out?

DORIS: Stopping time. For you time is stopped; for the rest of us it goes on and on but you stay young. You're dead now longer than I knew you. Longer than I knew you and not a day goes by—

MARSHA: So show me your dress for the bar mitzvah.

DORIS: I'm afraid now.

MARSHA: Show me.

DORIS *(Starts to go)*: You're not gonna like it.

MARSHA: Shut your trap; let me see.

DORIS: Well . . . *(She goes and returns with the dress)*

MARSHA: Oh, Doll . . .

DORIS: I don't know, I thought the color . . .

MARSHA: It's you.

DORIS: Yeah?

MARSHA *(Holds the dress against Doris)*: Oh, yeah, that's swell!

DORIS: Really? You don't think the color maybe—

MARSHA: Are you kidding, I love it.

DORIS: Oh, Marsh. . . . You don't know how many shops. . . . Finally, on Kings Highway. . . . You really like it?

MARSHA: I'm knocked out.

DORIS: I knew you would be. When I bought it, I said to my-self—it's so good to see you.

MARSHA: You think I would miss your kid's bar mitzvah?

DORIS *(A beat; getting something off her chest)*: I gotta tell ya, Marsh: I don't want you to get the wrong idea. I have two boys, you know.

MARSHA *(Pleased)*: Doll! Two?

DORIS: Mitchell I named for you. I would've named my first af-ter you but I was holding out for a girl.

MARSHA: Makes sense. Thanks, kid.

Marsha continues exploring the room; Doris watches her.

DORIS: You still got the greatest legs in the world.

MARSHA: That's me, Betty Grable. *(Looking out the window)* How high up are we, I lost count.

DORIS: Ten stories, ten luxurious stories up in the air and thirteen on top of that. This is modern luxury.

MARSHA: Well, Doll, to tell you the truth . . . I had in mind for you a place with trees.

DORIS: There are trees, way down there. See? They're little stick trees 'cause they were just planted, but they're still trees. One day their trunks'll be big and thick. Everything's new, Marsh. Clean and new. We're the first. We moved in and the walls were white and the rooms still smelled of paint.

MARSHA: Whatever makes you happy.

DORIS: You should've seen the place we lived before. I don't know how we did it. A slum; the neighborhood was going to hell. But here! Hot water always. Rec room. Elevators that work. Security patrolled by German shepherds. A Waldbaums that delivers. This is a big step up for us. Luxury, I'm telling you. Like fancy people. I hope not too fancy.

MARSHA: To think this is Brooklyn . . .

DORIS: Oh, we worked hard for all this, Marsh, you don't know. This is progress. I love our high-rise ghetto. Look out there. I can't wait for Hanukkah; Hanukkah looks like Kristalnacht here: a bonfire of orange-flame menorah bulbs burning in thousands of windows. A brick wall of electric flame! We're not alone. You know how good that feels? They moved us up, closer to heaven. Jews upon Jews who are glad to be here, who came as far as we did, from Flatbush, from Williamsburg, from East New York. Jews who escaped the Nazis, who escaped their relatives, who fled the *schvartzes*. Millions of miles of wall-to-wall carpeting that, if placed end to end, would reach from here to Jupiter and back. Instead of stoops they built us these little terraces. Sometimes I have to restrain myself from doing the cha-cha over the edge just to see what it would feel like going down.

(A beat; a confession) I hung my last sconce today. I'm done decorating, Marsh. I bought my last *tschatchke*. My life is over.

MARSHA: Hey, don't talk like that.

DORIS: It is. My life is over, Marsh.

MARSHA: I'm not gonna sit here and listen to you talking like some sad sack. Now, I don't know about you, but I want to have some fun! *(Pulls Doris to her feet)*

DORIS *(Protests girlishly)*: Marsh. . . . What are you doing?

MARSHA: Come on, I'm not gonna take no for an answer . . .

DORIS: I don't believe you!

Marsha leads Doris in a swing step and hums/sings "Shaking the Blues Away." Doris's ambivalence subsides and, laughing, she throws herself into the dance. Soon, Mitchell appears in his pajamas, roused by the sounds. He watches for a moment.

MITCHELL: Mom?

DORIS *(Stops dancing)*: Mitchell! Sweetheart! Come here, there's somebody I want you to meet. *(To Marsha)* This is my baby, Mitchell.

MARSHA: Oh!

MITCHELL *(Going to her)*: Mommy, it's the middle of the night.

DORIS: Mitchell, do you know who this is?

MITCHELL *(Shyly)*: No.

DORIS: This is my Aunt Marsha.

MITCHELL *(Recognizing her)*: Oh, yeah.

MARSHA: Hello, handsome.

MITCHELL: Hello. You look like your picture.

MARSHA *(Charmed)*: I do? So, you know who I am?

MITCHELL: Uh-huh.

MARSHA: I was your grandma's baby sister.

MITCHELL: I know. You were only like eight years older than my mother. Like a big sister to her. She talks about you all the time.

MARSHA: Oh, yeah?

DORIS: See? It's true, I talk about you constantly.

MARSHA: What does she say?

MITCHELL: I don't know. She tells us how nice and beautiful you were and everything.

MARSHA: Oh, yeah?, what else?

MITCHELL: How popular you were. And how being popular is one of the most important things in life 'cause otherwise you'll be alone. And, also how you really knew how to have a good time.

MARSHA: She told you all that, huh.

DORIS: Isn't he something? Doesn't forget a thing.

MARSHA: And what else did she tell you?

MITCHELL: Oh, yeah: how when you were twenty-three you slipped in the shower and got a concussion and died.

MARSHA *(Beat)*: Is that what she told you?

DORIS: Well . . .

MITCHELL: Yeah, so now I'm extra careful when I take a shower 'cause I don't want to slip in the bathtub and die like you.

DORIS *(A beat)*: Mitchell, honey, why don't you go back to bed? You have to get up for school in the morning. Say good night to Aunt Marsha.

MITCHELL: Good night, Aunt Marsha.

MARSHA: Good night.

MITCHELL: Nice meeting you, finally.

MARSHA: Nice meeting you, too, handsome.

He waves and goes back to bed. Pause.

What did you tell them?

DORIS: What do you mean?

MARSHA: You told your boys I slipped in the shower? Is that what you told them?

DORIS: What was I supposed to tell them?! They're children! *(Pause)* Oh, Marsh, I just tried to keep the good stuff alive, that's all.

MARSHA: Oh, yeah, sure. Sure you did, Doll. You did. We were pals, you and me; great pals.

DORIS: You ruined me, Marsh.

MARSHA: Just myself. I ruined myself.

DORIS: And me. You took a part of me with you I never got back, never.

MARSHA *(A beat)*: Yeah? Did I do that? Sorry, kid. I didn't mean it. I wasn't thinking, you know? I thought I was indestructible. Who doesn't when they're my age? I took a trip to the wrong side of the tracks and got lost there, accidentally on purpose. The wrong side has its moments, you know, depends on where you're standing. I liked the parties. And the booze. I liked watching my *Yiddishe* Momma rip hair from her head.

DORIS: Poor Bubba.

MARSHA: I loved the men. Oh, the men. I ruined myself, kiddo. Nobody did me in but me. I didn't mean to take no casualties.

DORIS: I had to be the good girl for the both of us. I did all the right things. You missed my wedding, Marsh. You're eighteen years late. I love my life, Marsh, I love the way my life has turned out. Don't you love this room? Isn't it unusual? I want you to be proud of me. I love my life I love my life . . .

MARSHA: Shhh . . .

Marsha gently rocks Doris as the lights fade to black.

Scene Four

An alarm clock sounds during the blackout. The light of dawn illuminates a scrim through which we see the suggestion of Mitchell and Stewie's room. Stewie is in the top half of a bunk bed. Mitchell, in his pajamas, stands at the edge of the scrim looking in the living room at Herbie, who sits perfectly still, staring into space. Dressing for work, he's got one sock on and holds the other.

MITCHELL *(Whispers, to Stewie)*: He's staring again.

Stewie, in the top bunk, grunts.

Stewie, he's staring again.

STEWIE: What time is it?

MITCHELL: Look . . .

STEWIE: What time is it?

MITCHELL: Six something.

STEWIE: Six something?!

MITCHELL: One sock on, one sock off.

STEWIE: It's not even light out.

MITCHELL: Every morning now.

STEWIE: We could've slept another hour . . .

HERBIE *(To himself; trying to recall)*: What did I dream?

MITCHELL *(Overlap; to Stewie)*: Shhh. He's talking.

STEWIE: To who?

MITCHELL: No one.

STEWIE: Oh, great.

HERBIE *(Still musing out loud)*: I know I dreamed something . . .

STEWIE: Why do you get up for this?

MITCHELL: I don't know . . .

HERBIE: Maybe not . . .

STEWIE: You know he's crazy . . .

MITCHELL: Yeah . . .

STEWIE: Why do you have to wake me up all the time?

MITCHELL *(Genuinely)*: I'm sorry. . . . I thought you were interested . . . *(He begins dressing for school)*

HERBIE *(To us)*: Maybe I don't have dreams anymore. I mean I must, but I don't remember. I don't remember a thing. My childhood? The war? Show me a picture of me taken someplace and I couldn't tell you where. I won't remember the name of the buddy I had my arm around. Ask me what year my kids were born, I couldn't tell you. Either of them. I know I was married eighteen years ago 'cause that's what Doris told me; the other night was our anniversary. I know how old I am; I'm forty years old. I was born in '25, but the exact date they're not sure, and the midwife who signed the birth certificate put my sex down as female. So I don't know; I don't know. I remember Dame May Whitty was in *The Lady Vanishes* . . . but I don't remember my father even shaking my hand.

STEWIE *(To Mitchell)*: He's crazy. Let's face it. He's gone. Lost in action.

HERBIE *(To us)*: Did my father throw me a bar mitzvah? I don't even remember being bar mitzvahed. If I was you can be sure nobody thought twice about it. They say we were very poor when I was young. *(Shrugs)* I don't remember. Supposedly we were on relief. Six kids in three rooms. No doors. No privacy. Hand-me-downs from my brothers. . . . Nothing ever started with me, it ended with me. I didn't have much; that much I remember. You stop wanting, so what you don't have doesn't matter. This is the Depression I'm talking about. I got through those years with my eyes shut tight and holding my breath like when you're underwater. Got the hell outta there, straight to the Army. War was an improvement. Then I met Doris, then I married her, got this job, kids. . . . And I go through every day with my eyes shut tight and holding my breath, till the day is over and I can come home. To what? What kind of home is left to come home to by the time I come home?

MITCHELL *(To Stewie)*: What's he thinking when he seems to be thinking?

STEWIE: Hm?

HERBIE *(Shrugs; to us, but responding to Mitchell's query)*: I don't know; nothing. I'm thinking I don't know what to say. I'm thinking if I do say something, I hope it's not stupid, the wrong thing to say.

MITCHELL *(To Stewie)*: Was he always like this? Did he ever have anything to say?

HERBIE *(To us; as before)*: It seems to me, in the days when I would say what was on my mind, I'd be shot down an awful lot. The more shot down you get, the less likely you are to say what's on your mind.

MITCHELL: What would that be like?

HERBIE *(To us)*: It kills you after a while, thinking all the time how . . . *(A beat)* You don't even pay attention what's being said anymore 'cause you're too busy worrying how you might come off.

MITCHELL *(Sighs)*: Boy . . . *(He gathers his schoolbooks)*

HERBIE *(To us)*: So I shut up a long time ago. It was a decision I made after something happened, something I don't remember what. I remember deciding well, fuck-'em-all one day, and Doris has handled it ever since. I let her do the talking. What the hell, I save my breath.

STEWIE *(To Mitchell)*: Where you going?

MITCHELL: In.

STEWIE: Well. . . . Might as well practice . . . *(Stewie picks up his Haftarah book and sings softly through the rest of the scene)*

HERBIE *(To us)*: I'm still waiting for her, for somebody, to notice and ask: What's up, Herbie? We'll all drop dead first.

Mitchell, schoolbooks in hand, tentatively enters the living room. Herbie senses his presence and looks up and sees him. Pause.

MITCHELL *(In explanation)*: Cereal.

Pause. They continue to look at one another.

HERBIE *(Finally)*: That's good. It's good you eat breakfast.

A beat. Mitchell nods, starts for the kitchen, but stops.

MITCHELL: Um . . . Dad?

HERBIE *(Turns; expectantly)*: Yeah, son?

A beat. Mitchell shakes his head "nothing," shrugs, and exits to the kitchen. Herbie watches him go. We hear Stewie practicing his Hebrew as Herbie finishes dressing and leaves for work. Lights fade to black.

Scene Five

In the black: "The Pajama Game" is playing on the hi-fi.

At rise: Mitchell, singing along with the music (he knows every word by heart), stands by the hi-fi as he puts on a skeleton costume. Soon, Stewie, dressed as a hunchback with a stocking over his face distorting his features, sneaks up on him. He does a good Charles Laughton imitation. He attacks Mitchell and knocks into the console, causing the needle to skid across the record.

STEWIE: "Sanctuary! Sanctuary!"

Stewie gets Mitchell in a headlock. The two roughhouse for a while.

MITCHELL: Let me go!

STEWIE: "Sanctuary!"

More roughhousing.

MITCHELL *(No longer enjoying himself)*: Let me go!! Stewie!! Stop it!! *(Etc.)*

Their play degenerates into a real fight; Stewie knocks Mitchell to the ground and sits on him.

DORIS *(Off)*: I hear body-drops in there!!

The fight ends as abruptly as it began.

STEWIE *(Calls to Doris)*: Let's go already!!

DORIS *(Off)*: I'm not ready yet!

STEWIE *(To Doris)*: I don't want to wait!

DORIS *(Off)*: You will wait for your mother!! I gave you life!!

Herbie enters through the front door and doesn't bat an eye at his sons' costumes.

HERBIE: Daddy's home! *(Unpacks milk and orange juice)*

MITCHELL: Hi, Dad.

STEWIE: Hi, Dad. *(Calls)* Ma! He's home!

DORIS *(Off)*: Herbie?

HERBIE: It's my early night. Doesn't anybody remember my early night? I should've gone out to a movie or something. I could have a chippie on the side, no one would know the difference.

DORIS *(Off)*: I remembered, I remembered . . .

Pause.

HERBIE *(To the boys)*: So? What's new?

They shrug.

Any good news to tell me?

MITCHELL: No.

STEWIE: No.

HERBIE: No good news? Gee . . . I count on you guys . . . *(A beat; to Stewie)* Let me guess. Some sort of holiday, right?

STEWIE: Right.

HERBIE: Halloween I bet, right?

STEWIE: You got it, Dad.

HERBIE *(To Mitchell)*: You, I can tell what you are. *(To Stewie)* Who *you* supposed to be?

STEWIE *(Mumbles in exasperation)*: The Hunchbackanotredame.

HERBIE: The what?

STEWIE *(Enunciating carefully)*: The Hunchback of Notre Dame.

HERBIE: Oh, yeah. So you're gonna go trick-or-treating, hm?

MITCHELL: Yeah.

STEWIE *(Loudly)*: We're waiting for Mommy.

DORIS *(Off)*: Shut up in there, Stewart.

HERBIE: Your mother's going trick-or-treating? *(Calls)* You're going trick-or-treating, Doris?

DORIS *(Off)*: So?

HERBIE: So nothing.

STEWIE *(Calls)*: Hurry up, Ma! I'm suffocating under here!

DORIS *(Off)*: So take off the stocking!

HERBIE: Take off the thing, you won't suffocate!

Stewie stares at him for a beat, then silently goes to the terrace. Another beat.

Hey, Mitch. Wanna see something?

MITCHELL: What.

HERBIE: Come here.

Mitchell approaches. Herbie takes a business card out of his pocket and hands it to him.

MITCHELL: What's this.

HERBIE: What's it say.

MITCHELL *(Reads)*: "Fred Werner, Regional Supervisor, Southwest, House and Home Stores, Incorporated." *(Looks up at Herbie)* So?

HERBIE: Guy comes into the place. Out-of-town guy in a suit. 'Bout my age. Tall. Looks like Robert Young.

MITCHELL: Yeah, so.

HERBIE: Comes up to me. Can I help you?, I say. Looking for anything in particular?, bathroom, kitchen, dining room; fluorescent, chandelier, poles. My usual shpiel. I'm feeling good. I just had my chicken salad sandwich to go, and a Patio diet cola; I was just breaking into an orange, my fruit with lunch.

MITCHELL: Yeah . . . ?

HERBIE: The guy is there, talking to me, asking me this fixture, that fixture. I'm rattling off model numbers: You mean the B624? Comes in silver finish and also brass. Plated. K455? I'm afraid we're out of stock. Are you the manager here?, he asks me. Why, yes I am, the fixture showroom is my domain. I laid out the showroom with all the fixtures on so you can see what they look like. I believe you got to see what a fixture looks like lit 'cause that's how you're gonna use it; a light is meant to be on, giving off light. The guy is very impressed with my ideas. The thing is you never know who you're talking to, son; remember that in all walks of life. Guy could be a guy who runs a chain of restaurants nationwide; if he likes my style, my approach, I could land an order in the thousands. You never know who you're talking to and that's a fact.

MITCHELL: Uh-huh.

HERBIE: So, he says to me the guy, You really seem to know your stuff, Herb. And the fact is I do, I don't have to snow him. I been in home improvement my entire life, I tell him. Well, since after the war. I say "war," turns out to be the magic word, sets off a whole other thing, and half an hour goes by, we're talking. That's when he hands me his card.

MITCHELL: Okay, so.

HERBIE: You heard me talk about House and Home, right?

MITCHELL: I think . . .

HERBIE: They're the biggest. They're all over the country. They're putting guys like my boss out of business. Well. This guy— *(Takes back the card to look at the name)* Fred—wants me to manage—are you ready for this?—they've got four stores in and around Albuquerque—

MITCHELL: Albuquerque, New Mexico?!

HERBIE: Wait. And he wants me to manage all four lighting showrooms.

STEWIE *(Who's been listening from the terrace all along)*: New Mexico?!

HERBIE: Is that a compliment or what? You see what he thinks of your dad? That's a big responsibility.

MITCHELL: Well, yeah. Congratulations.

STEWIE: Ugh. Are we moving to New Mexico?

HERBIE: I didn't say yes, I said I would think about it.

STEWIE *(Calls)*: Ma, Daddy wants us to move to New Mexico.

HERBIE: I didn't say that, I said I would think about it.

DORIS *(Off; overlap)*: Not New Mexico. There are no Jewish people in New Mexico.

HERBIE *(Calls)*: This guy Fred Werner says the climate's gorgeous, year-round.

DORIS *(Off)*: Werner? That's a German name, Werner. There are Indians in New Mexico. And Germans.

HERBIE *(Calls)*: But isn't it nice that he wants me?

DORIS *(Off)*: We just furnished, Herbie. We're throwing a bar mitzvah. We have people here, our people are here.

HERBIE *(Calls)*: But isn't it nice he wants me to think about it?

DORIS *(Off)*: Very nice. *(Doris enters dressed in her tattered wedding gown, her hair teased wildly, her face monstrous with makeup. She presents herself with a flourish, laughing madly)* Ta dahhh!!

The boys love it and clamor around her.

STEWIE: Ma! Wow!

MITCHELL: You look great! Boy, everybody's gonna flip!

DORIS *(To us)*: I'm telling you, this is inspired. I'll go around with the boys to all the neighbors and they won't know who I am. They'll think I'm just another crazy kid out trick-or-treating. People always mistake me for their older sister, that's how young I look. When I take the boys to the movies, the matron makes us sit in the children's section; I don't even bother to argue. I was married young. Eighteen. Well, twenty. I'm not obsessed with age. *(To Herbie)* Would you've recognized me on the street? I bet not.

Herbie is hurt, incredulous; a beat.

HERBIE: You tore up your dress?

DORIS: I'm surprised you noticed. I ripped it good.

HERBIE: You tore up your wedding dress?

DORIS *(After a beat; meaning, "I shouldn't have?")*: No?

HERBIE: Your wedding dress?

DORIS: It was old; it was faded.

HERBIE: So you tear it up?

DORIS: It was ruined from day one. Remember the rain—?

HERBIE: How could you do it?

DORIS *(After a long pause)*: How? Why. *(Meaning, "Why do you ask?")*

HERBIE: You could just tear it up?

DORIS: It's a joke! A gag!

HERBIE: A gag?

DORIS: It's Halloween, Herbie, what's the matter with you?

HERBIE: You were married in that dress.

DORIS: But it's so old-fashioned now.

HERBIE: We were married, that's what you wore.

DORIS: A long time ago. Look how faded. It was white once. Remember the mud—?

HERBIE: This is a joke to you?

DORIS: No? *(Pause)* What is the big deal? It's not like I have a daughter to—

HERBIE: How do you do that?

DORIS: What?

HERBIE: The dress you wore to your wedding. It's supposed to mean so much. How does a girl rip up—

DORIS: I was never gonna wear it again. It was getting old and faded hanging at the back of my closet eighteen years; what's the matter with you?! All of a sudden you're gonna take it personal? "The Bride of Frankenstein." *(As she goes to the kitchen)* God, Herbie, where's your sense of humor? *(Returns with three shopping bags and hands one to each of the boys)* Here, boys, bags for your loot. Remember, no eating till we check for razor blades.

STEWIE *(A la Quasimodo)*: "Sanctuary! Sanctuary!"

Stewie goes, followed by Mitchell who walks backwards, his eye on his parents.

DORIS *(To Mitchell)*: Go ahead. Wait for me at the elevator. We'll go up to twenty-three and work our way down. How's that?

MITCHELL: Okay. *(He puts on his skeleton mask but lingers in the doorway, watching)*

DORIS *(To Herbie; meaning the dress)*: The thing still fits me, how do you like that? *(A beat)* Pulls a little bit 'cross the back, I had to use a safety pin, but not bad considering I had two kids. You can't tell, can you?

Herbie shakes his head; a beat.

HERBIE: Go ahead. The boys are waiting.

A beat.

DORIS: I made you a tuna plate. It's in the fridge.

HERBIE: Good.

A beat.

DORIS: We won't be back late.

Herbie shrugs, "I don't care." They look at one another for a long time, then:

Sing to me "Autumn Leaves."

HERBIE: What?

DORIS: Sing to me—

Stewie appears at the front door, pushing Mitchell aside.

STEWIE: Ma-a. . . .

Stewie goes, but Mitchell stays in the doorway.

DORIS *(Calls, while still looking at Herbie)*: I'm coming. *(She starts to go, stops; a beat)* You were kidding about New Mexico. Right?

HERBIE: Sure.

DORIS: That's what I thought. See ya later.

Doris steers Mitchell out, exits. Herbie is alone. In a moment, he goes to the kitchen, returns with his tuna plate, and sets it down on the table. He looks with disinterest at his dinner, picks at it with his fingers, then pushes the plate away disgustedly. He violently slams a chair against the table and storms off to the kitchen again. He soon returns with a half gallon of fudge swirl ice cream. He turns on the TV, sits in front of it, and eats the ice cream out of its container with a vengeance. Lights fade except for the bluish light of the television which illuminates Herbie. Mitchell steps out of the darkness to talk to us.

MITCHELL: There's this scene in my musical that's not in the original. All the Lomans go off on a picnic together to Prospect Park. I thought it would lighten things up a little bit. You know, a little up-tempo production number. *(A beat)* Everybody's young and happy. Biff's wearing his varsity T-shirt and he and Happy are tossing around the football, and Linda's setting the picnic table with laminated paper plates and potato salad and coleslaw, and Willy's at the barbecue in a "Kiss the Cook" apron, flipping the franks. He's got the day off for a change, and he sings something like "Oh What a Beautiful Morning," only that's already been done, but you know what I mean. "What a Picnic!," something like that. And Willy's dead brother Ben is there, and Charley and Bernard from next door. Even the woman from Boston is there, disguised as a park attendant and laughing all the time. *(A beat)* They're all happy. Everybody. And it's very sunny, but not too hot, and there's no wind blowing away the napkins, and no bees or ants, I mean the insect kind, 'cause there are aunts and uncles and cousins and grandparents. . . . It's a perfect day—maybe that's it: *(Sings)* "What a perfect day for a picnic!" Yeah, and the whole family sings in harmony, really beautiful, like on the *Sound of Music* record when they sing "How do you solve a problem like Maria?" *(A beat)* You know, this picnic idea I really like. I love picnics. *(A beat)* We never go on any picnics.

Fade to black.

ACT TWO

Scene One

The suggestion of a room in a fancy catering establishment. Flocked wallpaper, mirrors, chandeliers, etc. The family is dressed to the nines, posing for photographs at Stewie's bar mitzvah. Doris's hair is done up in elaborate curls and she proudly wears a chiffon dress with a fur wrap. Herbie and the boys are wearing rented tuxedos and yarmulkes; Stewie is also wearing a tallis. Off, in another room, a small band plays "Sunrise, Sunset."

DORIS *(To us)*: Do I look sensational, or what? Huh? Who would believe I'm the thirty-eight-year-old mother of a bar mitzvah boy? How can that be? Thirty-eight? Impossible. Look at this figure: I still get into my wedding dress. Oh, this is a great day. This is my coming out party. My graduation day. As Stewie becomes a man, I become a middle-aged lady. Middle-aged lady, ha! I'll show them middle-aged! I'm not in the least concerned with getting older.

Doris smiles. The photographer's flash goes off.

HERBIE *(To us)*: How the hell I'm gonna pay for this I don't know. I got docked for taking off a Saturday. Saturdays at the place are our biggest days.

Flash. Stewie and Mitchell step aside as Herbie and Doris pose together; they face us but talk to one another.

DORIS: It's your kid's bar mitzvah, they'll understand.

HERBIE: I take off enough Saturdays, they could fire me.

DORIS: It's your kid's bar mitzvah! Nobody's gonna fire you!

HERBIE: I don't know, Doris, if I lose my job . . .

DORIS: You're not gonna lose your job! You been there nineteen years!

HERBIE: They fire guys all the time! Dave Mendelsohn they fired!

DORIS: He was stealing!

HERBIE: I don't know, Doris . . .

Flash. Herbie steps aside as Doris poses with Stewie, pinning on his boutonniere.

DORIS *(To us)*: Dan, my hairdresser, came over this morning to do my hair? He flipped over me. He wanted to do my eyes like Cleopatra but that's where I draw the line. I don't want to look schmaltzy; I'm a mother.

Flash.

STEWIE *(To us)*: Thank God that's over. I'm free! No more Hebrew school. No more practicing. No more dreams about getting up there and disgracing myself. No more afternoons with Mr. Shlosh. Today my youth is handed back to me. I can play with my friends after school again. When I come home from school on Monday, I'm gonna celebrate: I'm gonna eat all the chocolate off every Mallomar, down to the marshmallow, pop it in my mouth, and dunk the cookie part in milk.

Flash. Doris and Stewie pose dancing.

DORIS *(To us)*: What a party this is gonna be! A hundred and sixty-seven people, including four of Stewie's closest friends.

Sandy Rose and His Orchestra—they're very good; you hear them? A separate rented room for the smorgasbord. Open bar. Swedish meatballs, cocktail franks, bite-sized knishes, little frilly toothpicks to go with them. Roast beef *au jus*. Julienne potatoes. Salad à la Stewie. Fruit-flavored sherbet shaped like fruit. Viennese table with sparklers, make your own non-dairy sundaes. And the linens! A solid mustard-colored tablecloth, topped with lace so the color peeks through. I went for the mustard because I thought it was masculine; you know, for Stewie.

Flash. Mitchell joins them; Doris bends over so that he and Stewie can kiss her cheeks.

And relatives are coming from all over. Jersey. The Island. This is a big event. A lot of these people, the last time I saw them was when I got married. Now they're seeing my son bar mitzvahed. Isn't it beautiful how life goes on?

Flash. Doris steps aside and Stewie and Mitchell pose shaking hands.

MITCHELL *(To us)*: I could never sing in front of all those people. There must have been five hundred people there! I don't know how I'm gonna do it. I'll never do it as good as Stewie. I'm gonna be a nervous wreck for two years. I wish I were dead.

Mitchell smiles. Flash.

STEWIE *(To us)*: My voice cracked only once, but it sounded like I did it for effect. I brought down the house.

Flash. Herbie joins his sons. He poses shaking Stewie's hand while Mitchell watches.

HERBIE *(To us)*: I never had anything like this, I can tell you that. Maybe my mother served a little dairy when we got back from *shul*, if that. I probably went to run deliveries for my father right after. Yeah, that sounds right.

Flash. Stewie poses reading a prayer book as Herbie and Mitchell look on.

STEWIE *(To us)*: My friend Jeffrey Smolowitz cleared twenty-two hundred dollars at his bar mitzvah. And his was smaller than this. I'm gonna buy an electric guitar and an amp, and a bunch of albums. I made a list last week in back of my science notebook. Twenty-two hundred bucks; that's a lot of albums.

Flash. Doris rejoins the family pose.

HERBIE *(To us)*: She wanted a big party? *(He shrugs)* Alright, we'll have a big party. You want tuxedos?, we'll rent tuxedos. Then you have to buy shoes to go with the tuxedos for me and the boys. And a fancy French razor cut, 'cause a regular haircut wouldn't look right with a tux.

DORIS: It just wouldn't.

HERBIE: And a dress for her—alright, it's gorgeous, but still, aren't we going a little overboard here?

DORIS: This is an event. A big deal. There's no cutting corners when you're putting together an event like this. You go all out, or why bother? *(To Stewie and Mitchell)* Oh, look, boys: People are starting to arrive. I don't believe it, look who's here. You know how I told you about Hitler murdering the Jews?

MITCHELL: Yeah . . . ?

DORIS: Well there's Grandma's Uncle Izzy. The one who died in the war.

STEWIE: Where?

DORIS: The one in the striped pajamas. *(Calls)* Uncle Izzy! Go in to the smorgasbord! You must be starving! *(Blows a kiss)* Mwa! Talk to you later! *Ess! Ess! (To Stewie and Mitchell)* Did you see who he was with? Cousin Rifka.

MITCHELL: Who?

DORIS: Remember I told you boys about the Triangle Factory Fire? Poor thing.

Marsha appears and stands beside Doris.

Boy, they're really coming out for Stewie's bar mitzvah!

Flash. The family freezes in a tableau. Blackout.

Scene Two

Lights up on the living room. That night. The front door bursts open and Stewie, his tallis flying like a cape, runs in, envelopes spilling out of his hands. Mitchell enters after him, picking up the envelopes that have fallen. They laugh wildly. Herbie enters holding an aluminum tray wrapped in foil, followed by Doris carrying a huge flower arrangement. She sets it down.

DORIS *(In constant, dance-like movement)*: I could've danced all night. My feet are swollen but I don't care; I can't feel them, I'm numb.

HERBIE: Take off your shoes.

DORIS: I don't want to. I like being in heels. I like the elevation. Puts me closer to the clouds where my head already is. *(She spins herself around)* What do you think of your old mom now?, huh, boys?

MITCHELL: You looked beautiful, Mom. *(Nudges Stewie)*

STEWIE: You looked beautiful, Mom.

DORIS: Yeah? Thank you.

STEWIE: Okay, here we go!

DORIS: Mitchell, honey? Undo me?

Mitchell unzips her dress, which flaps open. Stewie begins to tear open envelopes and read out loud the various gifts.

STEWIE: Herb and Betty Beckerman!

DORIS: How much?

STEWIE: Twenty-five-dollar check!

MITCHELL AND STEWIE: Yayyyy!

DORIS *(To Herbie, during the above)*: Is that what we gave them for Kevin?

Herbie shrugs.

I think we did.

STEWIE: Tommy and Mary Ann Sorrentino.

DORIS: Yeah . . . ?

STEWIE: Twenty bucks.

DORIS: Alright, they don't know from bar mitzvahs.

HERBIE: Gee, I got a stain on my shirt, Doris, you think the tuxedo place'll fine me? Roast-beef juice or something.

DORIS *(Correcting him)*: Roast beef *au jus.*

Herbie takes off his jacket and sits in front of the TV with the aluminum tray. He peels off the foil and begins eating chopped liver with his finger.

MITCHELL: And the winner is . . . Aunt Reba and Uncle Morris! Fifty-dollar bond!!

MITCHELL AND STEWIE: YAYYY!!!

DORIS: Are you writing this down? Write this down.

Mitchell does.

MITCHELL: Should I separate bonds from checks and cash, or add it all together?

DORIS: However you want to do it, sweetheart.

HERBIE: Greatest chopped liver in the world.

STEWIE: Jake and Lillian Frankfurter and Sons, the pigs in the blanket: forty bucks cash.

MITCHELL: Oooo!

DORIS: Acceptable.

STEWIE: Ross and Sylvia Hirsch: twenty-five!

MITCHELL AND STEWIE: Yayyy!

DORIS: Typical.

STEWIE: Marvin and Dorothy Klein, twenty-five-dollar check!

MITCHELL AND STEWIE: Yayyy!!

DORIS: Was this a party to remember or what?

HERBIE *(Meaning the liver)*: Oh! Is this good!

DORIS: When the lights went out and they wheeled in the Viennese table . . .

STEWIE *(A la Jerry Lewis telethon)*: Come on, folks, keep those checks coming, don't give up now.

DORIS *(To Mitchell)*: Didn't you love those sparklers?

MITCHELL: Uh-huh.

DORIS: It was like a roomful of fireworks.

STEWIE: Shelly and Suzy Levine . . .

DORIS: I felt like crying.

STEWIE: Twenty-five dollars! Thank you!!!

DORIS: Stewie, I'm sorry about the tablecloths, honey.

STEWIE: It's okay I said, Ma . . .

DORIS: I walked into the main ballroom, I almost died: cranberry they gave me.

STEWIE: Don't worry about it . . .

HERBIE *(Still about the liver)*: Mmm!

DORIS *(To Stewie)*: I ordered mustard for you. They said they were one short so they had to give me cranberry. I'm sorry, Stewie. I wanted it to be perfect.

STEWIE: I know, I know, it was, it was.

DORIS: Yeah? And what a band, huh?! Didn't you love the band? I can't stop dancing. What range!

STEWIE: "Hava Nageliah" to "Satisfaction."

HERBIE *(Still on the liver)*: What do they use that makes it taste so good? It's like cake.

STEWIE: Aunt Ida, Uncle Lou, and Cousins Jack and Phyllis: fifty-dollar bond!

Mitchell and Stewie start to cheer.

DORIS *(Cutting them off)*: Is that all? A fifty-dollar bond from two couples?

STEWIE: No?

DORIS: Thirty-seven fifty, that's how much a fifty-dollar bond costs.

MITCHELL: Really?

The boys look at one another; a beat.

MITCHELL AND STEWIE: Ssssss.

STEWIE *(Telethon voice again)*: Come on, folks, please, don't be cheap. Go to your wallets, go to your checkbooks, go to your piggy banks and give!

MITCHELL: Look, Jerry, this pledge just came in: Sandy and Murray Schwartzberg of Hicksville. Twenty-five dollars.

STEWIE: Thank you, Sandy and Murray!

DORIS (*Mostly to us*): I don't want to sleep tonight. I'll squish my hair. To wake up with flat hair after a day like this would be like dying. I don't want the day to end. I can't believe this is it. You look forward, you plan . . . over a year we've been planning this, and before you know it. . . . My life is over. I've got two years till Mitchell's. That's too far to put even a down payment. Now what? What do I do now? (*A beat; she thinks of something*) Thank-you cards! Yes! Table pictures with us posing at every table! Color glossies! What a souvenir!

HERBIE: Stewie? You ever tasted chopped liver like this in your life?

STEWIE: Never. Never in my thirteen years have I tasted liver like that.

HERBIE: I can't stop eating it.

DORIS: Stop eating it.

HERBIE: I can't.

MITCHELL: I've got a subtotal, you want to hear the subtotal?

STEWIE: Drumroll please . . .

MITCHELL: So far, with a bunch of envelopes to go, the subtotal is . . . four hundred and twenty-five dollars!!

Mitchell and Stewie cheer, etc.

STEWIE: That's beautiful, ladies and gentlemen.

MITCHELL: Wait, this just in: from Grandma Rose.

DORIS: My mother?

MITCHELL: Wow, you are not gonna believe this: two hundred and fifty dollars!

STEWIE AND MITCHELL: WOWWWW!!

DORIS: No kidding. How can she afford that?

HERBIE: Have you tried the chopped liver lately?

DORIS: Will you stop with the chopped liver?!

HERBIE: Don't tell me to stop! Who paid for it?!

DORIS: So eat it all up, I don't care! Don't stop! You wanted to take it into the place, you won't have any left!

HERBIE: So I'll buy some more!

DORIS: Buy some more! Do what you want! Dance with me, Herbie! Enough with the liver!

HERBIE: I don't wanna dance.

DORIS *(Pulling him by his arm)*: Dance with me!

HERBIE: Doris. . . . A whole day of this . . .

DORIS: A little fox trot?! That's gonna kill ya?!

HERBIE *(Tugging his arm free)*: I don't wanna I said . . .

A beat.

DORIS *(Hurt)*: Well, the hell with you . . .

HERBIE *(Reaching out to her)*: Doris . . .

DORIS: The hell with you you don't wanna dance with me . . .

MITCHELL: Mommy?

HERBIE: A whole day of dancing . . .

DORIS: Who's gonna dance with me? Hm? Hm, Bar Mitzvah Boy?

She tickles Stewie under his arms; he finds it both pleasurable and annoying.

STEWIE: Ma–a–a!

More tickling and protesting.

DORIS: Hm? How about a dance?

STEWIE: Ma–a, st–o–op . . .

He cackles with laughter; Mitchell looks on with vicarious interest.

HERBIE: Stewie. . . . Quiet!

STEWIE: She's tickling me!

DORIS *(Stops tickling him)*: Nobody'll dance with me!

MITCHELL: I will.

STEWIE: I'm doing something.

DORIS: You're all a bunch of killjoys.

MITCHELL: Ma, I'll dance. If you want.

A beat.

DORIS: Hm?

MITCHELL: I'll dance with you.

DORIS: You, baby?

MITCHELL: If you want.

DORIS: What a sweetheart. You hear that? Mitchell will dance with me.

STEWIE: Good. You dance with her.

Doris playfully jabs at him.

Hey!

DORIS *(To Mitchell)*: I'd be honored . . .

She begins to dance with Mitchell.

Ready?

Mitchell nods shyly; while looking down at their feet, Doris leads him in a cha-cha. She occasionally offers words of encouragement ("Good. . . . Watch . . . "). Herbie and Stewie, pretending not to care, soon find themselves looking at Mitchell and Doris with growing resentment; their eyes meet for a moment, but they look away in embarrassment. Doris playfully sticks her tongue out at Herbie. Fade-out.

Scene Three

Later that night. Herbie and Stewie are alone in the living room. Herbie has one eye on the TV and the other on Stewie, who is looking through his stack of checks. Long pause. Herbie gets up and turns off the TV.

HERBIE: You made a list?

STEWIE: Mitchell did.

HERBIE: Let's see. *(Stewie brings him the list)* Very efficient. Look at that. Such a nice handwriting he has, no?

STEWIE: Uh-huh.

HERBIE *(Squinting at the total)*: So, how much you got?

STEWIE: Two thousand three hundred and seventy-five.

HERBIE: Wow. Two thousand . . .

STEWIE: Three hundred and seventy five.

HERBIE: That's a lot of money, twenty-three seventy-five.

STEWIE: I know.

HERBIE: That's good.

STEWIE: Yeah. My friend Jeffrey . . .

HERBIE: You did good.

STEWIE: Yeah? Thanks.

HERBIE: Very good. *(Pause)* I'm . . . proud of you.

STEWIE: Yeah? *(Pause)* You are?

HERBIE: Twenty-three hundred bucks? Sure. I am.

STEWIE: The money?

HERBIE: No, not just the money. The money, sure. But not just the money. Of course not. The money, that's one thing. No, I mean . . . proud. You know.

Pause.

STEWIE: You were proud? Of me?

HERBIE: Today? Sure.

STEWIE: Yeah?

HERBIE: A father watching his son? Are you kidding? A father watching his son on a day like today? You feel things.

STEWIE: You do?

HERBIE: Oh yeah. A man watching his son become a man? That men stuff? You feel things.

STEWIE: Like what?

HERBIE: I don't know. Your life. You feel your whole life . . . *(A beat)* I can't explain it.

STEWIE: You feel . . . what.

HERBIE: I can't explain it I said. One day it'll happen to you. You'll know what I'm talking about, seeing your son.

STEWIE: Proud you said?

HERBIE: Did I say that?

STEWIE: Yeah. You said—

HERBIE: I know. That's true. You do feel that. You feel other things too. You'll see. A thing like this happening in your life. . . . It's complicated. You think. You wonder. I'm forty years old—that's no secret; you know how old I am.

STEWIE: Uh-huh.

HERBIE: You're forty years old, you're in the middle of things. You can see your life in both directions. You know what I mean? You're standing in the middle of a big field or something, and you look to your left and you see your whole life, everything up till now. You look to your right, and you can see where it ends, the end is in sight. This creates a feeling in you. You wish . . .

Pause.

STEWIE: What.

Herbie shakes his head "never mind"; a beat.

HERBIE: So let's see.

Stewie holds up the stack.

Let me see.

Stewie flips through the stack.

You're not gonna let me see?

STEWIE: I'm showing you.

HERBIE: I want to see it, I can't see it?

STEWIE: Look.

HERBIE: What are you gonna do with it?

STEWIE: There are things.

HERBIE: Things?

STEWIE: I want.

HERBIE: Twenty-three hundred bucks? What do you want?

STEWIE: I don't know.

HERBIE: What do you want? You see yourself spending all that money?

STEWIE: Not all . . .

HERBIE: What, on records?

STEWIE: I don't know. *(A beat)* I want a guitar.

HERBIE: A guitar.

STEWIE: An electric.

HERBIE: What, so you can blast it?

A beat. Stewie gathers his things.

Alright alright. Not what are you gonna do with it, where you gonna put it?

STEWIE: I guess in the bank.

HERBIE: How you gonna put it in the bank on a Saturday night? You can't put it in the bank till Monday.

STEWIE *(Over "in the bank till Monday")*: Oh, you mean tonight?, where I'm gonna put it tonight?

HERBIE: Yeah, where you gonna put it, in your room?

STEWIE: Yeah.

HERBIE: No you're not.

STEWIE: Why?

HERBIE: That kind of money?

STEWIE: I'll hide it.

HERBIE: From who?

STEWIE: I don't know, you're the one who's worried.

HERBIE: I'm not worried. I'm asking. What if something happens to it?

STEWIE: Over the weekend?

HERBIE: Yeah, you never know.

STEWIE: I'll go to the bank Monday morning.

HERBIE: What if you lose it?

STEWIE: On the way to the bank?

HERBIE: Yeah, that too. What if you're mugged?

STEWIE: I won't be mugged.

HERBIE: How do you know? You know these things? You know that if you hide it in your room you won't misplace it?

STEWIE: I'll be careful.

HERBIE: You know for sure that someone won't break in tonight?

STEWIE: Dad . . .

HERBIE: No, answer me: You know this? You know that someone won't break in tonight and steal—

STEWIE: How they gonna break in? Through the window?

HERBIE: Possibly.

STEWIE: We're on the tenth floor!

HERBIE: Big shot! You know everything, hm?

Stewie starts to go.

Hey.

STEWIE: What.

HERBIE: Come here.

STEWIE: What.

HERBIE: Come here.

They look at one another for a beat. Herbie smiles.

Let me see all that. *(Extends his hand)*

STEWIE: I did.

HERBIE: Not like that. *(Pause. Jokingly)* You're really not gonna let me even touch it? My God, your own father . . .

Stewie hesitates, then gives it to him.

Thank you. Jesus, you'd think God knows . . . *(Hefts the stack)* Woww! Feel that! That's heavy! Boy!

STEWIE: Yeah. *(His hand is out, awaiting its return)*

HERBIE: So this is what twenty-three hundred bucks feels like.

STEWIE: Uh-huh. Now you know.

HERBIE: I don't think I ever in my life held this much money at once. Except for maybe a day's receipts.

STEWIE *(His hand still out)*: Uh-huh.

HERBIE: You know how many weeks it would take me to make that? Weeks. I take home a hundred and fourteen bucks a week. You figure it out. One-fourteen. Figure it out; you're smart.

STEWIE: Dad . . .

HERBIE: Figure it out. Ten weeks would be what?, eleven-forty. Twenty weeks . . .

STEWIE: Give me.

HERBIE: Twenty weeks is twenty-two-eighty.

STEWIE: Dad . . .

HERBIE: We're talking over twenty weeks. Half a year practically.

STEWIE: I want to go.

HERBIE: Where you going?

STEWIE: My room.

HERBIE: Tired?

STEWIE: I want to go to my room, yeah.

HERBIE: I can understand you're tired.

Pause.

STEWIE: Dad?

Stewie extends his hand for the money. Pause; they look at one another for a long time.

HERBIE: No, son.

STEWIE: No?

HERBIE: I'm gonna put it in my drawer.

STEWIE: Why?

HERBIE: It'll be safe there. You know my drawer, I got all my valuables.

STEWIE: Daddy . . .

HERBIE: What, you don't trust me? It'll be safe in my drawer, believe me. Safer in my drawer than under your pillow.

STEWIE: I wasn't gonna put it under my pillow . . .

HERBIE: Whatever.

STEWIE: It's my money.

HERBIE: It's not yours.

STEWIE: What do you mean not mine? It's my bar mitzvah! All the cards say my name!

HERBIE: I mean it's not yours to spend.

STEWIE *(Goes through discarded envelopes)*: "For Stewie," "For Stewart on his bar mitzvah."

HERBIE *(Overlap)*: I know, I know. I mean it's not your money, it's our money.

STEWIE: How is it ours? It's my bar mitzvah!

HERBIE: What we have to do: Sign the checks and I'll countersign them.

STEWIE: How is it ours?

HERBIE: You're a minor. A kid.

STEWIE: Today I am a man! You even said!

HERBIE: You don't understand something, son.

STEWIE: No, I understand.

HERBIE: We got a misunderstanding.

STEWIE: YOU'RE TAKING MY MONEY!

HERBIE: Oh, shut up. Who the hell you think is paying for this thing? Hm? You think Rockefeller?

Mitchell, in his pajamas, enters and watches from the foyer.

STEWIE: I thought you.

HERBIE: Me? With what?

STEWIE: I don't know. You're the father.

HERBIE: With what am I supposed to be paying for this with? Hm? Do I have the money for this kind of thing?

STEWIE: I don't know.

HERBIE: How would I have that kind of money? Schmuck. Think about it: I told you what I take home.

STEWIE: Yeah . . .

HERBIE: So where am I getting the money to throw you a fancy party?

Stewie shrugs. A beat.

The gifts!

STEWIE: You mean with the gifts?

HERBIE: Yeah. That's how we have to do it: What comes in has to go right out again. Didn't you know that?

STEWIE: No.

HERBIE: What, you thought I was gonna shell out all this money, to make you a party, just shell it all out out of the kindness of my heart? Is that what you thought?

STEWIE: I didn't think, I don't know.

HERBIE: Look at this bill. *(Takes it from his jacket pocket)* No, look at it. Thirty-two hundred sixty-four dollars and twenty-two cents. That's what just today cost. 32-64-22. Do you know what kind of money that is? And that doesn't count the hundred-buck deposit we had to put down a year ago, and your mother's dress, and these special suits we rented, and the photographer taking colored pictures. And the flowers. And the so-and-so. The band. We're talking four grand here. Four grand! You think your father has four thousand dollars? Where have you been? This is what I been trying to tell you! The gifts are only gonna cover half! I'm two grand in the hole! Even with your precious gifts! Two grand in the hole!

STEWIE *(With genuine innocence)*: I'll loan you some. You can borrow.

HERBIE: You're telling me?! You're telling me I can borrow?! Who's the father here?! Hm? Who pays the bills around here? Who hands out your allowance?! You don't tell me I can borrow!

STEWIE: Why didn't you tell me this before?! Why didn't you tell me I'd have to pay for my own bar mitzvah?!

HERBIE: Why didn't I tell you? I thought you'd figure it out for yourself.

STEWIE: So why did we do this? I didn't want it.

HERBIE: Why did we do this?, everybody does it.

STEWIE: My friend Jeffrey . . .

HERBIE: How would it look if we didn't throw you a bar mitzvah?

STEWIE: I don't know.

HERBIE: It would look very funny. Like something was wrong.

STEWIE: Isn't something wrong?

HERBIE: Hm?

STEWIE: You mean it would've looked like we couldn't afford it, so you made one anyway, even though we couldn't afford it!

HERBIE: Don't open a mouth like that to me.

STEWIE: But isn't it true?

HERBIE: Don't open a mouth.

STEWIE *(Overlap)*: We couldn't afford it. Say it. We couldn't afford it but you did it anyway and I have to pay for something I didn't even ask for in the first place!

HERBIE *(Enraged, he shakes Stewie violently)*: YOU THINK I WANT YOUR MONEY?!!

MITCHELL *(Approaches timidly)*: Daddy ...

HERBIE *(To Mitchell)*: Get outta here. *(To Stewie, while shaking him)* YOU THINK I LIKE HAVING TO DO THIS?!!

DORIS *(Calls from offstage)*: I hear body-drops in there!

STEWIE *(Overlap)*: YOU MADE A MISTAKE AND I HAVE TO PAY FOR IT!

MITCHELL: Daddy, stop ...

HERBIE *(To Mitchell)*: Get away I said.

STEWIE *(Overlap)*: WHY SHOULD I HAVE TO PAY FOR YOUR MISTAKES? IT ISN'T FAIR!—

DORIS *(Off)*: I hear body-drops!

STEWIE: ... I'M JUST A KID!

HERBIE: UH!, NOW YOU'RE A KID! NOW YOU'RE A KID!

MITCHELL *(Tugging on Herbie)*: Daddy ...

HERBIE *(To Mitchell)*: I TOLD YOU— *(Pushes him)*

STEWIE *(Adrenaline rushing madly)*: HEY! DON'T YOU TOUCH HIM. YOU HEAR ME? *(Swipes at Herbie with his fist)* DON'T YOU TOUCH MY BROTHER!

HERBIE: YOU WANT TO FIGHT? HM? YOU WANT TO KILL ME?

Stewie and Herbie are throwing punches; Doris comes in.

DORIS: Boys! What the—Herbie! Stop that!

HERBIE *(Still sparring)*: I should stop?! He started!

DORIS: Herbie! What's the matter with you?!

STEWIE *(Throwing punches; nearly hysterical)*: HE HATES US, MOMMY! HE HATES US!

HERBIE *(That did it; he's going berserk)*: YOU THINK I DON'T LOVE YOU?!! YOU THINK I DON'T LOVE YOU?!!

Doris puts her arms protectively around the shaken boys.

DORIS: Herbie, shush! The house is shaking!

HERBIE *(Jabbing at Stewie)*: I DON'T LOVE YOU?!!

DORIS *(Shielding Stewie)*: DON'T HURT HIM!

HERBIE: LOOK AT YOU WITH YOUR PRECIOUS BOYS!

WHAT DO I GET, HM?! *(Storms off to bedroom, screaming)* WHAT DO I HAVE! WHAT DO I HAVE!

Doris has her arms around both whimpering boys when Herbie returns carrying a dresser drawer.

(Now at a terrifying pitch) EVERYTHING I HAVE IS HERE IN THIS DRAWER! EVERYTHING I OWN IS RIGHT HERE! I COULD GET THE HELL OUT OF HERE LIKE THAT!

DORIS: Herbie, shhh . . .

HERBIE *(Overlap)*: WHAT DO I HAVE?! WHAT'S MINE?! THIS MUCH SPACE IN THE CLOSET?! One suit?! You can keep the suit; I don't give a damn about that suit; I hate suits; you made me buy that suit.

DORIS *(Quietly)*: I thought you needed—

HERBIE: DONATE IT TO GOODWILL! MAKE BELIEVE I DIED! WEAR IT FOR HALLOWEEN! WHAT DO I HAVE! I HAVE NOTHING! I HAVE SHIT! I HAVE THE TOILET FOR TEN MINUTES IN THE MORNING! I DON'T EVEN HAVE YOU!

DORIS: Herbie . . .

HERBIE: LOOK AT YOU! LOOK WHO GETS YOU!

DORIS: That's not true—the boys . . .

HERBIE *(Overlap)*: WHAT DO I HAVE! I DON'T EVEN HAVE THE TV! KEEP THE TV! THE HELL WITH THE TV! I'll buy myself a new TV. Top of the line! Color! Yeah, I'll buy myself a color! The boys can have the old one, watch whatever the hell they want! WHAT DO I GET?! WHAT DOES DADDY GET? *(Shaking the drawer violently)* EVERYTHING IN THE WORLD THAT'S MINE IS RIGHT HERE IN THIS DRAWER! EVERYTHING! What do I have? Underwear? This underwear is shot. Do I buy myself any? Do I buy myself anything? Look at these socks! Holes! Holes burned through 'em but I wear 'em anyway, tearing up my feet! My feet are torn up! Do I go to a foot doctor?! Look at all these single, lost socks I hold on to hoping the other'll show

up! Look at this! The hell with them? Garbage! LOOK
AROUND THIS HOUSE! WHAT'S MINE?! NOTHING!
(Rummaging through the drawer) I got my coin collection! My
silver dollars! What am I? Cufflinks? Tie clips? Skins? Under-
shorts with shot elastic? T-shirts with holes under the arms?
THIS IS ME?! THIS IS MY LIFE! THIS DRAWER IS MY
WHOLE LIFE, RIGHT HERE; THIS DRAWER! *(He
throws the drawer down and storms out of the apartment)*
DORIS: HERBIE!

*A sudden burst of music punctuates the action, signaling the start of
a musical number. Doris and Stewie exit; Mitchell is alone. The
following lines are all sung.*

MITCHELL:
Hey, why don't we
Get away from all this?
We all could use a little
Change of scene.
Let's go somewhere
A little green in places,
Where a little breathing space is,
And the air is clean.
Let's go
Where we can show
Off our sunglasses.
Yeah, let me take you all
To where the grass is!

With the tempo change, painted scenery moves in and lighting shifts.

What a perfect day
For a picnic!
We'll toast marshmallows
In the sun!

What a perfect day
For a fam'ly picnic!

Roasting chicken,
Having fun!

Stash the Slinky!
Pack Parcheesi!
Fill the football
Up with air!
We'll play catch in the park
Till it starts to get dark,
And take mem'ries home to share!

As Mitchell sings the following, Stewie enters broodingly, wearing a yarmulke, a varsity sweater over his tuxedo and reading his Haftarah booklet. Mitchell tries to get his attention.

It's a perfect day
For a picnic!
For the sky wouldn't dare turn gray!
What do you say, Brother?
Let's get away, Brother.
Stewie, what do you say?
What do you say, Brother?
We're on our way, Brother!
Stewie, let's all go out and—

STEWIE:
What is it that I do?
It's nothing I can name.
It doesn't matter what I do,
It's my fault all the same.

MITCHELL:
A picnic!
A picnic, Stewie!

STEWIE:
What is it that I say
That makes me feel ashamed?

253

It doesn't matter what I say,
I know that I'm to blame.

MITCHELL:
A picnic!
Think picnic, Stewie!
Think sunshine!

STEWIE:
It's always something.
It's always something.

(A little soft-shoe)

Something funny's going on.
Something funny with our dad.
I don't mean something funny ha-ha,
I mean it's something funny-sad.

MITCHELL: There's nothing we can do about it, Stewie. Nothing.

During the following, Mitchell follows Stewie's steps and dances with him.

STEWIE:
Dad's a little weird,
He's in a daze.
Could it be he's going nuts?
Or is it just a phase?

MITCHELL:
You're right.
Dad's weird.

STEWIE:
Dad's a little off,
He's feeling pain.
Is it that he's overworked
Or just a bit insane?
He's strange.

MITCHELL:
Dad's strange.

STEWIE:
Something funny's going on.

MITCHELL:
Something funny's going on.

STEWIE:
Something funny with our dad.

MITCHELL:
Something funny with our dad.

STEWIE AND MITCHELL:
I don't mean something funny ha-ha,
I mean it's something funny-sad.

Doris enters.

DORIS:
Attention!
Attention!
You must pay attention
To such a man as your dad.
In his soul I know where
Ev'ry nook and cranny is.
You just don't understand
The sort of man
He is.

He's not a bad man
He's not a great man.
Yes, he may even be a truly
Second-rate man.
Call him good, call him bad,
That's just fine—
He's mine.

He's not a kind man,
But—not a mean man.
Guess you could say
He's just your av'rage
In-between man.
I don't care, I don't cry,
I don't whine—
He's mine!

He's not a loser.
He's not a winner.
And, yes, I wish he were
A little thinner.
Or maybe once a week
Get home for dinner
Before nine.

He's not a dreamboat,
No Casanova.
But he will be my man
Until my life is over.
Am I right? Am I wrong?
Am I blind?
He's mine!

Don't mock him, Mitchell!
Don't snicker, Stewie!
For though you may believe
He's dull, or dumb, or screwy,
When he walks through that door,
It's a sign—
He's mine!

The front door opens and Herbie enters wearily in a hat and over-coat, carrying two large valises.

DORIS: Herbie!
HERBIE: Oy!

MITCHELL AND STEWIE: Dad!
HERBIE: Ugh!

You shoulda seen me today, boys!
I was clever! I was quick!
The world was going my way, boys!
I was lightning! I was slick!
Boy, was I hot, boys!
Boy, was I bright!
Bright as any shooting star
That lights up the night!
You shoulda seen how I handled the crowd—
If you'da seen me today, boys,
You woulda been proud!

Mitchell throws him an umbrella and he uses it as a song-and-dance man would a cane. His routine becomes more and more frantic.

You shoulda seen me
Answering calls,
Order after order,
Till I'm bouncing off walls.

You shoulda seen me
Going for broke,
Shaking all those clammy
Hands and cracking bad jokes.

You shoulda seen me
Faking and lying,
Shpieling and dealing,
Nobody buying.
Schmoozing and losing,
Never stopped trying.
Fretting and slipping
And sweating and schlepping
And yelling and crying

But knowing I'm dying.

(He collapses) I'm dead . . .

DORIS: *(Goes to him)*
Give me your feet,
I'll rub them.
Take off your socks and shoes.
Hand me your feet, I'll scrub them,
I'll scrub away your blues.
I know your soles are hurting,
I know your soul can sing!

ALL *(Including Marsha, who has entered during the above)*:
AHHHH!

DORIS:
Put your feet in my hands,
Oh they're sweet in my hands,
Put your feet in my hands,
With your feet in my hands,
You'll never walk alone!

ALL *(Variously; with great urgency)*:
Seems to me it's time
For a picnic!
We can still get our share of sun.
What a perfect day
For a fam'ly picnic!
Playing mah-jongg,
Having fun!
Fold the chairs up!
Pack the peanuts!
Fill the ice chest
With dry ice!
You can nap in the shade,
Maybe drink lemonade—
It's a steal at any price!

Thunder. Herbie, Stewie, Doris and Marsha disperse and exit.

MITCHELL:
It was a perfect day
For a picnic,
Till the clouds made the sky turn dark.
There'll be another day
We'll have our chance to play.
Hey, folks, what do you say?
Maybe some other day
I'll take us all away
To a picnic
In the
Park!

The scenery disappears. Fade-out.

Scene Four

Late that night. Doris paces fretfully. Marsha lights two cigarettes
Now, Voyager style.

DORIS: I saw this movie. Pure Lana Turner, I know. But this is what's happened to my life, Marsh. My life is a B-movie.

Marsha hands her a cigarette.

Thanks. I don't know what to do.
MARSHA: You gotta leave the bum.
DORIS: He's not a bum, Marsh, don't call him a bum.
MARSHA: Bum or no, you gotta leave him.
DORIS: How?
MARSHA: One foot in front of the other.
DORIS: Just like that? How? How do I do that?
MARSHA: Look, you said yourself: The guy's lost his marbles.
DORIS: Completely. Yes. You should have seen him. The way he
shook—

MARSHA: So what's the problem? Kiddo, this is your life, too. Take it from me. Time is short. It's rare, too good to waste on a dead-end proposition and that's what you got here.

DORIS: Oh, but, Marsh, people where we come from, it's unheard of. You know that. You of all people should. Jewish people don't go their separate ways, they stick it out even if they're miserable. We're like Catholics that way. Only I'm not worried about the Pope excommunicating me; my mother will sit shiva for me. She'll cover the mirrors and sit close to the ground. I'll call her on the phone and say, "Ma, it's me, your daughter, Doris," and she'll say, "My daughter Doris is dead" and hang up.

MARSHA: You gotta break out, kiddo. Grab your little boys and walk into the sunset. You gotta do it, Doll. If not you, send him out on his can. The party's over. You can do it. You gotta.

A key turns in the front door.

DORIS: Marsha, please, I . . .

MARSHA: You gotta, kid. It's the only way.

Marsha exits as Herbie enters through the front door. He and Doris look at one another for a long beat before he speaks.

HERBIE: I went to the movies. Anything. *Born Free*. The lions. Africa. Lots of growling, jumping around the fields. About lions yearning to breathe free or something. Dumb picture. I fell asleep.

Doris gets up.

Don't worry about my supper. I ate Bon Bons.

DORIS: Herbie.

A beat.

HERBIE: Yeah?

A beat.

DORIS: This is it, Herbie.

A beat.

HERBIE *(A nervous smile)*: Wha?

DORIS: I don't care anymore, Herbie. I can't be the good little girl anymore, the good daughter, the good wife. I can't live like this anymore, Herbie, the silence is deafening. I'm bored, Herbie, I'm dying. What am I saying? I hear myself talk and I can't believe how Harold Robbins I sound. I married for life, I know. I bought the whole *megillah*: love, honor, protect, till death. But I take it all back. Sorry for the inconvenience. They should have you take the vow: I'll love you forever or till I'm all used up, whichever comes first. I'm used up alright, Herbie, like a tube a toothpaste all squeezed out, but you don't stop squeezing. We've become one of those couples we'd see in restaurants, who go through a whole meal and don't say a word to each other.

HERBIE: We're talking now.

DORIS: Me. I'm talking. I do all the talking for both of us. I do all the thinking. It's gotten so I don't bother to say anything 'cause I know your half of the conversation.

HERBIE: Isn't that good? Isn't that knowing a person so well . . .

DORIS: No, it's just knowing the other half of the conversation. I'm very sorry, Herbie. You're a sweet man. You'll find someone. I'm used up. I can't prop you up and make you feel good when you should feel lousy. I can't cover for you and make excuses. I can't run your public relations anymore, Herbie. Eighteen years; that's not so bad. Nothing to be ashamed of. Who says you have to be married to just one person your whole life? Yeah, at this rate you still have time to squeeze in another couple eighteen-year marriages. You and the next eighteen-year lady, the two of you'll have a great time, I promise, Herbie. She'll either pick up where I left off and be your mother all over again or, if you're lucky . . . *(A beat)* I can't make up for your childhood anymore. And neither can the boys. I'm sorry, my job is done. I quit. *(A beat)* I packed up your drawer in the American Tourister like I'm sending you off to camp for the last time. Kiss the boys goodbye. We'll be in touch.

Lighting shifts. Doris and Herbie resume their places at the top of the scene and begin it again.

HERBIE: I went to the movies. *Born Free.* The lions. Africa. About lions yearning to breathe free or something. Dumb picture. I fell asleep.

Doris gets up.

Don't worry about my supper. I ate Bon Bons.

DORIS: Herbie.

A beat.

HERBIE: Yeah?

A beat.

DORIS: This is it, Herbie.

A beat.

HERBIE *(A nervous smile)*: Wha?

DORIS: My life is over, but it's still going on. I always wanted to go down in a blaze of glory, young and beautiful like my Aunt Marsha. What tragedy! What drama! Frozen gorgeous. Never forgotten. Never old. All that promise, all that youth, wasted. People never stop wondering what might've been. Forever twenty-three. Not bad. I want to be frozen in your mind, forever thirty-eight. *(A beat)* My life is over, Herbie. I have the boys, but I don't have them; they won't be mine much longer. They'll survive; children do. Children never remember the good stuff anyway, they only remember the shit. My life is over, stop the projector. It's the going on that's painful, not the going. There's no place left for me to go. We worked so hard to get to where we are, Herbie, to this luxury, but this is as far as they'll let us go. This is it for us: the top, the last stop. We have arrived. I'm stuck, Herbie. I'm stuck up here on the tenth floor. There's nowhere to go but out the window. Goodbye, Herbie. Kiss the boys goodbye.

She opens the door to the terrace, puts one foot over the railing and jumps. Lighting shifts. Doris and Herbie resume their places at the top of the scene and begin it again.

HERBIE: I went to the movies. *Born Free.* About lions yearning to breathe free or something. Dumb picture. I fell asleep.

Doris gets up.

Don't worry about my supper. I ate Bon Bons.

DORIS: Herbie.

A beat.

HERBIE: Yeah?

DORIS *(Runs into his arms; tearfully)*: Don't ever run out on me like that again, you hear me?! I never felt so lonely in my life! How dare you do that to me?! When I married you I thought, here is a man who'll never leave me, and when you did, it was like a part of me was stolen, my leg, my child. I need you to take care of. Who'm I gonna take care of if you leave me? The boys need me less and less; what happens when they don't need me at all? I need you, Herbie. Don't let me go. Please don't let me go.

Herbie sways with Doris in his arms. He gently sings the first verse of "Autumn Leaves." Mitchell and Stewie run out of their room.

STEWIE AND MITCHELL: Daddy! Daddy! *(Etc.)*

They embrace Herbie. Lighting shifts. The boys exit. Doris and Herbie resume their places at the top of the scene and begin it again.

HERBIE: I went to the movies. Anything. *Born Free.* The lions. Africa. Lots of growling, jumping around fields. About lions yearning to breathe free or something. Dumb picture. I fell asleep.

Doris makes a move.

Don't worry about my supper. I ate Bon Bons.

DORIS: Bon Bons? That's why I bust my chops making you Weight Watchers? I made you a tuna plate for when you got home. Eat it and eliminate your fruit today and tomorrow. Bon Bons! *(As she goes to the kitchen)* Sit.

Herbie does; Doris returns with his tuna plate, sets it down in front of him, and sits beside him as he begins to eat. Mitchell watches them. Finally, Herbie speaks.

HERBIE *(Sheepishly)*: Doris, look, I'm sorry about—
DORIS: Don't. *(A beat. Quietly)* Don't.

A beat. Herbie resumes eating, and Doris watches him in silence, as the lights fade very slowly.

SIGHT UNSEEN

▢ ▢ ▢

This play is for
Jonathan Alper
(1950–1991)
and
Laura Kuckes
(1961–1990)

Jonathan and Patricia are American, Nick is English. Grete is German; her English is excellent, if accented. Jonathan has maintained his working-class Brooklyn accent; Nick's rural, working-class speech finds its way into his university accent, particularly when he's been drinking; and Patricia's dialect suggests that of an expatriate New Yorker living in England.

ACT ONE

Scene One

Lights up: The kitchen of a cold farmhouse in England. Dusk. Jonathan, an overnight bag on his shoulder, stands at the open door. Nick is eating a hard roll.

JONATHAN: You must be Nick.
NICK: Mm.
JONATHAN: Jonathan Waxman.

He extends his hand. Nick doesn't shake it but takes a bite of his roll instead.

Is Patricia . . . ?

Nick shakes his head.

Oh. You *were* expecting me?
NICK: Mm.
JONATHAN *(Meaning, "Where is . . . ?")*: Patricia . . . ?
NICK: A lamb roast.

267

JONATHAN: Ah. Well! Nick! Nice to meet you.

Nick says nothing. A beat.

I left the car right outside. That alright?

Nick looks out the door, shrugs.

'Cause I'll move it.
NICK: No no.

A beat.

JONATHAN: Uh, I think I'm kind of freezing. You mind if I—

Nick gestures for him to come in.

Thanks. *(A beat)* I made really good time, by the way. Left London 'round one; not bad, huh?

Nick shrugs. A beat.

Her directions were really good Patricia. *(A beat)* Boy, this driving on the wrong side of the road stuff! —Ever drive in America?

Nick shakes his head.

Ever been to America?

Nick shakes his head again.

Uh-huh, well it's *weird* cars coming at you like that. A simple thing like the way you perceive the flow of traffic, the way you're used to seeing, gets challenged here, it all gets inverted. You've got to keep reminding yourself, over and over, remember what side of the road you're on. 'Cause all you need's to zone out for one second on the M4 and that's it, you're fuckin' wrapped in twisted metal.

Nick just looks at him. A beat.

Will she be long Patricia?
NICK: God, I hope not.

JONATHAN: Oh, I'm sorry, am I interrupting something?

NICK *(Gestures to a room)*: Well . . .

JONATHAN: Please. Do what you have to do. I want to hear all about your work, though.

NICK: Hm?

JONATHAN: Your work. I really want to hear about it.

NICK: Oh.

JONATHAN: Archeology's one of those things I've always found fascinating, but I don't know much about it.

NICK: Well, I . . .

JONATHAN: Not now. Whenever. Over dinner. I brought you some good wine; we should drink it. *(Takes out bottles of wine)* Maybe later I'll get you to show me the dig you're working on.

NICK: Uh . . .

JONATHAN: No, really, I'd like to see it. Hey, I know how obnoxious it is when people say they want to see my studio and then I show them and they're not really into it?, all they're thinking about is *after*, telling their friends they were there? No, I mean it, I'd really love to see it.

NICK: It's. . . . It's rather dull.

JONATHAN: I'm sure it isn't. What are you working on right now?

NICK *(A beat)*: A Roman latrine.

A beat. Patricia enters wearing a bulky sweater and carrying a bag bursting with groceries.

PATRICIA: Well! You're here!

JONATHAN *(Over "You're here")*: Hi. Yeah.

She moves around the room, unpacks groceries, prepares dinner.

PATRICIA: Fancy car.

JONATHAN: Rented. *You* know. What the hell.

PATRICIA: Must be fun whipping 'round these country roads in a thing like that.

JONATHAN: Yeah, as a matter of fact I was just telling Nick . . .

NICK: Um . . .

PATRICIA: What.

Nick gestures to his office.

Go.

He hesitates, goes. A beat.

He has work.

Jonathan nods. A beat.

So. Arrived in one piece I see.
JONATHAN: Your directions . . .
PATRICIA: What.
JONATHAN: Excellent. Just terrific.
PATRICIA: Oh, good. I'm glad you liked them.
JONATHAN: Great spot.
PATRICIA: Yeah? Looks like a lot of mud most of the time.

Pause.

JONATHAN: Good to see you, Patty.
PATRICIA: Is it? Well, good.

Pause.

JONATHAN: So you got a lamb roast?
PATRICIA: Ground veal, actually. It was on special. I've become
quite a resourceful little cook over here, you know.

Nick returns, gets a bottle of scotch, gestures offstage, exits.

Nick is painfully shy. Was he shy with you?
JONATHAN *(Lying)*: Nick? No. *(A beat)* So you've become a
good cook you said?
PATRICIA: I didn't say good, I said resourceful. No one's a good
cook here, so no one notices. Stews are the answer, I've discovered. The meat quality is so awful, you stew the stuff for hours
till it all falls apart and it's unrecognizable as meat. Bet you
can't wait for dinner, hm? *(She puts on water for tea, putters
around the kitchen, etc.)*
JONATHAN: Mmm. Can I help with anything?

PATRICIA *(Over "with anything")*: No. Sit. Pretend you're comfortable. Take off your coat.

JONATHAN *(Meaning the cold)*: No, I'll keep it if you don't mind . . .

PATRICIA: It's so funny having Americans visit, watching their teeth chatter.

JONATHAN: I think it's warmer out*side*.

PATRICIA: Probably. You get used to the cold and the damp, strangely enough. You get used to anything.

JONATHAN: You've kept your accent.

PATRICIA: For the most part. You'll notice little things here and there.

JONATHAN: It struck me on the phone; I thought by now you'd sound totally . . .

PATRICIA: I don't know, I like sounding American. It works to my advantage, really. You have no idea how hard it is being a woman running an excavation.

JONATHAN: I'll bet.

PATRICIA: The sexism here. . . . If you think the *States* are bad. . . . Being an *American* woman gives me license to be rude, aggressive, demanding. It comes in handy.

JONATHAN: Don't you ever miss it?

PATRICIA: What?

JONATHAN: Home.

PATRICIA: This is my home.

JONATHAN: What, you don't miss Disneyland, or the Grand Canyon, or Zabar's?

PATRICIA: No.

JONATHAN: You don't miss Zabar's? Now I know you're full of it.

PATRICIA: I don't. I don't get choked up when I see the flag, or Woody Allen movies. I've stopped reading about politics. Reagan, Bush, they're interchangeable. No, I prefer my bones and coins and petrified cherry pits.

JONATHAN: You must miss *something*. Insulated housing, *something*.

PATRICIA: No. I'm an expatriate now.

JONATHAN: An expatriate.

PATRICIA: Yes.

JONATHAN: Gee, I've never known an expatriate before, someone who could just turn their back . . .

PATRICIA: On what. I've turned my back on what? America? VCRs and microwaves? If that's what I've "turned my back on. . . . " We work hard here. It's not like the States. Everything is a struggle. It shows on our faces, on our hands. I haven't bought myself new clothes in years. We have to save for everything. The electric fire started smoking?

JONATHAN: Yeah . . . ?

PATRICIA: It'll be weeks before we can buy a new one. Everything's a struggle. The weather is hard. Leisure is hard. Sleep is hard.

JONATHAN: Do you ever think about leaving?

PATRICIA: God! What have I been saying! I like it!

JONATHAN: Oh.

PATRICIA: You're just like my mother! I *like* it here! I *like* the struggle! I *like* surviving obstacles. Hell, I survived *you*, didn't I.

He reaches for her hand, she pulls away. Pause.

Who are you to talk about turning one's back.

JONATHAN: What do you mean?

PATRICIA: You with your shiksa wife in Vermont.

JONATHAN: Upstate.

PATRICIA: Whatever.

JONATHAN: I don't understand. What does my wife have to do . . .

PATRICIA *(Over "have to do")*: You're an expatriate, too, and you don't even know it.

JONATHAN: How?

PATRICIA: You made a choice. When you married your wife, you married her world. Didn't you? You can't exist in two worlds; you've got to turn your back on one of them.

JONATHAN: I hadn't thought of it like that.

PATRICIA: See? We're more alike than you thought. *(Pause)* God, when I think of all the angst, all the, what's the word?, "cirrus"?

JONATHAN: *Tsuris.*

PATRICIA: After all the tsuris our young souls went through. . . . Your wife should thank me.

JONATHAN: You're right; she should.

PATRICIA: I laid the groundwork. I was the pioneer.

JONATHAN: Yeah.

PATRICIA: The sacrificial shiksa.

JONATHAN: You're looking beautiful, Patty.

PATRICIA: Stop.

JONATHAN: You are.

PATRICIA: I look fat.

JONATHAN: No.

PATRICIA: All the meat and potatoes, and nights at the pub. Don't look at me. I'm afraid this place is perfect for women like me, who've let themselves go.

JONATHAN: You haven't.

PATRICIA: We can blend right in with the mud.

JONATHAN: You look beautiful.

PATRICIA: And *you* look rich.

JONATHAN: I don't even. I'm the same old Jonathan.

PATRICIA: Don't be coy. You're rich and famous. How does it feel to be rich and famous?

JONATHAN: It's meaningless. Really.

PATRICIA: Oh, yeah, right.

JONATHAN: No, the whole scene is meaningless bullshit. You know that. It's all timing and luck.

PATRICIA: Timing and luck.

JONATHAN: Yeah. The party's over for me already; I'm not making now what I made two years ago.

PATRICIA: But you still have your millions to keep you company.

JONATHAN: The numbers don't mean anything. I mean, I'm not crying poverty or anything . . .

PATRICIA: Oh! Well!

JONATHAN: My gallery takes fifty percent. Okay? Remember that. Fifty. And then the government on top of that . . .

PATRICIA: Don't you think you're protesting just a little too much?

JONATHAN: Okay, so maybe I've enjoyed a little recognition—

PATRICIA: "A little recognition"?! Jonathan! You're "it—"

JONATHAN: No, no, not anymore.

PATRICIA *(Continuous)*: —the cat's pajamas. You can't fool me. I read all about you in the *Times*.

JONATHAN: The *New York Times*? You read the *New York Times*? Hypocrite. You were just telling me how you . . .

PATRICIA *(Over "telling me how you")*: My mother sent it to me.

JONATHAN: You talking about the Sunday magazine piece? Couple of years ago?

PATRICIA: "Jonathan Waxman: The Art Scene's New Visionary."

JONATHAN: Oh, please . . .

PATRICIA *(Laughs)*: Is that what it was? "New Visionary"?

JONATHAN: "Bad Boy or Visionary?"

PATRICIA: "Bad Boy or Visionary," excuse me.

JONATHAN: What do you want from me?

PATRICIA: Cover story and everything. Wow, Jonathan, how'd you manage that? I was quite impressed. You on the cover, the very model of messy, Jewish intensity.

JONATHAN: They shot me in my studio. That's how I look when I'm working.

PATRICIA: I know how you look when you're working.

They look at one another. Pause.

My mother's always sending me clippings about you.

JONATHAN: Oh, yeah? Why?

PATRICIA: I don't know, I'd say she's trying to tell me something, wouldn't you? The *Vanity Fair* piece was fun. "Charlatan or Genius?"

JONATHAN: I don't believe this.

PATRICIA: Every time she sends me something, I take it as some sort of indictment, some sort of accusation: *"See what you could've had? See what could've been yours if you weren't so crazy?"*

JONATHAN: Is that what *you* think or is that what *she* thinks?

PATRICIA: Me? No. *(Pause)* So tell me about your show. How's it going in London? *(That English inflection slips in)* Is it going well?

JONATHAN: Yeah. Pretty much. Oh, I brought you a catalogue.
(Hands her one from his bag)

PATRICIA: Hefty.

JONATHAN: There are a couple of gaps I'm not too happy about.
Particularly in the early stuff. It's supposed to be a retrospective.

PATRICIA: A retrospective? At your age?

JONATHAN: Are you kidding? I'm almost passé.

PATRICIA: You know, I still have that very first painting you did
of me, remember?

JONATHAN: Of course I remember. Where is it?

PATRICIA: Over the mantle. Go and see.

JONATHAN: No shit. You didn't just haul it out of the attic,
knowing I was coming?

PATRICIA: There is no attic. And, no, Jonathan, I wouldn't do
anything at this point to feed your ego.

*He goes to the doorway leading to the living room and sees his
painting; it's like seeing a ghost. She watches him in silence while
he looks at the painting.*

JONATHAN: Jesus. Look at that. I can't believe you saved it.
How old could I have been? Twenty-two tops?

She nods; a beat.

You know? It's not bad. I threw out most of my student work
years ago. I couldn't stand looking at anything. But this, this
one's different. It's really not bad.

PATRICIA: When do you open?

JONATHAN: What? Oh. Tuesday. *(Re: the painting)* Look at
that: See what I was doing with the picture plane?, how it's
sort of tipped? I didn't think I started doing that till like much
later.

PATRICIA: Nervous?

JONATHAN: No. I don't know. What can I do? It's my first solo
show outside of North America, okay?, my European debut.

PATRICIA: Yeah . . . ?

JONATHAN: So the critics are salivating, I'm sure. Ready to chomp into me like their next Big Mac.

PATRICIA: And what if they do?

JONATHAN: I don't know, I can't worry about it. Press is press. Good or bad. My father, God!, my father *loved* seeing my name in print.

PATRICIA: Oh, yeah?

JONATHAN: *My* last name, after all, was *his* last name. Got such a kick out of it. Eight pages in the Sunday *Times*. He couldn't believe the *New York Times* could possibly have that much to say about his kid. "All these words," he said, "are about *you*? What is there to say about *you*?"

She laughs.

He was serious; he wasn't just teasing. Oh, he was teasing, too, but it threatened him. No, it did. It pointed up the fact that he could be my father and still not know a thing about me. Not have a clue. What did the fancy-schmancy art world see that he didn't? What were those big dirty paintings about, anyway? So then when all the hype started . . .

PATRICIA: "New visionary"?

JONATHAN: Yeah, and that's very seductive in the beginning, I got to admit. Vindicating, even: "Ah ha! See? I *am* a genius. *Now* maybe my father will respect me." But it had the opposite effect on him. It didn't make him proud. It bewildered him. It alienated him. How could *he* have produced a "visionary"? It shamed him somehow. I can't explain.

PATRICIA: How's he doing?

JONATHAN: Oh. Didn't I tell you on the phone?

PATRICIA: What.

JONATHAN: He died.

PATRICIA: Oh, no.

JONATHAN: Right before I flew to London.

PATRICIA: You mean last week?

JONATHAN: What's today? Yeah, last Thursday it happened.

PATRICIA: Oh, Jonathan. . . . What happened?

JONATHAN: It was long in coming. Did I not mention this on the phone?

PATRICIA: No.

JONATHAN: Sorry, thought I did. Strange to think, four days ago I was in Flushing, Queens, burying my father under the Unisphere.

Pause.

PATRICIA: *He* was sweet to me, your dad.

JONATHAN: Yeah, I know.

PATRICIA: What about shiva? Didn't you have to sit shiva?

JONATHAN: There was no time.

PATRICIA: Oh.

JONATHAN: I mean, they were mounting the show.

PATRICIA: Couldn't they have waited? I mean, your *father* . . .

JONATHAN: No. I had to be here. I mean, there was nothing more I could do; he was dead. What could I do?

PATRICIA: I don't know.

JONATHAN: It was good for me, getting away, I think. Therapeutic. Bobby's doing it, though, shiva. He wanted to. I don't know, I just couldn't. It didn't seem like the thing to do. It's like I'd been sitting shiva for him for fifteen years, since my mother. I'd done it already. *(A beat)* I wasn't a very good son.

PATRICIA: That's not true; I'm sure you made him very proud.

JONATHAN: No no, that's not what I need to hear. I wasn't. *(A beat)* I went to pack up his house the other day? My parents' house? All his clothes, my old room, my mother's sewing machine, all those rooms of furniture. Strange being in a place where no one lives anymore.

PATRICIA: I know; I do that for a living.

JONATHAN: Yeah, I guess you do.

A beat.

Anyway, what I found was, he'd taken all the family pictures, everything that was in albums, shoved in drawers—hundreds of them—and covered an entire wall with them, floor to ceiling, side to side. I first saw it years ago, when he'd started. It was his Sistine Chapel; it took him years. He took my hand (I'll never forget this) he took my hand—he was beaming: *"You're* an artist," he said to me, *"you'll* appreciate this." He was so proud of himself I thought I was gonna cry. Proud and also in a strange way competitive?

PATRICIA: Uh-huh.

JONATHAN: So, there was this wall. The Waxman family through the ages. Black-and-white, sepia, Kodachrome. My great-grandparents in the shtetl, my brother's baby pictures on top of my parents' courtship, me at my bar mitzvah. Well, it was kind of breathtaking. I mean, the sweep of it, it really was kind of beautiful. I came closer to examine it—I wanted to see how he'd gotten them all up there—and then I saw the staples.

PATRICIA: What?

JONATHAN: Staples! Tearing through the faces and the bodies. "Look what you've done," I wanted to say, "How could you be so thoughtless? You've ruined everything!" But of course I didn't say that. How could I? He was like a little boy. Beaming. Instead I said, "Dad! What a wonderful job!"

A beat.

So, there I was alone in his house, pulling staples out of our family photos. These documents that showed where I came from. Did they *mean* anything to him at all? I mean as artifacts, as proof of a former civilization, when my mother was vibrant and he was young and strong and we were a family?

A beat.

That's all gone now, Patty. It's all gone.

Pause.

PATRICIA: You have your wife.

He nods. Pause.

She must trust you a lot.

JONATHAN: Why?

PATRICIA: Letting you pop up to see how the old lover made out? Or, ah-ha!, you didn't tell her you were coming!

JONATHAN: No, I told her.

PATRICIA: Too morbid for her taste, huh?, she decided to stay in London?

JONATHAN: No. Actually, she didn't come over.

PATRICIA: Oh?

JONATHAN: She stayed home. Up near New Paltz. We moved out of the city a couple of years ago.

PATRICIA: I know. The article said. I thought it said Vermont.

JONATHAN: No. We bought a farm.

PATRICIA: I know. Some "turn of the century" thing; here we have to ask "turn of *which* century?" So why isn't she here *with* you, your wife? Your big European debut.

JONATHAN: She wanted to. *(A beat)* She's pregnant.

PATRICIA *(A beat)*: Ah. Well. A baby. My! Aren't *you* full of news!

JONATHAN: She's pretty far along.

PATRICIA: Congratulations.

JONATHAN: Thanks. I mean, flying was out of the question. Third trimester.

PATRICIA: Of course. So I've heard. Well. Isn't that nice. You'll be a father soon.

JONATHAN: Yeah. Nine weeks or something, yeah.

PATRICIA: Well. This is something: Jonathan Waxman a father. Just as you've lost your own.

JONATHAN: Yeah. The irony hasn't escaped me. *(A beat. Going to his wallet)* Would you like to see a picture?

PATRICIA: Of the child already?

JONATHAN: No, of Laura.

PATRICIA *(Continuous)*: My God! American technology . . .

JONATHAN *(Over "technology")*: I *did* have a sonogram I carried around. It's a boy.

PATRICIA: A boy.

JONATHAN: You can tell. You can see his, *you* know, his scrotum.

PATRICIA: Yes.

JONATHAN: I meant a picture of Laura. Would you like to . . .

PATRICIA: I've already seen her.

JONATHAN: How?

PATRICIA: The article.

JONATHAN: Oh, right.

PATRICIA *(Continuous)*: Remember? Gazing at you like an astronaut's wife?

JONATHAN *(Returns the picture to his wallet)*: Oh, well, I thought you might've liked to . . .

PATRICIA: No, I will, show me.

JONATHAN: It's okay.

PATRICIA: *Show* me.

He shows her the photo. A beat.

JONATHAN: That was our wedding.

PATRICIA: I figured, white dress and everything. How long ago was that?

JONATHAN: A year ago May. We waited a while. How about you?

PATRICIA: Me?

JONATHAN: You and Nick, you've been married *how* long?

PATRICIA: I don't know, eight or nine years?

JONATHAN: Eight or nine?, what do you mean?

PATRICIA: We didn't have much of a wedding. I like her dress. She's so thin. A dancer, right?

He nods. She returns the photo.

She seems nice.

JONATHAN: Yeah, thanks, she is, you'd like her.

PATRICIA: I'm sure.

JONATHAN: And Nick seems . . .

PATRICIA: Don't do that.

JONATHAN: What.

PATRICIA: I tell you I like *your* spouse, you tell me you like *mine*. You don't have to do that.

JONATHAN: I wasn't.

PATRICIA: The fact is . . . Nick may seem . . . odd . . .

JONATHAN: No . . .

PATRICIA *(A small laugh)*: Yes. But he absolutely adores me.

JONATHAN: That's *good*. I'm glad he does. He should.

A beat. They look at one another.

And you?

PATRICIA: Look, what do you want?

JONATHAN: What do you mean?

PATRICIA: Do you have some sort of agenda or something?

JONATHAN: No.

PATRICIA: You just happened to be in the neighborhood?

JONATHAN: I wanted to see you again.

PATRICIA: Why?

JONATHAN: I don't know, it felt somehow . . . incomplete.

PATRICIA: What did?

JONATHAN: We did. I did. *(A beat)* I came. . . . I wanted to apologize.

PATRICIA *(Smiling)*: Not really.

JONATHAN: What did you think when I called?

PATRICIA: I don't know, I was nonplussed. I buried you years ago, then all of a sudden a call from London. You caught me off guard.

JONATHAN: So why did you invite me up?

PATRICIA: You caught me off *guard*, I said. I don't know, what *should* I have done?

JONATHAN: You could've said it was a bad time, you were busy, you had other plans . . .

PATRICIA: None of which was true.

JONATHAN: You could've said you had no interest in seeing me again. *(Pause)* Patty . . .

He makes a conciliatory gesture; she rebuffs him.

PATRICIA: I'll give you dinner and a place to spend the night, but, no, Jonathan, I won't forgive you.

Pause. He goes for his bag.

JONATHAN: Look, maybe this wasn't such a good idea. I should go to a hotel.

PATRICIA: No! *(A beat)* Hey, no one here calls me Patty. It's a novelty.

He drops his bag. She picks up a basket.

PATRICIA: I'm going foraging in my garden for dinner.

JONATHAN: I'll come with you.

PATRICIA: You aren't invited. *(A beat)* You're cold. I think it actually is warmer inside.

She puts on her jacket and goes. Jonathan soon gravitates toward the painting and looks at it for a while. Nick enters, the depleted bottle of scotch in his hand.

NICK: Oops.

Jonathan sees him. A beat.

You've spotted your painting.

JONATHAN: Yes.

NICK: I can't tell you how many nights I've stared at the fire and imagined that painting in the flames.

JONATHAN: Excuse me?

NICK: Oh, I wouldn't dream of damaging it. It's a work of art. And I am a preservationist by nature. *(A beat)* It makes Patricia happy to have a piece of you on the wall. Did I say *a piece of you*? I meant a piece *from* you. Or perhaps I *meant* a piece *of* you. A piece of *yours*, at any rate. She gazes at it sometimes, when we're sitting by the fire. It doesn't move me in the same way. No, the eye of the beholder and all that. Drink?

JONATHAN: No. I painted it a long time ago. When Patty and I were at school. It's strange seeing something I did like twenty years ago and see all these things I couldn't possibly have seen when I painted it.

NICK: You're rich now, aren't you?

JONATHAN: What?

NICK: Patricia tells me you're rich.

JONATHAN: Oh, God.

NICK: Read it in some magazine.

JONATHAN: Well, we talked about that. Actually, I . . .

NICK *(Over "Actually, I")*: She said you're rich. You're successful.

JONATHAN: Those are two different things, really.

NICK: Are they?

JONATHAN: Yes, I think—

NICK: How much do you make in a year?

JONATHAN: Well, I don't—

NICK: Am I out of line?

JONATHAN: Well, maybe.

NICK: How much then?

JONATHAN: It's difficult to say. I've had years in which I've made almost nothing. It's only in the last couple of years—

NICK *(Over "couple of years")*: How much would you get for something like that, for instance? *(Meaning the painting on the wall)*

JONATHAN: A student painting? I have no idea.

NICK: Guess.

JONATHAN: I really don't know.

NICK: Come on. A pivotal work. You said so yourself. A seminal work. How much would a seminal work, given your current currency, if you will, your current notoriety, how much would an old, young Waxman bring?

JONATHAN: I really have no idea.

NICK: Come on, guess.

JONATHAN: In the thousands, certainly. I don't know.

NICK *(Over "I don't know")*: Oh, I would think more than that.

JONATHAN: Look, I really don't pay much attention to this stuff.

NICK: Don't pay attention to money? Surely you must.

JONATHAN: No, I let my gallery worry about it.

NICK: Art for art's sake, eh? Well, even I, even I who know, or for that matter, *care* very little about contemporary values in art, or, even, the value *of* contemporary art, even I would guess you're being awfully stingy on yourself. Considerably more than in the thousands, I would say. More like in the *tens* of thousands, wouldn't you agree?

JONATHAN: Maybe. I really don't know.

NICK: Oh, I would think. A pivotal, precocious painting like this? A seminal masterpiece?

JONATHAN: I don't know. What do you want to hear? Whatever you want to hear.

NICK: You.

JONATHAN: What.

NICK: I feel as though I've known you all along.

JONATHAN: Oh, yeah?

NICK: Your picture. She has this snapshot.

JONATHAN: What snapshot?

NICK: A Polaroid. The two of you. Patricia the co-ed. The party girl. Lithe and sunny. Her tongue in your ear. You, squirming like a boy caught in a prank. With gums showing. You don't look at all handsome. She assured me you were. A costume party of some kind.

JONATHAN: A costume party?

NICK: Mm. Patricia in a swimsuit dressed as Miss America. You're dressed like a jester. A clown. A clown or a pimp.

JONATHAN: A what?

NICK: Loud clashing plaids, a camera 'round your neck. Sunglasses.

JONATHAN: Oh. Halloween. I was a tourist.

NICK: Hm?

JONATHAN: A tourist. I went dressed as a tourist.

NICK: A tourist.

JONATHAN: A visitor, a stranger. An observer. The camera, the Hawaiian shirt.

NICK: It doesn't read.

Jonathan shrugs.

You look like a pimp.

JONATHAN: The idea was a tourist.

NICK: Hm?

JONATHAN: Never mind.

NICK: Patricia had forgotten what you'd dressed up *as*. She thought a pimp.

JONATHAN: No.

NICK: Mm. *(A beat)* What was the idea?

JONATHAN: The idea?

NICK: What did it mean? Was there some symbolic value?, dressing as a tourist?

JONATHAN: I don't know . . .

NICK: Symbolic of your perception of yourself at that time, perhaps? A transient person? Dislocated?

JONATHAN: That's interesting. I wonder if—

NICK: Rubbish. Now, that picture, that photo. Was all I had to go on. For years. Until that *New York Times* article. That one Polaroid she keeps in a box with letters. *(Confidentially)* I've snooped. There's a postal card from you in that box. One picture postal card. No letters.

JONATHAN: I didn't write much.

NICK: Hm?

JONATHAN: There was no need to write. We were in school together. We saw each other all the time.

NICK: No, I imagine there *were* letters. Painful collegiate prose. Heartsick poems. Declarations of lust.

JONATHAN: Sorry.

NICK: I imagine there *were* letters, but she burned them. Like Hedda Gabler or somebody. Watched with glee while the missives went up in flames.

JONATHAN: No.

NICK: I think there *were*. I prefer to think there *were*. And all that remains is an innocuous postal card. From Miami Beach, Florida or someplace.

JONATHAN: Yes. A visit to my grandparents. Fort Lauderdale.

NICK: Then there are the stories. Tales of Waxman. The Jonathan Stories. Faraway sounding, exotic. Like from the Old Testament, if you will. Patricia's voice becomes especially animated

while telling a Jonathan story. She achieves a new range in a
different key. A new tune, a new music entirely. Fascinating. I
watch her face. The dimples that sprout! The knowing smiles!
Remarkable behavioural findings. *(A beat. He drags his chair
closer)* I've become a Waxmanologist, you see. A Waxmanophile.
No, a Waxmanologist. It's my nature. Beneath this reticent exte-
rior lies a probing, tireless investigator. A detective. An histo-
rian. And I'm good at my work. I'm compulsive. I'm meticu-
lous. I study the past in order to make sense of the present.

JONATHAN: I understand.

NICK: You're smaller in person than I imagined. I held out for
a giant. A giant among men. Instead, what's *this*? You're
medium- sized. Compact. Razor burn on your neck. Pimple on
your cheek. She said you were handsome; you're alright. Perhaps your appeal lies below the belt, but I doubt I'd be surprised.

JONATHAN: Look, I think I'll— *(Pointing to the door)*

NICK: Circumcision isn't common practice in the U.K., you
know.

Jonathan stops.

Jews still do it the world over, don't they. On religious grounds.
Here the risk is too great. Too many accidents. Too many boy
sopranos. Here we hold on to our overcoats.

Patricia returns with her basket filled with vegetables and herbs.

PATRICIA: Oh. Good. You're getting acquainted.

Jonathan and Nick look at one another.

Scene Two

*In the black, we hear the din of people chatting in a large room.
Lights up: four days later. An art gallery in London. A polished
wood floor and a white wall upon which "Jonathan Waxman" is
spelled out in display letters. It is after Jonathan's opening; plastic*

cups of wine are scattered about. Grete, an attractive, European New-Wave-looking young woman, arranges two Mies van der Rohe-style chairs and sets up a mini tape recorder on a table between them. Jonathan enters.

JONATHAN: Can we do this quickly?

GRETE: Yes. Please. Sit down.

JONATHAN: It's just I promised Antony—

GRETE *(While setting up her recorder)*: No, no, sit, let us start immediately.

JONATHAN *(Over "immediately")*: There's another reception for me in Hampstead, I really—

GRETE *(Over "Hampstead... ")*: I am ready. Please. We can begin.

She gestures for him to sit; he does. She takes a deep breath.

Now: First may I congratulate you, Mr. Waxman, on such a provocative exhibition.

JONATHAN: Thank you.

GRETE: It has been eagerly awaited and does not disappoint.

JONATHAN: Thank you very much. Can we get to the questions?

GRETE: Of course.

JONATHAN *(Overlap)*: I really don't have time to schmooze, I'm sorry.

GRETE: You were kind enough to agree to—

JONATHAN: Well . . .

GRETE: It is a thrill and an honor to finally meet—

JONATHAN: Thank you. Really, could we please—?

GRETE *(Takes out a stack of index cards)*: Forgive me, I have prepared some questions. . . . I will begin with the more important ones first.

JONATHAN: However you want to work it.

GRETE *(After a deep breath)*: Mr. Waxman.

JONATHAN: Yes.

GRETE: Your depictions of the emptiness and spiritual deadness of middle-class American life in the closing years of the twentieth century have earned you both accolades and admonishment in your own country. Your large, bold canvases of nude men and women who seem as alienated from one another as they do from their environment have been generating controversy in the art community in the United States for the better part of the last decade. They have also been commanding huge price tags in the art market. How do you reconcile the success of your work with its rather bleak subject matter?, and, b) do you think your work speaks as effectively to the rest of the world?, or, like a joke that loses something in translation, is its popularity purely an American phenomenon?

JONATHAN *(A beat)*:   Your English is very good.

GRETE: Thank you. I was a year at NYU.

JONATHAN: Ah. Now: Do I think my work is intrinsically American? Yes. Do I think that it's the equivalent of an inside joke that excludes the rest of the world? Definitely not. Whether the rest of the world *likes* it is another question. I'm not gonna worry too much about it. What was the first part of your question? How do I, what?, reconcile . . .

GRETE: . . . the success of your work with its rather bleak subject matter.

JONATHAN: Right. Well, I like to think that people are responding to good art. By good art I mean art that effectively tells the truth, effectively *reflects* the truth, and the truth is often rather bleak, so. . . . I mean, you're German, right?

GRETE: Yes . . .

JONATHAN: Germany's been way ahead of us on this. American art is just starting to get politicized again. Before AIDS, it was all about style and cleverness; we didn't know what to make art *about.* Your country, in Germany, you had guys like Beuys, and Kiefer, making art that terrified and revolted you. *Because they knew what they were making art in response to.*

GRETE: To . . . ?

JONATHAN: To the most horrible event of our time. Yeah, *that* old thing. They were dealing with a society that had literally gone to hell. They were looking for clues among the ashes, looking for answers.

GRETE: Yes, but is it not arguable that events such as America in Vietnam, America in Central America, the failure of the American civil rights movement, to name a few, should have been sufficiently powerful premises for making art during the last generation?

JONATHAN: Yeah, but we're talking about the Holocaust. The horror by which all other horrors are judged.

GRETE: Horror is horror, is it not? How can you say that one horror is more terrible than another? All societies are guilty of injustice—

JONATHAN: Whoa. Look, maybe we shouldn't get into this. Let's just talk about the work. Okay? Let's talk about the work.

GRETE: Very well.

JONATHAN: Um. . . . What was I gonna say? Oh, yeah. So anyway, I don't really see my work as bleak. I'm responding to situations that exist in American society that are bleak, maybe, but I'm presenting them in allegorical ways that I hope are provocative and entertaining, even. I mean, I don't set out by saying to myself, "I'm gonna make this really *bleak* painting of an interracial couple trying to make love in a vandalized cemetery." Bleak never comes into it. It's just an image. Just a story.

GRETE: I'm glad you brought up that painting. *Walpurgisnacht*, no? 1986. A very shocking painting. Some critics have suggested that the couple isn't making love but that the woman is being raped.

JONATHAN: That's what some critics have said, yes. They've accused me of being racist for showing a black man raping a white woman, but I say it's *their* problem 'cause *they're* the ones who can't fathom a naked black man on top of a naked white woman without calling it rape.

GRETE: Yes, I've read that explanation before. Some people have suggested that you were being disingenuous in your protestations.

JONATHAN: Some people would be wrong.

GRETE: But wouldn't you agree that the title, which means "Witches' Night," could easily mislead?

JONATHAN: No. If those people were to look beyond their own fears and knee-jerk attitudes toward miscegenation and actually look at the painting, they'd see that the lovers are in a Jewish cemetery that's been desecrated. Stones are toppled, spray-painted with swastikas. That's what the title refers to. I thought I was really hitting people over the head but I guess not. Everyone saw red and failed to see the painting. Just when things quieted down, *feminists* got on my case 'cause the man was on top of the woman!

A beat.

GRETE: While *Walpurgisnacht* is probably your most famous work—certainly it is your most controversial—and, fittingly, the centerpiece of this exhibition, the talk of the show here today seems to be a painting that to my knowledge has never before been shown.

JONATHAN: Yes.

GRETE: A student work. *The Beginning*, it is called.

JONATHAN: Uh-huh.

GRETE: Painted while you were in your early twenties.

JONATHAN: Yeah. I only recently came across it again. I'd figured it must've gotten lost or destroyed; student work is *supposed* to get lost or destroyed. But when I found it again, this thing I thought I'd lost, it was like a rush. Every painting I ever did suddenly made sense.

GRETE: Hm. It is the only painting from your personal collection, I see.

JONATHAN: Yes.

GRETE: A very curious painting, Mr. Waxman.

JONATHAN: Curious how?

GRETE: On the surface, it appears to be a fairly commonplace, rather youthful study of a seated figure.

JONATHAN (*Over "of a seated figure"*): Yeah, but you can't fault the painter for being young. The painting may not be brilliant, but it is inspired. I mean, I look at it and I feel the excitement and the, the *danger* of that day all over again.

GRETE: What was it about that day?

JONATHAN: I don't know, it was one of those days artists kill for. The kind we always hope we're waking up to, but which rarely comes to pass. I wish I knew what I'd had for breakfast that day or what shirt I was wearing or what I'd dreamed the night before. Burning leaves; I remember the room smelled of burning leaves. Whatever it was, something clicked that day. I was born. My life began. I started seeing things I'd never seen before.

GRETE: There *is* a kind of . . . *openness*, yes?, present in this painting that is virtually absent in your later work. The way the model *engages* the viewer, for instance. Her penetrating, unwavering eye contact. Nowhere else in your work does one find that kind of . . . connection.

JONATHAN *(A beat. She's right)*: Hm.

GRETE *(Rhetorically)*: I wonder about the model. Who *was* this woman? What role did *she* play? I wonder where she is today?

JONATHAN *(A beat)*: I have no idea.

Scene Three

The farmhouse. An hour before the start of Scene One. Patricia is sweeping the floor. Nick watches while preparing tea for the two of them. A long silence.

PATRICIA: We'll give him our bed.

He doesn't respond.

Nick?

NICK: Yes?

PATRICIA: We'll give him our bed. Alright?

NICK: Fine.

Pause.

PATRICIA: I'll *offer* it. How's that? I'll *offer* him the bedroom. It'll be up to him. Alright?

NICK: Alright.

PATRICIA: We can sleep on the futon down here. Don't you think?

Nick shrugs. A beat.

Don't you think it would be easier?

NICK: Fine.

PATRICIA: *Do* you? Do you think it would be easier?

NICK *(Over "would be easier")*: Fine. Whatever.

PATRICIA: *Tell* me.

NICK: Yes, I think it would be easier.

Pause.

PATRICIA: God, I should change the sheets. Don't you think?

NICK: Patricia . . .

PATRICIA: I really just changed them, should I bother to change them?

NICK: For one night?

PATRICIA: That's what *I* thought: It's only one night. No, I'm not going to change them.

NICK: Don't.

PATRICIA: We can get away with it. He doesn't have to know.

NICK: No.

PATRICIA: They're clean. Tomorrow I'll change them. When he leaves. In the morning.

NICK: Yes. Bright and early. When he leaves. In fifteen hours, eight of which will be spent sleeping. Come have tea.

Pause. She continues sweeping.

Patricia, come have your tea.

PATRICIA: Do you mind about the bed?

NICK: What do you mean?

PATRICIA: Do you mind about us giving him the bed?

NICK: Mind?

PATRICIA: I mean, don't you think it would be more comfortable? It's warmer in the bedroom. He'll be cold. Americans are always cold. *(Pause)* Nick? Do you mind about the bed.

NICK: Have your tea.

PATRICIA: *Do* you? Tell me.

Pause.

NICK: It's only for one night. *(A beat. He reminds her)* Tea.

She continues puttering.

We'll be fine downstairs. We'll light a fire. Warm it up. We've spent nights downstairs in front of the fire before. Right? Haven't we?

PATRICIA: What am I going to do with him?

NICK: What do you *mean* what are you going to do with him? You should have thought about that before.

PATRICIA *(Over "You should have . . . ")*: I mean it's been fifteen years. What am I going to *do* with him? What do I say?

NICK: Patricia. Really.

PATRICIA: This is foolish. Stupid. Let's go and leave a note.

NICK: Alright, love. Let's.

PATRICIA: "Called away suddenly."

NICK: Yes. Okay. "Dramatic findings in Cotswolds require our presence."

PATRICIA *(Laughs, then)*: What time is it?

NICK: Nearly half-past four.

PATRICIA: Damn. I've got to get to the butcher.

NICK: Have your tea. He's not bloody royalty, you know.

She puts on her coat.

Where are you going?

PATRICIA: To get a lamb roast.

NICK: Why don't I come *with* you?

PATRICIA: Someone has to be here.

NICK: You don't expect *me* to . . .

PATRICIA: I'll be right back.

NICK: *I* shouldn't be the one who . . .

PATRICIA: Please, Nick. Please.

NICK: Wait for him to get here.

PATRICIA: Nick . . .

NICK: No, take him with you. Show him the town. He'll be here any time.

PATRICIA: The butcher will be closed.

NICK: *I'll* go to the butcher, you stay.

PATRICIA: You won't know what to get.

NICK: A lamb roast, you said. Let *me* go. You can be here when he arrives. He's *your* friend.

PATRICIA: You're mad about the bed.

NICK: I am not mad about the bloody bed!

PATRICIA *(Over "the bloody bed")*: If you don't want him to have our bed, *tell* me! *Tell* me you don't want him to!

Pause.

NICK *(Simply)*: He has it already.

Pause.

PATRICIA: Why didn't you tell me not to invite him?

NICK: Me? Tell you? What do you mean?

PATRICIA *(Over "What do you mean")*: Why didn't you forbid me from seeing him again?

NICK: Forbid you? How, Patricia? How could I forbid you? *Why* would I? I wouldn't presume to forbid you to do anything.

PATRICIA: *Why. Why* wouldn't you.

They look at one another. Pause. She starts to exit.

NICK *(He calls)*: Patricia.

She stops and turns. Pause.

Come home soon?

Scene Four

*Fifteen years earlier. Spring. Late afternoon. Blinds drawn.
Jonathan's bedroom in his parents' house in Brooklyn, complete
with the artifacts of a lower-middle-class boyhood, the notable ex-
ception being a sewing machine. Wearing a vest, suit trousers and
socks, Jonathan is curled up on a bed. His hair is long. There is a
tentative knock. Patricia enters. A beat.*

PATRICIA *(Whispers)*: Jonathan? *(She waits, whispers again)*
Jonny?

*She looks around the room, gravitates toward the bookshelf and
begins scanning the titles. After a while, he sits up and sees her looking at a paperback.*

I love your little-boy handwriting. So round. The loopy *J* in
"Jonathan," the *o*, the *a*'s. "This book belongs to Jonathan
Waxman." *(Laughs, shows him the book) The Man from
U.N.C.L.E.* I wish I knew you then, Jonny. *(She returns the
book to the shelf and continues looking)*

JONATHAN: What are you doing?

PATRICIA: I love looking at people's books.

JONATHAN *(Still awaiting a response)*: Patty . . . ?

PATRICIA: It's like looking into their brain or something. Everything they ever knew. Everything they ever touched. It's like
archeology. Lets you into all the secret places.

JONATHAN: Patty, what are you doing here?

PATRICIA: Only took me two years to get in the front door. Hey,
not bad. —Why isn't *Franny and Zooey* at your place?

JONATHAN: It is. I have doubles.

PATRICIA: Oh.

Pause. They look at one another.

PATRICIA: You look handsome in your suit.

JONATHAN *(He begins to put on his shoes)*: Thanks.

PATRICIA: I don't think I've ever seen you in a suit. Have I? I must have. Did you wear a suit at graduation? No, you wore a cap and gown. What did you wear underneath it? Anything?

JONATHAN: What time is it?

PATRICIA: I don't know. *(A beat)* Your dad kissed me. When I came in? He kissed me. On the lips. He's very sweet, your dad. Said he was glad to see me, he was glad I came. See? He wasn't upset to see me. I told you you were overreacting. He's always kind of had a crush on me I think. *You* know the Waxman men and their shiksas. They're legend.

JONATHAN *(Fixing his shirt)*: I should go back down.

PATRICIA: No. Why? Stay.

She tries to touch his hair, he moves away.

(On his rebuff) So this is where you and Bobby grew up. *(She sits on a bed)*

JONATHAN: That's right . . .

PATRICIA: Funny, it's just how I pictured it. Like one of those Smithsonian recreations? *You* know: those roped-off rooms? "Jonathan Waxman's Bedroom in Brooklyn, Circa 1970." "The desk upon which he toiled over algebra." "The bed in which he had his first wet dream . . . "

JONATHAN: That one, actually.

PATRICIA *(She smiles; a beat)*: I loved the oil-painting bar mitzvah portraits of you and Bobby over the sofa by the way.

JONATHAN: What can I tell ya?

PATRICIA: Oh, they're great. *(A beat; she sees the incongruous sewing machine)* Sewing machine?

JONATHAN: She moved it in when I moved out.

PATRICIA: Ah.

JONATHAN: The only woman on record to die of empty-nest syndrome.

PATRICIA *(She goes to him and hugs him)*: Oh, Jonny, I'm sorry . . .

JONATHAN *(Trying to free himself)*: Yeah. You know, I really should go back down. My father . . .

They kiss, again and again; he's bothered as her kisses become more fervent.

JONATHAN *(Protesting)*: Patty. . . . Patricia . . .

She tries to undo his belt.

JONATHAN: Hey! What's the matter with you?

PATRICIA: Lie down.

JONATHAN: Patricia, my father is sitting shiva in the living room!

PATRICIA: Come on, Jonny . . .

JONATHAN: NO, I SAID! Are you crazy?! What the fuck is the matter with you?!

PATRICIA: You won't let me *do* anything for you.

JONATHAN: Is this supposed to cheer me up?!

PATRICIA: I want to *do* something.

JONATHAN: I don't want sex, Patricia.

PATRICIA: I've never known anyone who *died* before; tell me what I should do.

JONATHAN: This isn't *about* you. Do you understand that? This is *my* problem, *my* . . . loss, *mine*.

PATRICIA: But I'm your friend. Aren't I? I'm your lover, for God's sake. Two years, Jonathan . . .

JONATHAN *(Over "for God's sake . . . ")*: I thought we went *through* this . . .

PATRICIA: I want to be with you. I want to help you.

JONATHAN: You can't help me, Patty. I'm beyond help.

PATRICIA: Don't say that.

JONATHAN: It's true. I am beyond help right now. You can't help me. Your *blow* jobs can't help me.

PATRICIA: You don't know how I felt not being at the funeral.

JONATHAN: I'm sorry.

PATRICIA: No you're not. I was in agony. Really. I couldn't concentrate on anything all day. Knowing what you must've been going through? What kind of person do you think I am? I wanted to be with you so much.

JONATHAN: So you came over.

PATRICIA: You didn't say I couldn't. You said the funeral. I came over *after*.

JONATHAN: I meant the whole thing.

PATRICIA: What whole thing.

JONATHAN: The funeral, shiva.

PATRICIA: You mean I was supposed to keep away from you during all *this*?, like for a *week*?—isn't shiva like a week?

JONATHAN: Patty . . .

PATRICIA: Do you know how *ridiculous* this is? Don't you think you're taking this guilt thing a little too far? I mean, your mother is dead—I'm really really sorry, Jonny, really I am—and, okay, we know she wasn't exactly crazy about me . . .

JONATHAN: I'm so burnt out, Patty. . . . My head is . . .

PATRICIA *(Continuous)*: Not that I ever did anything to *offend* the woman personally or anything. I just happened to be born a certain persuasion, a certain incompatible persuasion, even though I'm an atheist and I don't give a damn *what* religion somebody happens to believe in. But did she even bother to get to know me, even a little bit?

JONATHAN: Oh, Patty, this is—

PATRICIA: It's like I was invisible. Do you know how it feels to be invisible?

JONATHAN: What do you think?, my mother's dying wish was keep that shiksa away from my funeral?! Come on, Patty! Grow up! Not everything is about *you*. I know that may be hard for you to believe, but not everything in the world—

PATRICIA *(Over "in the world")*: Oh, great.

JONATHAN *(A beat)*: Let's face it, Patricia, things haven't exactly been good between us for months.

PATRICIA: What do you mean? Your mother's been *sick* for months. How can you make a statement like that?

JONATHAN: What, this is a surprise to you what I'm saying?

PATRICIA: Hasn't your mother been dying for months.

JONATHAN: I don't really have the strength for this right now.

PATRICIA: Hasn't she? So how can you judge how things have been between us? Her dying has been weighing over us, over both of us, for so long, it's colored so much . . .

JONATHAN *(Over "it's colored so much")*: Look . . . if you *must* know—

PATRICIA: What.

JONATHAN: If you *must* know . . . *(A beat) I* was the one who didn't want you there. It wasn't out of respect to my mother or my father or my grandmother, it was me. I didn't want to see you. I didn't want you there, Patty. I didn't want to have to hold *your* hand and comfort *you* because of how cruel my mother was to you, I didn't want that. . . . I didn't want to have to deal with your display of—

PATRICIA: *Display?*

JONATHAN: Your display of love for me. Your concern. It was all about *you* whenever I thought about how it would be if you were with me! I didn't want you there, Patty. I'm sorry. *(A beat)* I guess when something catastrophic like this happens . . . you get to thinking.

PATRICIA: Yes? Well?

Pause.

JONATHAN: I don't love you, Patty.

He smiles lamely and reaches for her as if to soothe her as she goes to get her bag. She groans, lashes out at his arm with a single punch, and goes. He stands alone for a long time before moving slowly over to the sewing machine. He clutches a pillow and gently rocks himself. As he begins to cry, the lights fade to black.

ACT TWO

Scene Five

Lights up: the farmhouse. A few hours after the end of Scene One. Patricia and Jonathan are seated at the table after dinner. Nick is standing nearby, looking through the exhibition catalogue. The wine is nearly finished; they are all somewhat disinhibited.

JONATHAN: Drive down with me tomorrow.

PATRICIA: I don't *go* to London, I try to *avoid* London.

JONATHAN *(Over "avoid London")*: You can take the train back Tuesday night, after the opening.

PATRICIA *(Over "after the opening")*: The crowds, tourists, everything so bloody expensive.

JONATHAN: Don't worry about money; everything is on me.

PATRICIA: Why should everything be on you? I don't want everything to be on you.

JONATHAN *(Over "I don't want everything . . . ")*: What, you think I'd invite you down and make you pay for it?

PATRICIA: God, Jonathan . . .

JONATHAN: Let me treat you to a couple of days in London!

PATRICIA: You sound like such an American!

JONATHAN: Come on, we'll hang out for a couple of days, it'll be fun.

PATRICIA: What are you talking about?

JONATHAN: We'll do the museums, you'll come to the opening, I'll introduce you to people . . .

PATRICIA: I don't need to meet people, I know enough people.

JONATHAN *(Over "enough people")*: I mean artists. Writers, actors. You wouldn't believe the people coming.

PATRICIA: Uh-huh.

JONATHAN: Hey, I'll take you to Caprice.

PATRICIA: Is that a restaurant?

JONATHAN: *Yes*, it's a restaurant.

PATRICIA: I *told* you, your name-droppings are wasted on me.

JONATHAN: Patty, let me do this. I want you to be my *guests*, both of you.

PATRICIA: Well, I don't know about Nick; he *completely* falls apart in London, don't you, Nick.

NICK: Hm?

PATRICIA *(Continuing, to Jonathan)*: That's never any fun, holding his hand as we brave the crush on the pavement. Besides, he couldn't get away.

JONATHAN: Then *you* come.

PATRICIA: No. I couldn't. What are you saying? I don't like big cities anymore either, they get me nervous. I don't even remember the last time I was there.

JONATHAN: Then you're due for a visit. It's really changed, London. Even in the five or six years since I was last over.

PATRICIA: You were here? Five or six years ago?

JONATHAN: Yeah, just a . . . quick thing, *you* know. Passing through.

PATRICIA: Uh-huh. *(A beat)* I know: must have been a year ago Christmas. Whenever my mother comes, she drags me to every bit of crap on the West End; Lloyd Webber's latest ditty. Do you know what they get for that slop?

JONATHAN: Patty.

PATRICIA: I can't just take off and go; some of us have to *work* for a living, you know.

JONATHAN: Oh, well! Excuse *me*!

PATRICIA *(Over "Excuse me")*: I have data to collect. I have responsibilities, people who count on me; I can't just come and go as I please.

JONATHAN: I'm not asking you to quit your job and run away with me. Two or three days!

PATRICIA: Two or *three*? A minute ago it was a couple.

JONATHAN: Patty...

PATRICIA: I can't get away. This is a very exciting time for us. Has Nick told you about the project?

JONATHAN: A Roman latrine?

PATRICIA: Is that all he told you? Nick! *Tell* Jonathan.

NICK: What.

PATRICIA: About the project. *(To Jonathan)* He loves to minimize.

Jonathan nods.

(To Nick) Tell him what you found.

NICK: Patricia...

PATRICIA: Oh, you! *(To Jonathan)* He's impossibly modest. Nick found, not only the latrine, but a late-medieval rubbish pit.

JONATHAN: A garbage dump?

PATRICIA: Yes!

NICK: *I* didn't find it, Patricia, we *all* found it...

PATRICIA: Do you have any idea what a valuable find that is, medieval rubbish? Seriously. Shoes, rags, broken plates. It was one of those happy accidents and Nick led us to it.

NICK: I *didn't*. I wish you wouldn't...

PATRICIA: Everything you need to know about a culture is in its rubbish, really. What they wore, what they ate. It's a treasure trove. Tons of it. I sift through parcels of ancient rubbish every day, analyze it, catalogue it. That's what I do. Every day. Now you know. I shouldn't have told you.

JONATHAN: Why not?

PATRICIA: Sounds fascinating.

JONATHAN: No, it does.

She gives him a look. He laughs.

It does. Come to my opening.

PATRICIA: Stop it.

NICK: Um . . .

They look at him. A beat.

(Referring to the catalogue) I'm looking at your paintings . . .

JONATHAN: Yes . . . ?

NICK: And, honestly . . . I don't get it.

JONATHAN: What don't you get?

NICK: I don't get. . . . What's all the fuss about?

JONATHAN: What fuss?

PATRICIA: Oh, Nick. Be nice.

NICK: You're supposed to be something of an iconoclast, aren't you?

JONATHAN: An "iconoclast"?

NICK: I mean, is this all it takes to set the art world ablaze?

PATRICIA: Nick's idea of art is the Mona Lisa.

NICK: My idea of art, in point of fact, Patricia, begins and ends with the Renaissance. Everything before it was ceremonial, arts and crafts—hardly "art," really; everything since, well, everything since has been utter rubbish.

JONATHAN: Are you kidding? How can you say that? *(To Patricia)* All of modern art, he's dismissing just like that?

NICK *(Over "just like that")*: But it's all been done, hasn't it. The so-called modern age, as far as I can tell, has been one long, elaborate exercise, albeit a futile one, to reinvent what had already been perfected by a handful of Italians centuries ago.

JONATHAN: But the world is constantly reinventing *itself.* How can you say that Leonardo's world-view expresses *our* world, or Picasso's even?

NICK: Picasso. Now *there* was an energetic little bloke.

JONATHAN: Am I supposed to shrink in the shadow of the great masters and pack it all in? Say the hell with it, why bother?

NICK: If you had any sense? Yes.

Patricia giggles naughtily.

Absolutely. Why bother, indeed? *(To Patricia)* How is it that all the artists I've ever known feel that what they do is so vital to society?

She laughs some more.

Does it ever occur to them that if they were wiped off the face of the earth the planet would survive intact?

JONATHAN *(To Patricia)*: Gee, you didn't tell me you'd married such an art lover.

NICK: Art was devised as a celebration of beauty, was it not. I mean, does *this* celebrate beauty? *(Waving the catalogue)* This, this . . . pornography?

PATRICIA: Nick!

JONATHAN *(Smiling, to Patricia)*: That's okay.

NICK *(Over "That's okay")*: Because as far as I can tell that's precisely what this is. And not very *good* pornography at that.

JONATHAN: Really. Well.

PATRICIA: Nick was raised by a puritanical mother.

NICK: *Fuck* that, Patricia. I look at this . . . "art" and I see pornography. Tell me what's there that eludes me.

JONATHAN: I'm not gonna *tell* you what to see. If you see pornography . . .

NICK: I don't *get* it, is what I'm saying. If I don't get it, is it my failure or yours? Enlighten me. Help me see.

JONATHAN: You know, you usually don't have the luxury of painters whispering in your ear when you're looking at their paintings, telling you what to see. That's not the job of the artist. The job of the artist is not to spell everything out. *You* have to participate.

NICK: Participate.

JONATHAN: Yes. You play an active role in all this; it's not just me, it's not just the artist.

NICK: Alright . . . what's this, then? *(Flips the catalogue to a particular painting)*

JONATHAN: You can't judge the work like *that*, black-and-white reproductions in a catalogue . . .

NICK *(Over "in a catalogue")*: What is this if not pornography?

JONATHAN: Come on, Nick, use your head a little. What do you see?

NICK: You actually want me to tell you?

JONATHAN: Yeah. Describe to me what you see.

NICK: Alright. I see what *appears* to be a painting—

JONATHAN: Oh, man . . .

NICK *(Continuous)*: —executed with minimal skill in terms of knowledge of basic anatomy—

JONATHAN: You really have to see the *painting* . . .

NICK *(Continuous)*: —of what *appears* to be a couple of mixed race fornicating in what *appears* to be a cemetery, is it?

JONATHAN: Don't be so literal! Yes, that's what it appears to be on the surface, but what's it really saying?

PATRICIA: Let me see.

Nick shows it to her.

JONATHAN *(Continuous)*: What's going on there? It's an allegory, it's telling a story. Use your imagination!

PATRICIA: The woman is being raped.

JONATHAN: Ah ha. Is she?

PATRICIA: Well, yes, look at her hands. They're fists.

NICK: They aren't necessarily fists; they're just poorly drawn hands.

JONATHAN: Jesus.

NICK: That's what I mean by the apparent disregard for basic traditions in art like knowing the skeletal structure of the human hand.

JONATHAN: But you know what hands look like.

NICK: What?! Is that your response?, I *know* what hands . . . ?

JONATHAN: What I'm saying is, it's not my job to photographically recreate the skeletal structure of the human hand.

NICK: What *is* your job? You keep talking about what isn't your job; what *is* your job? Is it your job to paint well, or not?

JONATHAN: What do you mean by "paint well"? You obviously have very limited ideas about painting. I'm telling you, if you guys came down to London, I'll take you around, we'll look at art, I could *show* you . . .

NICK: If one were to *buy* one of these . . . paintings—presuming, of course, one could afford to—where would one put it?

JONATHAN: What?

NICK: I mean, they're quite large, aren't they.

JONATHAN: Fairly.

NICK: One would have to have quite a large wall on which to hang such a painting and, preferably, an even larger room in which to view it properly. (Art *is* meant to be seen, no?) And that room would undoubtedly have to sit in an even more capacious house. Not your standard taxpayer, I take it.

JONATHAN: No.

NICK: Say *I* wanted to buy one of these.

JONATHAN: You? One of those?

NICK: Mm. What would I do?

JONATHAN: Well, for starters, you couldn't; they're already sold.

NICK: *All* of them?

PATRICIA *(Leafing through the catalogue; sotto voce)*: "Saatchi Collection," "Union Carbide Collection," "Mobil Corporation Collection . . . "

JONATHAN: All of the existing ones, yes.

NICK: The "existing" ones?

JONATHAN: Yes. And there's a waiting list for the paintings I have yet to paint.

PATRICIA: A waiting list? You're joking.

JONATHAN: No.

NICK: You mean there are people on Park Avenue or in Tokyo, who have walls in their living rooms especially reserved for the latest Waxman, Number 238?

JONATHAN: Yeah.

NICK: It doesn't matter which painting, as long as they get their Waxman?

JONATHAN: It's not like this is new, you know; artists have always lived off of commissions.

NICK: So, wait, these art lovers, these poor, unsuspecting—rather, *rich*, unsuspecting—patrons of the arts have bought, sight unseen, a painting you have not yet painted?

JONATHAN: Yes.

PATRICIA: Amazing, Jonny. Pre-sold art.

NICK: What happens if they don't like it?

JONATHAN: What?

NICK: The painting. Say it doesn't please them. The colors clash with the carpet; the image makes madam blush. What then? Are they entitled to a refund? Can they hold out for the next one off the line?

JONATHAN: If they really dislike it, I guess, but it hasn't happened.

NICK: So how many can you expect to do in a year?

JONATHAN: One every five or six weeks? Figure ten a year.

NICK: Ten a year. At roughly a quarter million dollars per painting . . .

JONATHAN *(Over "per painting")*: Now, wait a minute. What is this fascination with my finances? Ever since I got here you've been hocking me . . .

NICK *(Over "Ever since I got here . . . ")*: Patricia, are you aware of how fortunate we are to be the proud owners of our own, actual, *already painted* painting by Jonathan Waxman? And a seminal Waxman at that!

JONATHAN: Look, why should I have to *apologize* for my success?

PATRICIA: Nobody's asking you to.

JONATHAN *(Continuous)*: What am I supposed to do? Reject the money? Lower my price? What would *that* accomplish? Would it make me a better artist if I were hungry again?

NICK: I don't know. Would it?

PATRICIA *(A beat; looking at the catalogue)*: They *do* look like fists, Jonathan.

JONATHAN: What if they are fists? What difference does it make?

PATRICIA: It makes a very big difference. It changes everything. If they're fists, then that suggests that she's being taken against her will. If they're not. . . . Is the painting about a black man raping a white woman, or is it about a couple screwing in a cemetery?

JONATHAN: Oh. You're saying it's ambiguous.

PATRICIA: I'm saying it's confusing. You can't have intended both things.

JONATHAN: Why not? I've got you thinking about it haven't I?

NICK: But thinking about what? What does it *mean*? If *you* can't say, unequivocally . . .

PATRICIA *(To Jonathan)*: He has a point. It's all about shock, then. Effect. You can't *mean* "What difference does it make," Jonathan, that just isn't good enough.

JONATHAN *(Over "isn't good enough")*: You know I don't entirely mean that. I mean, *my* intention is irrelevant; it's all about what you make of it.

NICK: Either way you look at it, it has about as much impact as a smutty photo in a porno mag.

A beat.

JONATHAN: You can't get past the flesh, can you.

NICK: What.

JONATHAN: This is very interesting. All you see is the flesh. Of course! You surround yourself with bones all day. I mean, here you are, freezing your asses off—

PATRICIA: Jonathan . . .

JONATHAN *(Continuous)*: —cataloguing bones whose flesh rotted away centuries ago. No wonder my paintings scare you!

NICK: Scare me, did you say?

JONATHAN: Yes. They're . . . voluptuous, dangerous. They deal with unspeakable things, fleshy things. *That's* what's going on in my paintings. The lengths people go to, living people go to, in order to feel something. Now. Today.

Pause.

PATRICIA: We thought we'd put you in our bedroom.

JONATHAN: What?

PATRICIA: We thought we'd put you . . .

JONATHAN: In *your* room? No, you don't have to do that.

PATRICIA: No bother.

JONATHAN: Where are *you* gonna sleep?

PATRICIA: Down here.

JONATHAN: No no, I'll sleep down here.

PATRICIA: The bedroom is actually warmer.

JONATHAN: I don't mind.

NICK: Are you sure?

JONATHAN: Yeah.

PATRICIA: No, trust me, the bedroom, it's really no problem.

NICK *(Over "no problem")*: Patricia, he said he doesn't mind.

JONATHAN: I don't.

NICK: See? *(To Jonathan)* Yes, why *don't* you stay downstairs?

JONATHAN: Fine.

PATRICIA: But the electric *blanket* is upstairs. He's going to need the electric blanket.

JONATHAN *(Over "electric blanket")*: Don't worry about me.

NICK: I'll bring it down.

PATRICIA: The mattress-warmer, actually. It's under the sheet. You'll have to strip the bed. It really would be easier . . .

NICK *(Over "easier")*: So I'll strip the bed. The bed needs stripping anyway.

PATRICIA *(A beat; to Nick)*: Are you sure?

NICK: Yes. I'll take care of it. Leave it to me.

JONATHAN: Thank you.

Nick goes. Pause.

I hope I'm not . . .

PATRICIA: You hope you're not what?

JONATHAN: I don't know, it seems that my being here . . .

PATRICIA: Yes?

JONATHAN: *You* know. . . . Things seem a little, I don't know . . . prickly, maybe? I mean with Nick?

PATRICIA: I haven't seen this much life in him in years.

JONATHAN: Really.

Pause.

PATRICIA: I married Nick to stay in England.

JONATHAN *(A beat)*: Oh.

PATRICIA: They would've deported me. After my degree.

JONATHAN: Ah.

PATRICIA: My visa, *you* know, it was a student visa. It expired. I couldn't go home. How could I go home? Back to my broken-down mother? I couldn't. My skeptical father, who humored me through all my crazy pursuits? I had no one to go home to. No, this made sense. I found that I could survive here. I had to stay.

JONATHAN *(A beat)*: Does he know?

PATRICIA: I'm sure he does. You mean why . . . ?

Jonathan nods.

I'm sure he knows. It was certainly no secret. He knew I needed a way to stay.

JONATHAN: I don't understand you. How can you be so cool about this?

PATRICIA: What?

JONATHAN: The man is obviously crazy about you; he's like a blushing *schoolboy* around you . . .

PATRICIA: I know.

JONATHAN: How can you do this? I never thought you'd be *capable* of something like this. You were such a passionate girl, Patty . . .

PATRICIA: Oh, God, spare me . . .

JONATHAN: You were the "student of the world"! Remember? No, really, how do you. . . . I mean, passion, sex, love. . . . You just decided, what, you don't need those things anymore?, you just shut that part of you all out?

PATRICIA: Yes. Exactly. My "passion" nearly did me in, now, didn't it.

JONATHAN: Oh, come on, don't lay this on me. That's bullshit. You call yourself an expatriate? You're no expatriate, you're just hiding!

PATRICIA: Who the hell are *you* to judge—?!

JONATHAN: Why do you live with him?

PATRICIA: Why? He's my husband.

JONATHAN: That's not a reason. Why do you live with him if you don't love him?

PATRICIA: Who said I don't love him?

JONATHAN: You just said yourself, you married Nick . . .

PATRICIA: *This is the best I can do!*

Pause.

JONATHAN: Don't say that. It isn't even true. I know you too well.

PATRICIA: *Knew* me. You *knew* me. You don't *know* who I am.

A beat. Nick appears with a bundle of bedding. They look at him. Pause.

NICK: Um. . . . Shall I. . . . Would you like me to make your bed?

Scene Six

The gallery in London. This scene is the continuation of Scene Two.

GRETE: You just said your definition of good art is "art which effectively reflects the truth." Do you think it is your responsibility as an artist to always tell the truth?

JONATHAN: In my work? Yes.

GRETE: And in your personal life?

JONATHAN: My personal life is my personal life. Look, if my work tells the truth, then I think people are compelled, they *have* to deal with it, they can't not. I like to shake 'em up a little, I admit it. People see my stuff at a gallery, a museum, and the work *competes* for their attention. They're preoccupied, overstimulated. All I can hope is maybe—*maybe*—one night, one of my images'll find its way into their unconscious and

color their dreams. Who knows? Maybe it'll change their perception of something forever. I mean, in art, as in life, we tend
to affect people in ways we can't always see. You can't possibly
know what that other person has taken away with her. *(A beat)*
You can't see it. And just 'cause you can't see it doesn't mean it
didn't happen.

GRETE: Hm. Getting back to "good art . . . "

JONATHAN: Okay, let me ask you something: When *we* talk about
good art, what are we talking about? Stuff we like? Stuff our
friends make? We're talking about value judgments. Most people, do you think most people, most Americans—my *father*—
do you think most people have any idea what makes good art?

GRETE: Hm.

JONATHAN: The little old lady who paints flowers and pussycats
at the YMCA—and *dazzles* her friends, I'm sure—I mean,
does that little old lady make good art? I mean, why not?, her
cat looks just *like* that. I'm not putting her down; I think it's
great she's got a hobby. But is what she does good art? See,
most people . . . I remember, years ago, the big van Gogh show
at the Met?, in New York? The place was packed. Like Yankee
Stadium. Buses emptied out from all over; Jersey, Westchester.
All kinds of people. The masses. Average middle-class people.
Like they were coming into the city for a matinee and lunch at
Mamma Leone's. Only this was Art. Art with a capital A had
come to the shopping-mall generation and Vincent was the
chosen icon. Now, I have nothing against van Gogh. Better
him than people lining up to see the kids with the big eyes. But
as I braved that exhibit—and it was rough going, believe me—
I couldn't help but think of Kirk Douglas. Kirk Douglas
should've gotten a cut of the house.

A beat.

See, there's this Hollywood packaging of the artist that gets
me. The packaging of the mystique. Poor, tragic Vincent: He
cut off his ear 'cause he was so misunderstood but still he
painted all these pretty pictures. So ten bodies deep they lined

up in front of the paintings. More out of solidarity for Vincent (or Kirk) than out of any kind of love or passion for "good art." Hell, some art lovers were in such a hurry to get to the post-cards and prints and souvenir place mats, they strode past the paintings and skipped the show entirely! Who can blame them? You couldn't *experience* the paintings anyway, not like that. You couldn't *see anything.* The art was just a backdrop for the *real* show that was happening. In the gift shop!

GRETE: Hm.

JONATHAN: Now, you got to admit there's something really strange about all this, this kind of *frenzy* for art. I mean, what is this thing called art? What's it for? Why have people histori-cally drunk themselves to death over the creation of it, or been thrown in jail, or whatever? I mean, how does it serve the masses? *Can* it serve the—I ask myself these questions all the time. Every painting I do is another attempt to come up with some answers. The people who crowded the Met to look at sunflowers, I mean, why *did* they? 'Cause they *thought* they should. 'Cause they thought they were somehow enriching their lives. Why? *'Cause the media told them so!*

GRETE: You seem to have such contempt—

JONATHAN: Not contempt; you're confusing criticism with contempt.

GRETE *(Continuous)*: —for the very same people and the very same system that has made you what you are today.

JONATHAN: What I am today? What *am* I today? I just got here. People like *you* suddenly care what I have to say.

GRETE: I *do* care.

JONATHAN: I know you do. It cracks me up that you do; it amuses me. You know, up till like eight or nine years ago, let's not forget, I was painting *apartments* for a living. Apartments. Walls. Rooms. I was good at it, too. I'd lose myself all day while I painted moldings, then I'd go home and do my *own* painting all night. A good, simple, hardworking life. Then, like I said, like nine years ago, my world started getting bigger. I couldn't even retrace the steps; I can't remember how it happened. All I know is I met certain people and got a gallery and a show and the public started to discover my work. The night of my first opening, it's like these strangers witnessed a birth, like the work had no life before they laid eyes on it. We know that's ridiculous, of course, but this is what happens when you take your art out of your little room and present it to the public: It's not yours anymore, it's *theirs*, theirs to see with their own eyes. And, for each person who sees your work for the first time, you're discovered all over again. That begins to take its toll. You can't be everybody's discovery. That gets to be very demanding. Who *are* these people who are suddenly throwing money at you and telling you how wonderful and talented you are? What do *they* know? You begin to believe them. They begin to want things from you. They begin to expect things. The work loses its importance; the importance is on "Waxman."

GRETE: Would you prefer to have remained an outsider?

JONATHAN: Preferred? No. It's cold and lonely on the outside.

GRETE: And yet being cozy on the inside—

JONATHAN: "Cozy"?

GRETE *(Continuous)*: —seems to make you uncomfortable as well. Is this not an illustration of that Jewish joke?

JONATHAN: What Jewish joke?

GRETE: Forgive my paraphrase: not wanting to be a member of a club that would also have you as a member?

JONATHAN: That's not a Jewish joke, that's Groucho Marx.

GRETE: Groucho Marx, then. Is he not Jewish?

JONATHAN: Yeah, so?

GRETE: Well, does not that joke apply to the problem Jews face in the twentieth century?

JONATHAN: What problem is that?

GRETE: The problem of being on the inside while choosing to see themselves as outsiders?—

JONATHAN: Is that a Jewish problem?

GRETE *(Continuous)*: —even when they are very much on the inside?

JONATHAN: "Very much on the inside"? What is this?

GRETE *(Over "What is this")*: Perhaps I am not expressing my-self well.

JONATHAN: No, I think you're probably expressing yourself *very* well.

GRETE: All I am suggesting, Mr. Waxman, is that the artist, like the Jew, prefers to see himself as alien from the mainstream culture. For the Jewish *artist* to acknowledge that the *contrary* is true, that he is *not* alien, but rather, *assimilated* into that mainstream culture—

JONATHAN *(Over "mainstream culture")*: Wait a minute wait a minute. What is this *Jewish* stuff creeping in here?

GRETE: You are a Jew, are you not?

JONATHAN: I don't see what that—

GRETE *(Over "what that")*: *Are* you?

JONATHAN: Yeah; so?

GRETE: I am interested in the relationship between the artist and the Jew, as Jonathan Waxman sees it.

JONATHAN: Who *cares* how Jonathan Waxman sees it? I'm an *American* painter. *American* is the adjective, not *Jewish, American*.

GRETE: Yes, but your work calls attention to it.

JONATHAN: How?

GRETE: The Jewish cemetery in *Walpurgisnacht*—

JONATHAN: *One* painting.

GRETE: One *important* painting—the depictions of middle- class life, obviously Jewish—

JONATHAN: How can you say that? "Obviously" Jewish.

GRETE: I have studied your paintings, I have done research on your upbringing—

JONATHAN: Oh, yeah?

GRETE *(Continuous)*: —I have written many critical studies for art journals in my country. The middle-class life you ex-plore—. It is safe to say that your paintings are autobiographi-cal, are they not?

JONATHAN: In what sense? Of course they're autobiographical in the sense that they come from *me*, they spring from *my* imagination, but to say that the subjects of my paintings are *Jewish* subjects, because a Jew happened to paint them, that's totally absurd!

GRETE: Mr. Waxman, I cannot tell to what you have most taken offense: the suggestion that was made, or that it was made by a German.

JONATHAN *(A beat)*: Look, maybe we should . . .

GRETE: Please, just one more question . . .

JONATHAN: Can we please move on? Let's move on.

GRETE: Of course. *(A beat)* Mr. Waxman, you speak with charming self-effacement about your much-celebrated career. You say you are amused by your sudden fame—

JONATHAN: Yes.

GRETE *(Continuous)*: —and seem to view it as an unwanted but not unwelcome bonus, that making good art is all you have ever wanted to do.

JONATHAN: Yes.

GRETE: And yet—forgive me, Mr. Waxman—I am confused. If, as you claim, you had no interest in celebrity, why would you hire a public relations firm?

JONATHAN: This is how you change the subject?

GRETE: There have been whispers, Mr. Waxman. *(She says "vispers")* Why would you hire a publicist if—

JONATHAN: You think I'm the only painter who has a publicist? This is the reality. You reach a certain point in your career, an *artist* reaches a certain point, where he achieves a certain amount of recognition—

GRETE: Yes, I know, you said. I do not question that.

JONATHAN: Will you let me finish please? If you're gonna make a statement like that—

GRETE: I am sorry.

JONATHAN *(Continuous)*: —then at least let me make my point.

GRETE: Please.

JONATHAN: An artist who's achieved a certain amount of celebrity, very quickly, there are suddenly all these demands being placed on him. I've talked about that.

317

GRETE: Yes.

JONATHAN: People want you. Interviews, parties, schools. The problem becomes *time*. Where do you find the time to work?, to do the thing that made you famous? This is where having a publicist comes in. The publicist helps manage your social obligations. And if the painter doesn't have one, the gallery does, so what's the big deal?

GRETE: No, no, I understand. Perhaps I did not phrase my question correctly.

JONATHAN: Cut the crap, Miss; your English is impeccable.

GRETE: Mr. Waxman, the whispers I have heard . . .

JONATHAN: Again with the "vispers"!

GRETE: Is it true that you hired a public relations firm *two years before* your first success—

JONATHAN: Oh, come on. What is this, the Inquisition? Art is a business, you know that.

GRETE: Two years *before*, to promote your standing in the art community—

JONATHAN: My "standing"—?

GRETE *(Continuous)*: —more importantly, in the art-buying community.

JONATHAN: What are you saying?, I bought my career? I bought my reputation?, what?

GRETE: Mr. Waxman . . .

JONATHAN *(Continuous)*: What about the work? Why aren't we talking about the work? Why must it always come down to business? Huh? *I'm* not doing it, and yet you accuse *me* . . .

GRETE *(Over "and yet you accuse me")*: *Is* it true or is it *not* true?

JONATHAN: That's irrelevant. True or not true, who cares?

GRETE *(Over "who cares")*: It *is* relevant.

JONATHAN: How? How?

GRETE: It is relevant if you espouse to be a visionary of truth.

JONATHAN *(Over "visionary of truth")*: I espouse nothing! What do I espouse? I paint pictures! You're the one who comes up with these fancy labels, people like *you*!

GRETE *(Over "people like you")*: How can you talk about truth?

318

Mr. Waxman, how can you talk about truth when your own
sense of morality—

JONATHAN: What do *you* know about morality?

GRETE *(Continuous)*: —when your own sense of morality is so
compromised and so—

JONATHAN: Huh? What do *you* know with your sneaky little
Jew-baiting comments.

GRETE: I beg your pardon.

JONATHAN: Don't give me this innocence shit. You know exactly
what I'm talking about.

GRETE *(Over "what I'm talking about")*: No, I am sorry, I have no
idea.

JONATHAN: You think I haven't picked up on it? Huh? You think
I don't know what this is all about?

GRETE: Mr. Waxman, this is all in your imagination.

JONATHAN: My imagination?! I'm imagining this?! I'm imagining you've been attacking me from the word go?

GRETE: Mr. Waxman!

JONATHAN: You have, Miss, don't deny it. You expect me to sit
here another minute? What do you take me for? Huh? What
the fuck do you take me for? *(He abruptly goes)*

GRETE: Mr. Waxman . . .

*Pause. She presses a button on the tape recorder. We hear the tape
rewind.*

Scene Seven

*The farmhouse. A few hours after the end of Scene Five. The mid-
dle of the night. Jonathan, bag packed, his coat on, tears a sheet of
paper out of his sketchbook, turns off the tea kettle before its whistle
fully sounds and prepares a cup of tea. The painting, wrapped in
newspaper, leans against the kitchen table. He takes six fifty-pound
notes out of his wallet and leaves them under the honey pot on the
kitchen table. Nick has quietly come downstairs and lingers in the*

darkness. He emerges from the shadows. Jonathan is startled when he sees him and spills his tea.

JONATHAN: Oh. Shit. Hi.

NICK: Sorry.

JONATHAN: I didn't see you.

NICK: My fault. *(A beat)* Are you alright?

JONATHAN: A little wet; I'm alright.

NICK *(A beat)*: Couldn't sleep.

JONATHAN: No.

NICK: I mean *I* couldn't.

JONATHAN: Oh. Me, neither.

NICK: Was the futon . . . ?

JONATHAN: No, it's fine. Did the kettle—? I'm sorry if the whistle . . .

NICK: No. *(A beat)* Shall I get the fire going again?

JONATHAN: No, you don't have to do that, I could've done that. No, I think I'll just head back early.

NICK: Oh. I see.

JONATHAN: Yeah, I think I'll, *you* know . . .

NICK: Back to London.

JONATHAN: Yeah.

NICK: Hm. *(A beat)* You won't even wait until breakfast?

JONATHAN: No, I'd better not.

NICK: Patricia will be disappointed.

JONATHAN: Yeah, I'm sorry about that.

NICK: She had planned something, I think. Breakfast.

JONATHAN: Oh, that's too bad.

NICK *(A beat)*: So you won't get to see the dig.

JONATHAN: I guess not.

NICK: I was going to take you.

JONATHAN: Next time.

NICK: Yes. Next time.

JONATHAN *(A beat)*: It's just, I've got so much to do when I get back.

NICK *(Nods; a beat)*: Did *I* . . . ? Was *I* . . . ? I mean I hope I wasn't too . . . *(A beat)* You weren't . . . sneaking out, were you?

JONATHAN: Sneaking—? No. No, I just thought I'd get an early start.

NICK: It's half-past three. You'll be in London before seven. That's quite an early start you're getting.

JONATHAN: I couldn't sleep. I thought I might as well hit the road.

NICK: I see. Well. Patricia will be so disappointed. *(A beat)* You weren't sneaking out on Patricia.

JONATHAN: No. Of course not. I was gonna leave her a note.

NICK: I'll give it to her.

JONATHAN: I haven't written it yet.

NICK: Oh.

JONATHAN: I was just gonna sit down and write it.

NICK: Please. Carry on.

Jonathan sits. Pause.

What were you going to *say?*

JONATHAN: Hm?

NICK: In this note. What were you going to say?

JONATHAN: I'm not sure.

NICK: What were you going to tell her? That would be difficult. Finding the right words. Patricia will be *so* disappointed. She was so looking forward to breakfast. I don't know what she'll do. I might have to comfort her. *(A beat)* She doesn't sleep with me, you know.

JONATHAN: Oh.

NICK: Not that I was ever her type. There was a certain challenge to be found in that. I thought she would never, not with me. She was so . . . *attractive*, you know, so confident, so American. The first time she slept with me I thought it must have been because I was her supervisor. I'm sure that was why. When it happened a second time, well, I didn't know *what* to think; I chose to think there was hope. Yes, I opted for hope. In a moment of uncharacteristic brazenness, I asked her to marry me. She accepted. I don't know why. I have my suspicions. *(A beat)* From time to time, I'll fortify myself with stout and kiss her neck, feel her tit, lay with my head there.

JONATHAN: Nick.

NICK: Sometimes she'll let me. She'll even stroke my hair. Once she kissed my head. I wanted to reach up and kiss her mouth, but why get greedy and piss her off?

JONATHAN: Why don't you go back to bed?

NICK: Some nights she'd respond—oh, she'd respond, or initiate even—and I would rush into it foolishly, trying not to feel I was somehow being rewarded. I take what I can get; I'm English. *(A beat)* She succumbed to my charms tonight, though. Tonight she acquiesced. Did you hear us?

Jonathan shakes his head; he's lying.

Oh. What a shame. It was brilliant. *(A beat. He sees the money)* What's this?

JONATHAN: What.

NICK: Under the honey pot. Money is it? A gratuity? Leaving a gratuity?

JONATHAN: No. Just a little cash.

NICK: A little cash? This is three hundred pounds. Why are you leaving three hundred pounds?

JONATHAN: I thought . . .

NICK: What.

JONATHAN: I thought it could be useful.

NICK: Useful? Of course it could be useful. Money is always useful. Why are you leaving three hundred pounds?

JONATHAN: I thought I could help you out.

NICK: Me?

JONATHAN: You and Patricia.

NICK: With three hundred pounds?

JONATHAN: Yeah. I happened to have a lot of cash on me, I thought I . . .

NICK *(Over "I thought I")*: You thought you could help us out, unload some cash—

JONATHAN: You know what I mean.

NICK *(Continuous)*: —lend us a hand, by leaving three hundred pounds.

JONATHAN: I wanted to say thank you.

NICK: *Thank* you?! *Thank* you?!

JONATHAN *(Over "you")*: Don't be offended.

NICK: Who's offended? Who even *suggested* offense had been taken?

JONATHAN: I thought maybe. . . . You sounded . . .

NICK: Do you wish for me to be offended?

JONATHAN: Oh, please. Look, can we—

NICK: Do you *wish* for me—

JONATHAN: No. I'm sorry; you're taking it the wrong way.

NICK: Am I? You leave three hundred pounds under my honey pot . . .

JONATHAN: Nick. Jesus. I can't win with you, can I. Please. Just accept my thanks.

NICK: Your thanks for what?

JONATHAN: For letting me spend the night.

NICK: Three hundred pounds? For "letting" you? Three hundred pounds for letting you spend the night? If I'd known there was a price, I'd have charged you considerably more than three hundred pounds. Considering the damages to my home and happiness. Yes, like German reparations after the war.

I should thank *you.* Your proximity served as a welcome marital aid. Interesting going at it like that. Each for his or her own reasons, yet mutually satisfying just the same. It *is* kind of like war, isn't it.

JONATHAN: I never meant you any harm.

NICK: Never meant me . . . ?

JONATHAN: You act as if I'm to blame for your unhappiness. I'm sorry if you're unhappy. I never meant you any harm. We only met this afternoon . . .

NICK: Have I spoiled the surprise?

JONATHAN: What surprise?

NICK: Were we to awaken to find you gone but three hundred pounds in your stead, under the honey pot? Economic aid, is that it? Jonathan Waxman: Our American Cousin. Our Jewish uncle.

JONATHAN: Enough with the "Jewish," Nick.

NICK: You're right; cheap shot. A Robin Hood for our time, then. Stealing from the rich and giving to the poor. Hey, not entirely off the mark, is it?, stealing from the rich and giving to the——. You are quite the charlatan it turns out.

JONATHAN: Am I?

NICK: Oh, yes. You shit on canvas and dazzle the rich. They "oo" and "ah" and shower you with coins, lay gifts at your feet. The world has gone insane. It's the emperor's new clothes.

JONATHAN *(Reaching for it)*: Look, if you don't want my money . . .

NICK: Uh uh uh. Don't get me wrong: I will take your money. Gladly. *And* insult you. I will bite your hand. With relish. Your money is dirty, Wax Man. Hell, I don't care; I could use a few quid.

Patricia, awakened from a deep sleep, enters wearing a robe.

PATRICIA: What is happening?

NICK: Our guest is leaving. Getting an early start. He left a gratuity.

PATRICIA: What?

NICK *(Shows her the money)*: Three hundred quid.

JONATHAN: Look, I thought it would be best for everyone if I was gone in the morning.

PATRICIA: Is that what you thought? Why? Was the evening so unbearable?

JONATHAN: No . . .

PATRICIA: I thought it went pretty well, considering.

JONATHAN *(Over "considering")*: It did.

PATRICIA: It could have been excruciating.

JONATHAN: I know; it could've been. I was gonna write you a note.

PATRICIA: A note. You know, Jonathan?, you have this incredible knack for dismissing me whenever I've finished serving whatever purpose you've had in mind for me. Just incredible.

JONATHAN: Patty. . . . Look: It was really good to see you.

PATRICIA: What kind of shit is *that*?: "good to see you." I'm not one of your fucking patrons.

Nick slips out of the room.

JONATHAN: Alright, already! What do you want me to say? Did you think it was easy, calling you and coming up here like this?

PATRICIA: Nobody asked you to!

JONATHAN: I had to! Okay? I had to see you again; I had to face you.

PATRICIA: This is how you face me? By sneaking out? *(She sees the painting. A beat)* What are you doing with that? Oh, no you don't. Absolutely not.

JONATHAN: I'm only talking about a loan.

PATRICIA: Why?

JONATHAN: For the show.

PATRICIA: But it's my painting.

JONATHAN: I know.

PATRICIA: You gave it to me.

JONATHAN: I know I did. I'd like you to loan it to me. For the show. My gallery'll send you all the legal . . .

PATRICIA *(Over "all the legal")*: What the hell do you want with this painting? It isn't even that good.

JONATHAN: I don't care how good it is. It's missing something, the show. *I'm* missing something. I've been looking for a link, a touchstone. When I saw this painting . . .

PATRICIA: It's *me* in that painting, Jonathan. You gave it to *me*.

JONATHAN: Don't worry about privacy, the loan can be anonymous—

PATRICIA: I sat for that painting. The day we met. You gave me that painting.

JONATHAN *(Over "You gave me that painting")*: It'll be anonymous, nobody has to know your name.

PATRICIA: That's not the point. I don't want my painting hanging in a gallery!

JONATHAN: It's only for five weeks. In five weeks, they'll ship it back to you.

PATRICIA: It doesn't mean anything to anyone else; it means something to me. I don't understand—. Is *this* why you came?

JONATHAN: What? No.

PATRICIA: Hoping I'd provide the missing link?

JONATHAN: I wanted to *see* you. I had no idea you'd even have it. As far as I knew you'd hacked it to bits fifteen years ago.

PATRICIA: Why didn't I?

JONATHAN: You tell me.

PATRICIA: So, what was your plan, you were just going to pack it up and go?

JONATHAN: I was going to write you a letter. To explain.

PATRICIA: What, that you were stealing it?

JONATHAN: Borrowing it.

PATRICIA: Taking it. Without my knowledge. That's stealing! You were stealing my painting!

JONATHAN: I didn't think it would matter so much to you. I thought you'd be, I don't know, flattered.

PATRICIA: Flattered?!

JONATHAN: To be in the show.

PATRICIA: God, Jonathan, the arrogance! So you just take what you want now, hm? Is that what fame entitles you to? I don't understand what's happened to you, Jonathan, what's happened to your conscience? You had a conscience, I know you did. Guilt did wonders for you. It made you appealing. Now I don't *know*. You've lost your *goodness* or something. Your spirit.

Nick slips back in.

JONATHAN: You're right; I have. I *have* lost something. I've lost my way somehow, I don't know. . . . I've been trying to retrace my steps. . . . Ever since my father died. . . . I'm nobody's son anymore, Patty. They're all gone now, all the disappointable people. There's no one left to shock with my paintings anymore. When I saw this painting, though, it was like all of a sudden I remembered where I came from! There's a kind of purity to it, you know?, before all the bullshit. Patty, I just need to hold on to it.

NICK: How much is it worth to you?

JONATHAN: What?

NICK *(Gets the painting)*: Start the bidding. What's it worth?

PATRICIA: Nick. For God's sake . . .

JONATHAN: I'm only talking about borrowing it.

NICK: Borrowing is no longer an option. Either you buy it outright . . .

JONATHAN: You're not serious.

PATRICIA: Nick! This is none of your business!

NICK: None of my—? It most certainly is my business.

PATRICIA: It isn't yours to sell!

NICK: Oh, let him have the bloody painting and let's be on with it?

PATRICIA: No!

NICK: Please, love. Let him take it out of our home. At long last, please.

PATRICIA: It isn't for sale!

NICK: *Let* him, Patricia. Let him take it to London.

PATRICIA: No, Nick!

NICK: Let him buy it. Doesn't it make sense, love? Think of it: This one painting . . .

PATRICIA: No!

NICK: We'll make some money, love. Tens of thousands.

PATRICIA: This painting doesn't have a price!

NICK: It's our future, love! Our future was sitting on the wall all along. Think of it: We can *save* some money, we can pay our debts. We can get on with it. *(Pause. Softly)* Let him take the painting, love.

Nick and Patricia look at one another for a long time. She lets him take the painting; he gives it to Jonathan.

There you go.

JONATHAN *(To Patricia, who is facing away)*: You're sure this is what you want.

NICK: Yes. Absolutely. Send us a check. Pounds or dollars, either is acceptable. As long as it's an obscene amount.

JONATHAN: It will be.

NICK: Good. *(A beat)* Goodbye, Jonathan.
JONATHAN: Goodbye.
NICK *(To Patricia)*: I think I'll . . . go back to bed.

He starts to go. She takes his hand.

PATRICIA: Soon.

Nick leaves. Long pause.

I can't describe the pleasure I had being your muse. The days and nights I sat for you. It thrilled me, watching you paint me. The connection. The connection was electric. I could see the sparks. I never felt so alive as when I sat naked for you, utterly still, obedient. I would have done anything for you, do you know that?
JONATHAN: Patty . . .
PATRICIA: Isn't that shameful? A girl so devoid of self? I would have done anything. *(A beat)* You know, even after that last time in Brooklyn, I never actually believed that I'd never see you again.
JONATHAN: No?
PATRICIA: No, I always held out the *possibility*. But *this* time . . . *(A beat)* We won't be seeing each other again. Will we.

A beat. He shakes his head. A beat.

Hm. I wonder what that will be like.

They continue looking at one another as the lights fade.

Scene Eight

About seventeen years earlier. A painting studio at an art school. Easels in motley array. We can see the model dressing behind a screen. A class has just ended; a youthful, shaggier Jonathan continues to paint. Soon, the model, the young Patricia, enters and finishes dressing in silence.

PATRICIA *(Finally)*: How's it going?
JONATHAN: Hm?
PATRICIA: How's it—
JONATHAN: Oh. Fine.

Pause.

PATRICIA: You want me to shut up?
JONATHAN: What? No.
PATRICIA: Can I see?
JONATHAN: Uh . . .
PATRICIA: Please? I won't—
JONATHAN: It's. . . . It's really not there yet.
PATRICIA: Oh, come on . . .
JONATHAN: You'll get the wrong idea.
PATRICIA: I won't say anything.
JONATHAN: I don't know, I'm still . . .
PATRICIA: Not a peep.
JONATHAN *(A beat)*: Alright.

She goes to the easel, stands beside him for a long time trying not to show her reaction.

I'm playing around with the point of view. See how the—
PATRICIA: Shhh . . .

She takes a long beat, then walks away, resumes dressing. Pause.

JONATHAN: Well . . . ?
PATRICIA: What.

He looks at her expectantly.

You told me not to say anything.
JONATHAN: You can say *something* . . .
PATRICIA: I'm going on a diet effective immediately.
JONATHAN: I knew you'd take it the wrong way. It's purposely distorted. I'm trying something. You see how it looks like I'm looking *down* at you and *at* you at the same time? That's why the figure, your figure, looks a little . . .

PATRICIA: Huge. No, I'm kidding, it's good. Really. It's me. I have this mental image of myself . . . I think I'm a Botticelli, but I always come out Rubens. *(A beat)* You're very good, you know.

JONATHAN: I am?

PATRICIA: Oh, come on, you know it. I looked around during the break. You're the best in the class.

JONATHAN: Nah, I'm just having a good day.

PATRICIA: You want me to shut up so you—?

JONATHAN: That girl Susan's the best I think.

PATRICIA: She is not. Are you kidding?

JONATHAN: She's very slick, I know, but her color . . .

PATRICIA: I'm Patricia, by the way.

JONATHAN: I know.

PATRICIA: I mean, we haven't been formally introduced; you've been staring at my *bush* all *day* but we haven't . . .

JONATHAN: I'm Jonathan.

PATRICIA: I know.

They shake hands. Pause.

JONATHAN: You're a good model.

PATRICIA: Yeah? This is my first time ever.

JONATHAN: Is it really? I wouldn't have known.

PATRICIA: You mean it?

JONATHAN: Yeah. I really wouldn't have known. You're good.

PATRICIA: What makes a model good?

JONATHAN: I don't know. You're very steady.

PATRICIA: Steady.

JONATHAN: *You* know, you keep the pose.

PATRICIA: Oh.

JONATHAN: *You* know what I mean.

PATRICIA: So that's all it takes? Steadiness?

JONATHAN: No. I don't know, I mean, when you're working from a model—

PATRICIA: Yeah . . . ?

JONATHAN *(Continuous)*: —you kinda have to distance yourself.

PATRICIA: Uh-huh.

JONATHAN: I mean, just because one of you is naked, it's not necessarily a sexual thing.

PATRICIA: It's not?

JONATHAN: No. It's. . . . You have to maintain a certain objectivity, a certain distance. See, it's the whole *gestalt*.

PATRICIA: The gestalt.

JONATHAN: Yeah. It's the room and the pose and the canvas. It's the *moment*. The light, the way you look . . .

PATRICIA: You like the way I look?

JONATHAN *(A beat)*: Yes.

PATRICIA *(A beat)*: I can't believe I actually signed up to do this (my mother would *die*). It isn't hard, all I have to do is sit still and let my mind wander. I do that all the time anyway. Why shouldn't I get paid for it? I was watching them burn leaves out the window. The fire was beautiful. —Hey, you want me to get undressed?

JONATHAN: What?

PATRICIA: So you can work.

JONATHAN: No you don't have to do that . . .

PATRICIA: I don't mind . . .

JONATHAN: Your time is up; you don't get paid overtime.

PATRICIA: I don't care.

JONATHAN: No, really, I can paint from memory. Really.

PATRICIA: Why should you paint from memory? I'm *here*. . . . I mean, I *do* have my film history class . . .

JONATHAN: Is that your major? Film?

PATRICIA: No, I have no major. I'm a dilettante.

JONATHAN: Oh.

PATRICIA: You want to know what I'm taking this semester? I'm taking American Film Comedy from Chaplin to Capra, Women in Faulkner's South, Poetry Workshop (talk about dilettantes), Introduction to Archeology. And, you know what? It's wonderful, I am having such a wonderful time. I never thought being a dilettante could be so rewarding. I'm interested in a lot of different things so why should I tie myself down with a major, you know?

JONATHAN *(Humoring her)*: Uh-huh.

PATRICIA: You're humoring me.

JONATHAN *(Lying)*: No.

PATRICIA: My *father* always humors me; you're humoring me.

JONATHAN: I'm not.

PATRICIA: What's wrong with someone admitting she's a dilettante?

JONATHAN: Nothing.

PATRICIA: All it means is that I see myself as a student of the world. A student of the world. I'm young, I have time. I want to try a *lot* of things. Is that something to be ashamed of?

JONATHAN: No. It's just . . . I've never been able to do that. I mean, all I ever wanted to do was paint. I wanted to be an artist, ever since I was a little kid. I was like four and I could copy amazing. I don't know, if I could just paint all the time, maybe once in a while go out for Chinese food . . . that's all I want out of life.

Pause.

PATRICIA: You know?, you do this *thing* . . .

JONATHAN: What.

PATRICIA *(A beat)*: I've been watching you. While you work?

JONATHAN: You've been *watching* me?

PATRICIA: Uh-huh. There's this *thing* you do I've noticed. With your mouth.

JONATHAN: What do I do with my mouth?

PATRICIA: When you're painting.

JONATHAN: What do I *do*?!

PATRICIA *(A beat)*: You sort of stick your tongue out.

JONATHAN: Oh. So you're saying I look like an idiot?

PATRICIA *(Laughing)*: No, it's. . . . I'm sorry. . . . It's *cute* . . .

JONATHAN: Oh, great . . .

PATRICIA: It *is*. I mean, your concentration . . . *(A beat)* It's sexy.

JONATHAN: Oh, I'm sure. This dribbling down my . . . a real turn-on.

PATRICIA *(Laughing)*: It is . . .

She suddenly kisses his mouth.

JONATHAN *(Surprised, he recoils)*: Hey!

PATRICIA: Sorry. I'm sorry. . . . Look, why don't you just paint . . .
(Quickly gathers her things)

JONATHAN: No, wait . . . I didn't mean "Hey!" I meant "Oh!" It
came *out* "Hey!"

PATRICIA: Are you gay or something?

JONATHAN: No. . . . Surprised. I'm not used to having girls . . .

PATRICIA: What.

JONATHAN: I don't know. Come on so strong.

PATRICIA: Sorry. It won't happen again. *(She goes)*

JONATHAN: Oh, great . . .

PATRICIA *(Returning)*: Let me ask you something: If I hadn't
kissed you, would you have kissed me?

JONATHAN: No.

PATRICIA: What *is* it with you?! We're staring at each other all
day . . . I'm *naked*, totally exposed to you . . . your tongue is
driving me insane—the attraction is mutual, wouldn't you say?
I mean, wouldn't you say that?

JONATHAN: Yeah . . .

PATRICIA: Then what is it?

Pause.

JONATHAN: You . . . scare me a little.

PATRICIA: I scare you.

JONATHAN: You do. You scare me. . . . A lot, actually . . .

PATRICIA: How could I scare you? I'm the scaredest person in
the world.

JONATHAN: Oh, boy . . . *(Takes a deep breath; a beat)* You scare
me . . . 'cause of what you represent. I know that sounds . . .

PATRICIA *(Over "I know that sounds")*: For what I r—. What do
I represent? Dilettantism? Nudity? Film studies?

JONATHAN *(A beat)*: You aren't Jewish.

He smiles, shrugs. A beat.

PATRICIA: You're kidding. And all these years I thought I was.

JONATHAN: Look, this is hard for me. It's a major thing, you know, where I come from . . .

PATRICIA: What, your mother?

JONATHAN: Not just my mother. It's the six million! It's, it's the Diaspora, it's the history of the Jewish people! You have no idea, the *weight*. You got to remember I come from Brooklyn. People where I come from, they don't like to travel very far, let alone intermarry. They've still got this ghetto mentality: safety in numbers and stay put, no matter what. It's always, "How'm I gonna get there?"

She smiles.

No, really. "How'm I gonna get there?" and "How'm I gonna get home?" "It'll be late, it'll be dark, it'll get cold, I'll get sick, why bother? I'm staying home." This is the attitude about the world I grew up with. It's a miracle I ever left the house!

She laughs. They look at one another for a long beat.

PATRICIA: So now what do we do?

JONATHAN: What do you mean?

PATRICIA: This is it? No discussion? The end?

JONATHAN: I *told* you. I'm sorry. I can't . . . get *involved* with you.

PATRICIA: "Involved"? What does that *mean*, "involved"? You can't *look* at me?, you can't *talk* to me? What are you so afraid of?

JONATHAN: I don't even know.

PATRICIA: We're talking about a *kiss*, Jonathan, a kiss, some coffee, and maybe spending the night together.

JONATHAN: Uy.

PATRICIA: We are not talking about the future of the Jewish race.

JONATHAN: See, but I think we are.

PATRICIA: My God, they've got you brainwashed! Is this what they teach you in Hebrew school?

JONATHAN: This is how it starts, though, Patricia, a kiss.

PATRICIA: You make it sound like a disease!

JONATHAN: Well, maybe it is. Maybe it's wrong and destructive and goes against the natural order of things. I don't know. Maybe it just shouldn't be.

PATRICIA: And maybe it's the greatest adventure!

JONATHAN: Assimilation as Adventure. Sounds like one of your courses.

PATRICIA: *Don't humor me!* It's very condescending, Jonathan, it really is.

JONATHAN *(Over "it really is")*: I'm sorry I'm sorry.

PATRICIA: I come from a tribe, too, you know. Maybe not one with the same history as yours, but still. . . . You're as exotic to me as I am to you! You're an artist! An artist has to experience the world! How can you experience the world if you say "no" to things you shouldn't have to say "no" to?!

JONATHAN *(A beat. He smiles)*: Do me a favor?, get my mother on the phone?

He gestures to the easel with his brush, meaning: "I should get back to work." A beat. She kicks off her shoes.

(Quietly) No, no, don't, really. . . . What are you doing?

PATRICIA: Don't paint from memory. *I'm* here, Jonathan. *(A beat)* Paint *me*.

They're looking at one another. As she slowly unbuttons her blouse and he approaches, lights fade to black.

AFTERWORD

by the Playwright

Sometime in the early '60s, when I was around nine years old, my parents told me and my older brother that instead of spending my father's one-week summer vacation on a bus tour of the Berkshires or Pennsylvania Dutch country (as we had done before), this time we would be spending it in The City. To Brooklynites like us, The City meant Manhattan and, until my parents announced our vacation plans, I thought of it as a special place that existed solely for school trips to the Planetarium or the occasional family outing to Radio City.

"What are we gonna do in The City?" I asked. It was not, as far as I could tell, a place where people from Brooklyn spent the night, let alone a whole week.

"We're gonna see shows!" my parents told me, which meant, of course, Broadway. (We were cultural Jews; the only fervor that existed in our household wasn't centered on religion but on show business.)

So my mother and father and brother and I put on our nice clothes and, suitcases in tow, got on the Brighton local (we didn't own a car) and took the hourlong ride from Sheepshead Bay to Rockefeller Center. We checked into a cheap hotel in the West 50s and for the next six days saw every hit in town, shows like *Funny Girl, Fiddler on the Roof, Hello, Dolly!* As the house lights dimmed each night, plus matinees on Wednesday, Saturday and Sunday, I remember feeling almost unbearably excited by what lay ahead.

When I recently recalled my family's theatregoing vacations, they took on the mythic proportions of something we used to do all the time—until I realized that we probably did it only twice. Those two weeks, spent during two different theatrical seasons in the same funky midtown hotel, have blurred in my memory but their impact was powerful.

Herb Gardner's *A Thousand Clowns* was the first nonmusical play I ever saw, and I remember how the muscles in my face hurt from grinning in pleasure for two hours. I felt privileged being in a grand Broadway theatre packed with well-dressed adults and being let in on jokes they so obviously enjoyed; I was thrilled to add my small sound to all that laughter. For a boy like me, whose father worked all the time, it must have been invigorating to see a play about a man who preferred being home to toiling at a demoralizing job. In retrospect, it seems fitting that my first exposure to drama was a play about a complex father figure and his surrogate son, for the theme of fathers and sons has long figured in my plays and in my life.

The central character of my first full-length play, *Pals* (1979), had a lot in common with my father; I see now that I was trying to concretize my father's speech and thought processes as a way of understanding him. The grief-stricken father in *What's Wrong With This Picture?* was a further exploration of my own father, but it wasn't until after his death in 1987 (my mother had died nine years earlier) that I was able to truly uncover him.

My black comedy, *The Loman Family Picnic* (1989), is about a middle-class Jewish family in extremis over the oldest son's bar mitzvah. The cultural, economic and social pretensions surrounding that event lead to the beleaguered father's terrifying explosion. Giving voice to that inarticulate rage helped me find my father.

In *Sight Unseen*, the father is offstage, a shadowy figure whose recent death jolts the protagonist, the painter Jonathan Waxman, into examining his loss of cultural identity and artistic purpose. His journey leads him to Patricia, the woman with whom he long ago had a relationship, which symbolized the themes of his life and which remains unresolved. "I'm nobody's son anymore, Patty," he tells her. "They're all gone now, all the disappointable people."

My parents, Charlene and Bob Margulies, were of the generation of lower-middle-class Jews who were raised during the Depression and came of age during World War II. Like many married couples of that generation, my mother was the *balebusteh*, the powerhouse who embodied the cockeyed optimism and practicality of that time, while my father was the eternally haunted one who lived in fear of losing his job (even though he worked for the same people for forty years) and who was disturbed by change of any kind.

My father was a taciturn man, physically affectionate but prone to mysterious silences, who worked six, sometimes seven, days a week selling wallpaper in a store on Flatbush Avenue. His days routinely began at six in the morning and didn't end until eleven at night, but his rare days off were often devoted to playing records on the living room hi-fi. The great composers whose music wafted through our tiny apartment weren't Beethoven and Mozart but Loesser and Styne and Rodgers and Hammerstein. That was my father at his most content: playing his Broadway musical cast albums, dozens of them, on Sunday mornings throughout my childhood. I was the only kid in the sixth grade who knew by heart the entire score of *Happy Hunting*, an obscure Ethel Merman musical I heard countless times.

When I was small, my father and I would watch old movies on television together, the beloved movies of his youth, and he'd grill me on the character actors. "Donnie, who's that?" he'd ask, pointing to the wizened old woman on the TV screen. "Maria Ouspenskaya," I'd tell him, having learned my lessons well. But as my brother and I grew more intellectually and creatively curious, he began to distance himself. We were, no doubt, challenging sons for a stolid, unanalytical father; he responded by abdicating, by leaving our education entirely up to my mother. We were fortunate that she loved to read and instilled that love of books in her children.

As a youngster, I was troubled that my father showed no interest in reading anything but the *Daily News*. How could someone not read books? I took it as a personal affront, a form of rejection. Unconsciously, I began to search for spiritual fathers, creative men with whom I could commune intellectually, older men who could help me make sense of the world. My father's silence created in me a hunger for words that drew me to surrogate fathers, men I knew only through what they wrote. Herb Gardner may have been my earliest spiritual father, but Arthur Miller came into my life not long after.

I was eleven years old when I read *Death of a Salesman*, and I remember the guilt and shame I felt for recognizing in the Lomans truths about my own family: that my mother shared Linda's chauvinism and, most frightening of all, that my father, then barely forty, might turn out to be a Willy himself. But the play's uncanny reflection of my life and worst fears also exhilarated me and made me feel less alone. I studied it with great fascination, as if it were a key to understanding what was happening to the people I loved, so that I might somehow alter my family's fate. As a boy growing up in Trump Village (the Coney Island housing project built by Donald Trump's father), I imagined that our high-rise was one of the buildings that overshadowed the Lomans' modest house. Years later, in *The Loman Family Picnic*, I took that notion and made a play out of it.

After Miller, and as adolescence approached, I discovered in J. D. Salinger a spiritual father so empathic that he seemed to know how I felt about everything. Once I'd read *The Catcher in the Rye*, I devoured all of Salinger (just three slim paperbacks) and made a mission of tracking down the uncollected stories in old volumes of the *New Yorker*. I wanted more, but Salinger, who still writes but refuses to publish, proved to be the ultimate withholding father.

Philip Roth was not withholding. He was brainy, naughty and bursting with words: the cool daddy with whom one could talk about sex. I was fifteen when I first read *Portnoy's Complaint* and for all the wrong reasons; I was scanning for tales of sexy shiksas, but what I found were stunning insights into what it meant to be a Jew and a man. Even though he was nearly a generation older, Roth and I seemed to have grown up together, surrounded by many of the same relatives, sharing many similar experiences. He opened a window for me and let fresh air into a stuffy Brooklyn apartment and gave me (and still gives me) the courage to write what I know.

Because as a child I drew well, I was encouraged by my parents and teachers to pursue the visual arts. Art dominated my public school education and, when it came time to go to college, I was offered a scholarship to Pratt Institute. I lasted at Pratt for a year and a half. I was already itching to write (what, I had no idea), but I found no one there to guide me. I transferred to the State University of New York at Purchase, then the upstart liberal-arts college in the SUNY system, where I made mentors of literate and wise art professors like Abe Ajay and Antonio Frasconi. I found inspiration in Giacometti drawings, Schwitters collages and Diebenkorn paintings.

I was a disgruntled art major with literary aspirations when I walked into the office of Julius Novick, the theatre critic, who taught dramatic literature at Purchase. I boldly asked if he would be willing to sponsor me in a playwriting tutorial. He said yes and could not have imagined the impact that his decision was to have on my life: I was given permission to write. It was about this time that I discovered *The Homecoming* and *The Sound and the Fury*. On the face of it, Pinter's stark, nightmarish black comedy and Faulkner's gorgeously poetic family saga had little in common and yet, in my mind, they coexisted, thrillingly. If I was to be a writer, why couldn't I be an offspring of *all* these spiritual fathers, a son of Pinter and Faulkner—and Miller and Salinger and Roth and Giacometti and Schwitters?

After I graduated, I supported myself as a graphic designer while I wrote plays. My entry into the real world of New York the-atre in the early '80s eventually brought me into contact with the man who was the surrogate father to an entire generation of theatre people: Joseph Papp. Stories of his enormous heart (and his capriciousness) are now legend, and they're all probably true. When Joe loved you, he loved you extravagantly; when he loved you less, you could feel the drop in temperature.

At the peak of his affection, I'd run into him in the lobby of the Public Theater and he'd ask, "How's my Jewish playwright?" and I'd stand there and kibbitz with Joe Papp, as I would with any one of my relatives, and have the exciting feeling that there, in Joe's nurturing hands, under Joe's approving eye, at the age of twenty-nine, I had somehow arrived.

My father lived to see *Found a Peanut*, my Off Broadway debut, at the Public in 1984. The opening night party was pure Joe Papp: a bar mitzvah boy's dream come true, complete with brisket, potato pancakes, hot dogs, egg creams and loud rock-and-roll. I brought my father across the crowded room to introduce him to Joe. There was something exquisite in the meeting of these two men: my father, the working-class lover of theatre, the lifelong fan, meeting the self-made impresario. A crossing of the bridge at last, from Brooklyn to The City. Father of my childhood, meet father of my professional life. "Bob Margulies, meet Joe Papp."

"You've got quite a son here," Joe said as he shook my father's hand.

"Thanks to you."

"What do you *mean*, thanks to *me*," Joe Papp yelled at my father, "thanks to *you*!" as if to say, *"I'm not his father, you are! Take responsibility for what's yours once and for all and be proud!"*

Not until I was an adult did I understand that, in his lonely abdication, my father sought refuge from his demons, from the terrible fear that, not having had a relationship with his own father, he wouldn't know how to be a father himself; rather than try and fail, he simply retreated into silence. Years after I became a playwright, I realized that playwriting—the craft of dramatizing the unspoken—provided me with the tools I needed to get inside my father's head and figure out what he was thinking. Through the echoes of my father that occur in my plays, I have been able to give him a voice he only rarely used in life.

PRODUCTION CREDITS

Found a Peanut was originally produced in New York City at the New York Shakespeare Festival (Joseph Papp, Producer) in June 1984 with the following cast and creative contributors:

MIKE	Robert Joy
JEFFREY SMOLOWITZ	Evan Handler
MELODY	Robin Bartlett
JOANIE	Nealla Spano
LITTLE EARL	Peter MacNicol
SCOTT	Greg Germann
ERNIE	Jonathan Walker
SHANE	Kevin Geer
DIRECTOR	Claudia Weill
SETS	Thomas Lynch
LIGHTS	Beverly Emmons
COSTUMES	Jane Greenwood
MUSIC	Allen Shawn

⊡ ⊡ ⊡

What's Wrong With This Picture? was first presented in New York City by the Manhattan Theatre Club (Lynne Meadow, Artistic Director; Barry Grove, Managing Director) in January 1985. The cast and creative contributors were as follows:

MORT	Bob Dishy
ARTIE	Evan Handler

SHIRLEY	Madeline Kahn
CEIL	Marcia Jean Kurtz
SID	Salem Ludwig
BELLA	Florence Stanley
DIRECTOR	Claudia Weill
SETS	Adrianne Lobel
LIGHTS	Beverly Emmons
COSTUMES	Rita Ryack

The play made its West Coast premiere at the Back Alley Theatre (Laura Zucker and Allan Miller, Producing Directors) in Van Nuys, California in January 1988. The cast and creative contributors were as follows:

MORT	Allan Miller
ARTIE	James Stern
SHIRLEY	Phoebe Dorin
CEIL	Patti Deutsch
SID	Sandy Kenyon
BELLA	Lillian Adams
DIRECTOR	Stuart Damon
SETS	Don Gruber
LIGHTS	Larry Oberman
COSTUMES	Bob Miller

The Off Broadway premiere was at the Jewish Repertory Theatre (Ran Avni, Artistic Director) in June 1990 with the following cast and creative contributors:

MORT	Michael Lombard
ARTIE	Stephen Mailer
SHIRLEY	Lauren Klein
CEIL	Barbara Spiegel
SID	Salem Ludwig
BELLA	Dolores Sutton
DIRECTOR	Larry Arrick
SETS	Ray Recht
LIGHTS	Brian Nason
COSTUMES	Jeffrey Ullman

The play was produced on Broadway at the Brooks Atkinson Theatre in December 1994 by David Stone, the Booking Office, Albert Nocciolino and Betsy Dollinger in association with Ted Snowdon. The cast and creative contributors were as follows:

MORT	Alan Rosenberg
ARTIE	David Moscow
SHIRLEY	Faith Prince
CEIL	Marcell Rosenblatt
SID	Jerry Stiller
BELLA	Florence Stanley
DIRECTOR	Joe Mantello
SETS	Derek McLane
LIGHTS	Brian MacDevitt
COSTUMES	Ann Roth
SOUND	Guy Sherman/Aural Fixation

▢ ▢ ▢

The Model Apartment received its world premiere at the Los Angeles Theatre Center (Bill Bushnell, Artistic Producing Director) in November 1988 with the following cast and creative contributors:

LOLA	Erica Yohn
MAX	Milton Selzer
DEBBY/DEBORAH	Chloe Webb
NEIL	Zero Hubbard
DIRECTOR	Roberta Levitow
SETS	John Iacovelli
LIGHTS	Liz Stillwell
COSTUMES	Ann Bruice
SOUND	Jon Gottlieb

The Off Broadway premiere took place in October 1995 at Primary Stages Company (Casey Childs, Artistic Director) with the following cast and creative contributors:

LOLA	Lynn Cohen
MAX	Paul Stolarsky

DEBBY/DEBORAH	Roberta Wallach
NEIL	Akili Prince
DIRECTOR	Lisa Peterson
SETS	Neil Patel
LIGHTS	Paul Clay
COSTUMES	Katherine Roth
MUSIC AND SOUND	David Van Tieghem

☐ ☐ ☐

The Loman Family Picnic was originally produced in Manhattan Theatre Club's Stage II (Lynne Meadow, Artistic Director; Barry Grove, Managing Director) in June 1989 with the following cast and creative contributors:

DORIS	Marcia Jean Kurtz
MITCHELL	Michael Miceli
STEWIE	Judd Trichter
HERBIE	Larry Block
MARSHA	Wendy Makkena
DIRECTOR	Barnet Kellman
SETS	G. W. Mercier
LIGHTS	Debra J. Kletter
COSTUMES	Jess Goldstein
SOUND	Aural Fixation
MUSIC	David Shire
CHOREOGRAPHY	Mary Jane Houdina

The play was subsequently produced in Manhattan Theatre Club's Stage I (Lynne Meadow, Artistic Director; Barry Grove, Managing Director) in November 1993 with the following cast and creative contributors:

DORIS	Christine Baranski
MITCHELL	Jonathan Charles Kaplan
STEWIE	Harry Barandes
HERBIE	Peter Friedman
MARSHA	Liz Larsen
DIRECTOR	Lynne Meadow
SETS	Santo Loquasto

LIGHTS	Peter Kaczorowski
COSTUMES	Rita Ryack
SOUND	Otts Munderloh
MUSIC	David Shire
CHOREOGRAPHY	Marcia Milgrom Dodge

▯ ▯ ▯

Sight Unseen was commissioned by South Coast Repertory (Martin Benson, Artistic Director, David Emmes, Producing Artistic Director) in Costa Mesa, California where it received its world premiere in September 1991. The cast and creative contributors were as follows:

JONATHAN WAXMAN	Stephen Rowe
NICK	Randy Oglesby
PATRICIA	Elizabeth Norment
GRETE	Sabina Weber
DIRECTOR	Michael Bloom
SETS	Cliff Faulkner
LIGHTS	Tom Ruzika
COSTUMES	Ann Bruice
MUSIC	Michael Roth

The play received its New York premiere at Manhattan Theatre Club's Stage II (Lynne Meadow, Artistic Director; Barry Grove, Managing Director) in January 1992 and subsequently moved to the Orpheum Theatre for an extended run. The cast and creative contributors were as follows:

JONATHAN WAXMAN	Dennis Boutsikaris
NICK	Jon De Vries
PATRICIA	Deborah Hedwall
GRETE	Laura Linney
DIRECTOR	Michael Bloom
SETS	James Youmans
LIGHTS	Donald Holder
COSTUMES	Jess Goldstein
MUSIC	Michael Roth

DONALD MARGULIES was born in Brooklyn, New York in 1954. He has received playwriting fellowships from the New York Foundation for the Arts, the National Endowment for the Arts and the John Simon Guggenheim Memorial Foundation. *Sight Unseen*, a Pulitzer Prize finalist, won the Dramatists Guild/Hull-Warriner Award and the Obie Award for Best New American Play. Margulies's plays have premiered at Manhattan Theatre Club, the New York Shakespeare Festival, South Coast Repertory, Actors Theatre of Louisville and the Jewish Repertory Theatre, and have been produced throughout the United States and abroad. He is a member of New Dramatists and was elected to the council of the Dramatists Guild in 1993. He lives with his wife, Lynn Street, a physician, and their son, Miles, in New Haven, Connecticut, where he is a visiting lecturer in playwriting at the Yale School of Drama.